POCKET

NEW YORK CITY

TOP EXPERIENCES · LOCAL LIFE

ALI LEMER, ANITA ISALSKA,
MASOVAIDA MORGAN, KEVIN RAUB

Contents

Plan Your Trip   4

Manhattan Bridge, framing the
Empire State Building (p152)
MARTIN FROYDA/SHUTTERSTOCK ©

Explore
New York City 37

Worth a Trip

Survival
Guide   237

Special Features

COVID-19

We have re-checked every business in this book before publication to ensure that it is still open after the COVID-19 outbreak. However, the economic and social impacts of COVID-19 will continue to be felt long after the outbreak has been contained, and many businesses, services and events referenced in this guide may experience ongoing restrictions. Some businesses may be temporarily closed, have changed their opening hours and services, or require bookings; some unfortunately could have closed permanently. We suggest you check with venues before visiting for the latest information.

New York City's Top Experiences

Explore Central Park

NYC's most popular backyard. **p204**

BART SADOWSKI/GETTY IMAGES ©

ITZAVU/SHUTTERSTOCK ©

Wander the Galleries of the Metropolitan Museum of Art

Truly world-class art and antiquities. **p182**

SANGHAI KUMAR/SHUTTERSTOCK ©

Visit the Statue of Liberty & Ellis Island

Powerful symbols of America's multi-cultural history. **p40**

NYC RUSS/SHUTTERSTOCK ©

Catch the View at the Empire State Building

Cinematic icon with killer views. **p152**

Stroll through Times Square

The neon heart of NYC. **p150**

Crane Your Neck at One World Observatory

Manhattan's loftiest heights. **p48**

Cross Brooklyn Bridge

NYC's enduring masterpiece of engineering. **p44**

Explore Masterpieces at the Museum of Modern Art

Bliss for modern-art fans. **p154**

Visit the National September 11 Memorial & Museum

Moving commemoration of national loss. **p46**

LEFT: PIT STOCK/SHUTTERSTOCK © RIGHT: JOSEPH PERONE/SHUTTERSTOCK ©

Explore the Guggenheim Museum

Modern art and architecture. **p186**

LEFT: MATT MUNRO/LONELY PLANET LP MAGAZINE © RIGHT: DAN HERRICK/LONELY PLANET ©

Get a Bird's Eye View at the The High Line

Urban renewal at its best. **p108**

Visit MoMA PS1

Top avant-garde art museum in Queens. **p176**

Dining Out

From inspired iterations of world cuisine to quintessentially local nibbles, New York City's dining scene is infinite, all-consuming and a testament to its kaleidoscope of citizens. Even if you're not an obsessive foodie hitting the newest cult-chef openings and enclaves of global cuisine, an outstanding meal is always only a block away.

Market Munchies

Don't let the concrete streets and buildings fool you – New York City has a thriving greens scene. At the top of your list should be the Chelsea Market (p114), packed with gourmet goodies of all kinds. Also check out Gansevoort Market (p120-1); French-themed Le District (p55) in Lower Manhattan; Italy-inspired Eataly (p140) in the Flatiron District; and gourmet picnic paradise Essex Market (p97), rehoused on the Lower East Side. For self-catering or picnics, head to the Union Square Greenmarket (p137), open four days a week throughout the year. Check Grow NYC (www.grownyc.org/greenmarket) for a list of the other 50-plus markets around the city.

Food Trucks & Carts

Skip the hot-dog carts – mobile crews are dishing up unique fusion fare in NYC. Food trucks stop in designated zones throughout the city – namely around Union Square, Midtown and the Financial District. Among our favorites are Mad Sq Eats (p142), **Calexico Cart** (www.calexico.net), **MysttikMasaala** (www.facebook.com/MysttikMasaala), **Cinnamon Snail** (www.cinnamonsnail.com) and **Cool Haus** (www.cool.haus).

Best Fine Dining

Eleven Madison Park Arresting, cutting-edge cuisine laced with unexpected whimsy. (p139)

Le Bernardin The holy grail of NYC fine dining, starring a seafood menu. (p164)

LEONARD ZHUKOVSKY/SHUTTERSTOCK ©

Bâtard Classic, beautifully balanced continental cuisine in Lower Manhattan. (p56)

Modern Mouthwatering Michelin-starred morsels beside MoMA's sculpture garden. (p163)

Best Vegetarian & Vegan

Nix Michelin-starred vegetarian dishes in a modest West Village setting. (p117)

Hangawi Meat-free (and shoe-free) Korean restaurant in Koreatown. (p165)

Blossom on Columbus Tofu Benedict, shiitake risotto and other exemplary plant-based fare. (p215)

Best Old-School NYC

Barney Greengrass Perfect smoked salmon and sturgeon for more than 100 years in the Upper West Side. (p214)

Russ & Daughters A celebrated Jewish deli in the Lower East Side. (pictured; p103)

Zabar's Upper West Side store selling gourmet, kosher foods since the 1930s. (p214)

Margon Unfussy, unchanged Cuban lunch counter in Midtown. (p166)

Yonah Schimmel Serving up pillowy stuffed knishes for over a century. (p96)

Worth a Trip

Legendary pizzeria **Juliana's** (www.julianas pizza.com; 19 Old Fulton St, btwn Water & Front Sts, Brooklyn Heights; pizzas $20-32; ⊙11:30am-10pm, closed 3:15-4pm; S A/C to High St-Brooklyn Bridge) offers delicious, thin-crust perfection in both classic and creative combos. Try the No 1, with mozzarella, *scamorza affumicata* (smoked cow's cheese), pancetta, scallions and white truffles.

New York City on a Plate
The Best Pastrami Sandwich

Purists agree: rye bread (preferably seeded) is best.

Top the pastrami with spicy brown mustard.

LEONARD ZHUKOVSKY/SHUTTERSTOCK ©

Leave off the extra toppings: less is more.

A dill pickle on the side adds complexity.

★ Top Four Places for Pastrami Sandwiches

Katz's Delicatessen (p94)
The NYC deli of your dreams.

Zabar's (p214) King of the gourmet deli-supermarkets.

Barney Greengrass (p214) The Sturgeon King also knows pastrami.

Ess-a-Bagel (www.ess-a-bagel.com; 831 Third Ave, at E 51st St, Midtown East; bagel sandwiches $3.50-5.50; ⊙6am-9pm Mon-Fri, to 5pm Sat & Sun; S 6 to 51st St; E/M to Lexington Ave-53rd St) Humble but classic.

The Pastrami Sandwich Experience

Biting into a pastrami sandwich is a classic New York City experience. It's best eaten in one of the city's old-school Jewish delis – the kind with neon signs out front, counter seating inside and gruff but kind-hearted staff. The sandwich comes piled high with tender, juicy slices of lightly spiced meat contrasting with the crunch of toasted rye bread, and the zing of brown mustard binding it all together: a delectable work of art.

Katz's Delicatessen (p94)

LEONARD ZHUKOVSKY/SHUTTERSTOCK ©

Bar Open

You'll find all kinds of thirst-quenching venues here, from terminally hip cocktail lounges and historic dive bars to specialty taprooms and third-wave coffee shops. A legendary club scene spans everything from upscale celebrity staples to gritty, indie hangouts. Head downtown or to Brooklyn for the parts of the city that, as they say, truly never sleep.

Coffee Town

A boom in specialty coffee roasters continues to raise New York's caffeine culture to ever-greater heights. More locals are cluing-in to single-origin beans and different brewing techniques, with numerous roasters now offering cupping classes for curious drinkers. Many are transplants from A-list coffee cities, among them Portland and the Bay Area. An antipodean influence is also present, with a growing number of top cafes claiming Australian roots.

Craft Beer

The city's craft beer culture is equally dynamic, with an ever-expanding bounty of breweries, bars and shops showcasing local artisanal labels. Top local breweries include Brooklyn Brewery, Sixpoint, SingleCut Beersmiths, Coney Island Brewery and Bronx Brewery.

Retro Cocktails

Here in the land where the term 'cocktail' was born, mixed drinks are still stirred with the utmost gravitas. The city's top barkeeps create some of the world's most sophisticated and innovative libations. Often it's a case of history in a glass: New York's obsession with rediscovered recipes and Prohibition-era style continues to drive many a cocktail list.

Best Coffee

Stumptown Coffee Roasters Cool baristas serving Portland's favorite cup o' joe. (p124)

Bluestone Lane Aussie brewing prowess in the shadow of Wall St. (p58)

GUILLAUME GAUDET/LONELY PLANET ©

La Colombe Intense roasts for the downtown cognoscenti. (p59)

Best Cocktails

Bar Goto Lower East Side icon with New York's most famous mixologist at the helm. (p97)

Employees Only Award-winning barkeeps and arresting libations in the timeless West Village. (p121)

Raines Law Room Well-composed cocktails from serious mixologists in a Prohibition-style den near Union Sq. (p143)

Best Spirits

Brandy Library Blue-blooded cognacs, brandies

and more for Tribeca connoisseurs. (p59)

Rum House Unique, coveted rums and a pianist to boot in Midtown. (p168)

Dead Rabbit NYC's finest collection of rare Irish whiskeys in the Financial District. (p58)

Best Wines

Terroir Tribeca An enlightened, encyclopedic wine list in trendy Tribeca. (p59)

La Compagnie des Vins Surnaturels A love letter to Gallic wines steps away from Little Italy. (p78)

Buvette A buzzing, candlelit wine bar on a tree-lined West Village street. (p122)

Worth a Trip

Anything goes at warehouse venue **House of Yes** (pictured above; www.houseofyes.org; 2 Wyckoff Ave, at Jefferson St, Bushwick; tickets free-$60; ⏲ usually 7pm-4am Wed-Sat; Ⓢ L to Jefferson St), which offers some of the most creative themed performance and dance nights in Brooklyn. Costumes or other funky outfits highly encouraged.

New York City in a Glass
The Egg Cream

Pour ½ cup of cold whole milk into a tall glass.

Add 3 tbsps of chocolate syrup and stir. Authentic NYC egg creams use *only* Fox's U-Bet Chocolate Syrup.

Fill glass with soda water and stir to make a frothy head.

Egg creams can't be bottled so are always made fresh.

★ Five Top Places for Egg Creams

Gem Spa (131 2nd Ave, at St Marks Pl, East Village; 10am-1am) Widely hailed as NYC's best egg cream.

Yonah Schimmel Knish Bakery (p96) Great way to wash down your knish.

Katz's Delicatessen (p94) Enjoy with a giant pastrami sandwich.

Veselka (p94) Also serves vanilla egg creams.

Lexington Candy Shop (p194) The old-school diner atmosphere is key.

A Delicious Paradox

The egg cream: no eggs, no cream. This fizzy chocolate-milk soda was invented in the 1900s by Louis Auster, a Jewish candy store owner who served them from his shop at Second Ave and E 7th St, in the heart of the old Yiddish theater district. Be sure to drink it fast, before the fizz goes flat, and enjoy this cool, bubbly, milk-chocolatey glass of old New York.

Lexington Candy Shop (p194)

DAN HERRICK/LONELY PLANET ©

Treasure Hunt

Unsurprisingly for a capital of commercialism, creativity and fashion, New York City is one of the best shopping destinations on the planet. From indie designer-driven boutiques to landmark department stores, thrift shops to haute couture, record stores to the Apple store, street eats to gourmet groceries, it's quite easy to blow one's budget.

Vintage Adventures

As much as New Yorkers gravitate towards all that's shiny and new, it can be infinitely fun to riffle through unwanted wares and threads. The most popular flea market is the **Brooklyn Flea** (www.brooklynflea.com; 80 Pearl St, Manhattan Bridge Archway, Anchorage Pl, at Water St, Dumbo; ⊙10am-5pm Sun Apr-Oct; 🚌B67 to York/Jay Sts, Ⓢ F to York St), found in different locations on different days, April through October. The East Village is the city's go-to neighborhood for secondhand and vintage stores.

Sample Sales

While clothing sales happen year-round – usually when seasons change and old stock must be moved out – sample sales are held frequently, a way for high-end labels to get rid of overstock at wonderfully deep discounts. You'll find them mostly in the huge warehouses in the Fashion District of Midtown or in SoHo.

Best Department Stores

Bergdorf Goodman The most magical of NYC's legendary department stores, with stellar store displays. (p174)

Saks Fifth Avenue Home to the 'Shoe Salon,' NYC's biggest women's-shoe department. (p174)

Best Fashion & Accessories

Rag & Bone Beautifully tailored clothes for men and women, in SoHo and elsewhere. (p83)

John Varvatos Rugged but worldly wearables in a former downtown rock club. (p105)

DROP OF LIGHT/SHUTTERSTOCK ©

Opening Ceremony Head-turning, cutting-edge threads and kicks for the fashion avant-garde in SoHo. (p81-2)

Best Vintage

Screaming Mimis Lots of appealing clothes from decades past. (p131)

Beacon's Closet Get a new outfit without breaking the bank at this great vintage shop. (p132)

Resurrection Mint-condition pieces from couture labels. (p80)

Best Bookshops

Strand Book Store Hands-down NYC's best used bookstore. (pictured; p131)

Housing Works Bookstore Used books and a cafe in an atmospheric setting in Nolita. (p82)

McNally Jackson Great SoHo spot for book browsing and author readings. (p80)

Best NYC Souvenirs

New York Public Library Stationery, tote bags, library

lion bookends and literary-minded graphic T-shirts. (p159)

New York Transit Museum Store Transport-themed souvenirs and fun, map-emblazoned gifts. (p175)

Lower East Side Tenement Museum Books, jewelry, bags, scarves and more from the museum shop. (p90)

Sales Tax

Clothing and footwear that costs less than $110 is exempt from sales tax. For everything else, you'll pay 8.875% retail sales tax on every purchase.

Top NYC Souvenirs

New York Public Library Lions

Bibliophiles can get a New York Public Library lion paperweight and other bookish gifts at the NYPL gift shop (p159).

I ♥ NY Anything

Milton Glaser's iconic 1976 design has never gone out of style. Get the official classic logo on T-shirts, mugs, keychains, baby onesies, Christmas ornaments and more at CityStore (p63).

Coffee Shop Mug

A ceramic version of the classic 'Anthora' coffee cup – one of NYC's most enduring, and endearing, symbols – can be found at the MoMA Design Store (p173).

Local Fashion

Show off your hipster cred back home with some creative pieces from indie and streetwear shop Opening Ceremony (p81).

Diptyque Candle

The Madison Ave outpost of French *parfumerie* Diptyque (p199) will have your senses reeling with their lush natural aromas, also available in scented candles.

Under the Radar New York City

NYC has no shortage of big-ticket tourist favorites – Times Square, the Empire State Building, the Brooklyn Bridge etc – but though spectacular, they don't give much sense of the real New York. Take some time to explore the less famous parts of town for experiences you won't find on any postcard.

Get Outta (Mid) Town

Many visitors to New York City head straight for the lights of Times Square and don't see anything outside midtown Manhattan except from the window of their flight home. That's a real shame, as so much of the best of NYC can only be found north of 96th St and out of Manhattan entirely. While the more commercial areas of Manhattan have struggled with empty storefronts since the lockdown of 2020, local life has flourished in other neighborhoods.

Multicultural Queens has contemporary art and international enclaves like Astoria, Flushing and Jackson Heights, with vibrant, authentic dining experiences across dozens of different world cuisines. Cosmopolitan Brooklyn is home to some of NYC's most beautiful parks and tree-lined streetscapes, especially in the Park Slope area, as well as some of the city's best cocktail bars and beer gardens, eclectic restaurants, boutique and vintage shopping and live-music venues, especially in too-hip Williamsburg. And even if you don't have enough time to leave Manhattan, head north to Harlem for African American culture and shops, historic jazz clubs and mouthwatering soul food.

Buy Local

One of the best parts about exploring the nooks and crannies of New York is finding one-of-a-kind small businesses, where spending your dollars means supporting actual New York

DAN HERRICK/LONELY PLANET ©

communities, not just national corporate chains. Sites like **Made In NYC** (www.madeinnyc.org) and **Black-Owned Brooklyn** (www.blackownedbrooklyn.com) offer curated listings of dozens of locally owned shops, restaurants and bars all around town.

Best in Harlem

Sylvia's One of Harlem's most famous restaurants has been serving up heaping plates of authentic Southern soul food since 1962. (p201)

Minton's The legendary birthplace of bebop hosts jazz, Cuban, Afro beats and more, five nights a week. (p201)

Apollo Theater One of the world's most famous stages has launched the careers of countless Black musical legends. (pictured; p201)

Best in Brooklyn

Prospect Park Brooklyn's crown jewel: hundreds of acres of rolling hills, broad meadows, a serene lake and activities such as skating, bicycling and pedal-boats. (p226)

Bell House A repurposed Gowanus warehouse stages live music, comedy, The Moth Story Slams, podcast tapings and more. (p231)

Ample Hills Creamery Homegrown artisanal ice cream in the most ingenious flavor combinations, churned up right here in Brooklyn. (p228)

Best in Queens

MoMA PS1 The Queens offshoot of the midtown stalwart serves up razor's-edge contemporary art in a decommissioned public school. (p176)

Socrates Sculpture Park This four-acre waterside park and al fresco gallery has gorgeous views of Manhattan, as well as outdoor activities like live music, yoga and kayaking. (p179)

King Souvlaki Down some feta-topped Greek fries and a tender chicken souvlaki pita courtesy of this celebrated Astoria food truck. (p179)

Museums

The Met, MoMA and the Guggenheim are just the beginning of a dizzying list of art-world icons. You'll find museums devoted to everything from fin de siècle Vienna to medieval European treasures, and sprawling galleries filled with Japanese sculpture, postmodern American painting, Himalayan textiles and New York City lore.

Planning

Most museums close at least one day a week, often Monday or Tuesday. Many stay open late one or more nights a week – often on a Thursday or Friday.

Galleries

Chelsea is home to the highest concentration of art galleries (p110) in the entire city. Most lie in the 20s, on the blocks between Tenth and Eleventh Aves. For a complete guide and map, pick up Art Info's Gallery Guide, available for free at most galleries, or visit www.chelseagallerymap.com. Wine-fueled openings for new shows are typically held on Thursday evenings, while most art houses tend to close their doors on Sundays and Mondays.

For Free

Many museums offer free or reduced admission once a week – check the websites to find out when. Most gallery openings are on Thursdays, but you'll find gratis events throughout the week.

Best Art Museums

Museum of Modern Art (MoMA) Brilliantly curated galleries feature iconic modern works. (p154)

Metropolitan Museum of Art Heavyweight of the Americas, the Met even comes with its own Egyptian temple. (p182)

Whitney Museum of American Art World-class contemporary shows in a grand new space designed by Renzo Piano. (p114)

Guggenheim Museum The architecture is the real star at this Frank Lloyd Wright creation. (p186)

New Museum of Contemporary Art A cutting-edge temple to contemporary art in all its forms. (p90)

MANUEL HURTADO/SHUTTERSTOCK ©

Best New York Museums

Lower East Side Tenement Museum Fascinating glimpse of life as an immigrant during the 19th and early 20th centuries. (p90)

Merchant's House Museum Step back in time at this perfectly preserved Federal home from well over a century ago. (p70)

New-York Historical Society NYC's oldest museum runs historical exhibits filled with artifacts. (p211)

Museum of the City of New York Details of the city's past abound in thoughtful cultural curations. (p191)

Best Lesser-Known Treasures

MoMA PS1 Across the river in Queens are some of NYC's most cutting-edge exhibitions. (p176)

Frick Collection A Gilded Age mansion sparkling with Vermeers, El Grecos, Goyas, and a fountain. (p189)

Neue Galerie An exquisite collection in a former Rockefeller mansion. (p190)

Museum of Jewish Heritage Compelling exploration of Jewish culture and history before, during and after the Holocaust. (p52)

Worth a Trip

Overlooking the Hudson River, the **Met Cloisters** (pictured; www.metmuseum.org/cloisters; 99 Margaret Corbin Dr, Fort Tryon Park; 3-day pass adult/senior/child $25/17/12; ⏱10am-5:15pm Mar-Oct, to 4:45pm Nov-Feb; 🚇A to 190th St) is a curious architectural jigsaw of various European monasteries, built in the 1930s to house the Metropolitan Museum's medieval treasures.

With Kids

New York City has loads of activities for young ones, including imaginative playgrounds and leafy parks where kids can run free, plus lots of kid-friendly museums and sights. Other highs include carousel rides, puppet shows and noshing at markets around town.

Eating Out

Restaurants in the most touristy corners of the city are ready at a moment's notice to bust out the high chairs and kiddie menus. In general, however, dining venues are small, and eating at popular joints can be a hassle with the little ones in tow. Early dinners can alleviate some of the stress, as most locals tend to eat between 7:30pm and 9:30pm. In good weather, we recommend grabbing a blanket and food from one of the city's excellent grocers and heading to Central Park or one of the many other green spaces for a picnic.

Resources

If you're hitting the Big Apple with kids, you can check for upcoming events online at Time Out New York Kids (www.timeout newyorkkids.com) and Mommy Poppins (www.mommy poppins.com). For an insight into New York aimed directly at kids, pick up a copy of Lonely Planet's *Not for Parents: New York*. Perfect for children aged eight and up, it opens up a world of intriguing stories and fascinating facts about New York's people, places, history and culture.

Best Family Outings

American Museum of Natural History Dinosaurs, butterflies, a planetarium and IMAX, oh my! (p210)

Metropolitan Museum of Art A fun trip back in time – make sure to stop at the Egyptian Wing. (p182)

New York City Fire Museum Kids (and parents) can live out their firefighting dreams at this historical museum. (p71)

LEE O/SHUTTERSTOCK ©

Best Parks

Central Park Row a boat, visit the zoo and hit Heckscher playground, the best of the park's 21 playgrounds. (pictured; p204)

Hudson River Park Choose from mini-golf, a fun playground, a carousel, water features and a science-themed play. (p114)

Prospect Park Brooklyn's 585-acre park has a zoo and an ice-skating rink that's a water park in summer. (p226)

Best Shopping

Books of Wonder Storybooks, teen novels, NYC-themed gifts and in-house storytime make this rainy-day perfection. (p147)

Mary Arnold Toys A neighborhood toy store stuffed to the brim with toys and games, plus free monthly events. (p199)

Best Food

Smorgasburg A great family spot to grab snacks in Prospect Park. (p228)

Chelsea Market Assemble a picnic then munch in the nearby Hudson River Park or on the High Line. (p114)

Ample Hills Creamery Watch the ice cream being made as you choose from their singular flavors. (p228)

Worth a Trip

NYC has a few zoos, but best by far is the 265-acre **Bronx Zoo** (www.bronxzoo.com), one of the USA's oldest and largest. It features over 6000 animals and re-created habitats from around the world, from African plains to Asian rainforests.

Festivals

STEVE EDREFF/SHUTTERSTOCK ©

Lunar (Chinese) New Year Festival (pictured; http://betterchinatown. com; ⊘late Jan/early Feb) This display of fireworks and dancing dragons is one of the USA's biggest.

St Patrick's Day Parade (www.nycstpat ricksparade.org; ⊘Mar 17) A massive audience lines Fifth Ave for this popular parade of bagpipers and floats.

Tribeca Film Festival (www.tribecafilm.com; ⊘Apr–May) A major star of the indie movie circuit.

Cherry Blossom Festival (www.bbg.org; Brooklyn Botanic Garden, Prospect Park; ⊘late Apr/ early May) A celebration of pink flowering cherry trees in Brooklyn.

NYC Pride (www.nycpride. org; ⊘late Jun) Gay Pride Month culminates in a major march down Fifth Ave on the last Sunday in June.

HBO Bryant Park Summer Film Festival (www. bryantpark.org; ⊘mid-Jun –Aug) On Monday nights in summer, classic films are shown on a huge outdoor screen in Bryant Park.

Celebrate Brooklyn! (www.bricartsmedia.org; Prospect Park Bandshell, near Prospect Park W & 11th St, Park Slope; ⊘Jun–mid-Aug) A beloved open-air summer concert and events series.

July Fourth Fireworks (www.macys.com; ⊘Jul 4) The USA's Independence Day is celebrated with fireworks over the East River, starting at 9pm.

SummerStage (www. cityparksfoundation.org/ summerstage; Rumsey Playfield, Central Park, access via Fifth Ave & 69th St; ⊘May-Oct) A series of outdoor concerts in Central Park with a wide mix of cultural fare.

Village Halloween Parade (www.halloween -nyc.com; Sixth Ave; ⊘7-11pm Oct 31) The country's largest, a costumed mix of Mardi Gras and art project.

Thanksgiving Day Parade (www.macys.com; ⊘4th Thu Nov) Massive helium-filled cartoon character balloons soar overhead at this cold-weather event.

NYC Marathon (www. nycmarathon.org; ⊘Nov) This annual 26-mile run through the five boroughs on the first Sunday in November draws thousands of international athletes.

Rockefeller Center Christmas Tree Lighting (www.rockefellercenter. com; ⊘Dec) The massive Christmas tree in Rockefeller Center gets bedecked with more than 25,000 lights.

New Year's Eve (www. timessquarenyc.org/nye) A raucous, freezing party to watch the famous ball drop in Times Square.

For Free

It will come as no surprise that the Big Apple isn't a cheap destination. Nevertheless, there are many ways to kick open the NYC treasure chest without spending a dime – free concerts, theater and film screenings, pay-what-you-wish nights at legendary museums, city festivals, free ferry rides and kayaking, plus loads of green space.

ALREDOSAZ/SHUTTERSTOCK ©

Staten Island Ferry Hop on the free ferry bound for Staten Island for postcard-perfect views of southern Manhattan. (p242)

Chelsea Galleries More than 300 galleries are open to the public along Manhattan's West 20s. (p110)

New Museum of Contemporary Art Ethereal white boxes house a serious stash of contemporary art that's (almost) free for visitors on Thursday evenings after 7pm (suggested minimum donation $2). (p90)

Central Park New York's giant backyard, with acre after acre of tree-lined bliss. Go for a jog; relax on the lawn; or throw bread crumbs at the ducks in the pond. (p204)

The High Line This catwalk of parkland is great for a stroll and skyline ogling. (p108)

New York Public Library This grand beaux-arts gem merits a visit for its sumptuous architecture and free exhibitions. (p159)

MoMA The glorious Museum of Modern Art is free from 5:30pm to 9pm on Fridays – be prepared for massive crowds and long lines. (p154)

National September 11 Memorial The largest artificial waterfalls in North America are a spectacular tribute to the victims of terrorism. (p46)

SummerStage Free summertime concerts and dance performances in Central Park. (p26)

Neue Galerie This under-the-radar beauty is gratis from 5pm to 8pm on the first Friday of the month. (p190)

National Museum of the American Indian Beautiful textiles, objects and art are a vivid testament to Native American cultures at this gem. (pictured; p52)

African Burial Ground National Monument A moving memorial to the legacy of enslaved Africans in colonial New York. (p53)

Frick Collection Gaze at works by European masters for a pay-as-you-wish donation on Wednesdays from 2pm to 6pm. (p189)

Green-Wood Cemetery Also a gorgeous park, with historical battle sites and high harbor views. (p226)

LGBTIQ+

ARTURO HOLMES/SHUTTERSTOCK ©

School-Night Shenanigans

In NYC, any night of the week is fair game to paint the town rouge – especially for the gay community, who attack the weekday social scene with gusto. Wednesday and Thursday nights roar with a steady stream of parties, and locals love raging on Sunday (especially in summer). The NYC Pride March (pictured) is held in June.

Resources

Tons of websites are dedicated to the city's LGBTIQ+ scene. Check out what's on around town with **Get Out** (www.getoutmag. com). One of the best ways to be in on the party scene is to follow your favorite promoter.

Best Promoters

BoiParty (www.boiparty. com) Throws impressive weekly, monthly and annual dance parties.

Hot Rabbit (www.hotrabbit. com) This outfit hosts regular women-friendly queer dance parties in Manhattan and Brooklyn.

The Saint at Large (www. saintatlarge.com) Throws the annual Black Party, a massive circuit event in March.

Daniel Nardicio (www. danielsbigideas.com) Organizes dance parties and other fun events in NYC and Fire Island.

Best Classic Hangouts

Marie's Crisis One-time hooker hangout turned Village show-tune piano bar. (p123)

Duplex Camp quips, smooth crooners and riotously fun drag queens at a Village institution. (p128)

Best for Dancing Queens

Industry As night deepens, this Hell's Kitchen hit turns from buzzing bar to thumping club. (p167)

Therapy Small fun dancefloor when you need a break from the mega clubs. (p168)

Best Lesbian Bars

Cubbyhole A no-attitude Village veteran with jukebox tunes and chatty regulars. (p122)

Henrietta Hudson A fun, classic dive packed with super-cool rocker chicks. (p126)

Active New York City

EDDTORO/SHUTTERSTOCK ©

Although hailing cabs in New York City can feel like a blood sport, and waiting on subway platforms in summer heat is steamier than a sauna, New Yorkers still love to stay active in their spare time. Considering the city's reputation as a megalopolis of neck-craning skyscrapers, the range of outdoor activities is a terrific surprise.

Running & Cycling

The 1.6-mile path around the Jacqueline Kennedy Onassis Reservoir is for runners and walkers only; also try the paths along the Hudson River in Lower Manhattan or FDR Dr and the East River in the Upper East Side. Brooklyn's Prospect Park has plenty of paths.

NYC has added more than 250 miles of bike lanes in the last decade, but the uninitiated should stick to the less hectic trails in parks and along rivers.

Fitness

Yoga and Pilates studios dot the city. For a gym workout, try scoring a complimentary day pass from one of the major chains.

Best Spectator Sports

NY Yankees (pictured; www.mlb.com/yankees; 1 E 161st St, at River Ave; tours $20; B/D, 4 to 161st St-Yankee Stadium) Major League Baseball (MLB).

NY Mets (www.mlb.com/mets; 120-01 Roosevelt Ave, Flushing; S 7 to Mets Willets Point) MLB.

NY Knicks (p170) NBA basketball.

Brooklyn Nets (www.barclayscenter.com; cnr Flatbush & Atlantic Aves, Prospect Heights; S B/D, N/Q/R, 2/3, 4/5 to Atlantic Ave-Barclays Center) NBA basketball.

NY Rangers (p170) NHL ice hockey.

Online Tickets

Score seats for major-league sports from **Ticketmaster** (www.ticketmaster.com) or **StubHub** (www.stubhub.com).

Four Perfect Days

Day 1

Spend the morning in **Central Park** (p204), visiting **Bethesda Fountain** (pictured), **Conservatory Water** and **Strawberry Fields**. Take some time for a rowboat paddle at the **Loeb Boathouse** (p205).

Next, take in **Grand Central Terminal** (p158), the **Chrysler Building** (p159) and the **New York Public Library** (p159). Round the afternoon off with a visit to the **Museum of Modern Art** (p154).

Soak up the urban maelstrom of **Times Square** (p150). Pick up tickets for a **Broadway** show or check out something ahead of the curve at **Playwrights Horizons** (p171). Quaff cocktails at **Rum House** (p168) and then head to the **Top of the Rock** (p158) to bid the city goodnight.

Day 2

At the **Metropolitan Museum of Art** (pictured; p182), take in the Egyptian and Roman collections and the European masters; in summer head up to the roof for a view over Central Park. The nearby **Neue Galerie** (p190) offers a feast of German and Austrian art in a 1914 mansion.

Head down to SoHo for an afternoon of shopping along **Prince** and **Spring Streets** (p80), then rove Chinatown's **Mulberry Street** (p73) and visit the **Museum of Chinese in America** (p71). Head to **Madison Square Park** (p138) to admire the classic Flatiron Building.

After dinner finish up with Italian wine at Eataly's gorgeous rooftop bar, **Serra** (p142).

Day 3

SOLEPSIZM/SHUTTERSTOCK ©

Head to Brooklyn and wander beautiful **Prospect Park** (p226). Amble west to explore sedate **Park Slope** and gritty **Gowanus**. Rummage the racks at **No Relation Vintage** (p233) and devour melt-in-your-mouth pie at **Four & Twenty Blackbirds** (p227).

Catch a taxi to **Williamsburg** (p234) and stroll **Bedford Avenue**'s boutiques and cafes. Find unique souvenirs at **Artists & Fleas** (p235); see esoteric exhibits at the **City Reliquary** (p235); hit **Maison Premiere** (p235) for dinner and cocktails.

Walk off dinner by strolling down to **Domino Park** (pictured; p235), admiring magnificent views of Manhattan. A brisk **NYC Ferry** (p242) ride brings you back across the East River.

Day 4

OSUGI/SHUTTERSTOCK ©

Catch an early **Staten Island Ferry** (p242) and watch the sun rise over Lower Manhattan. Gape at marvelous views from the **One World Observatory** (p48), then see the moving **National September 11 Memorial & Museum** (p46).

Head to the Meatpacking District to visit the gorgeous **Whitney Museum of American Art** (p114). The **High Line** (p108) offers a wander along a once-abandoned elevated rail line; stop for snacks, coffee and intriguing streetscape views.

Explore the lovely streets of Greenwich Village for dinner and then an evening of intimate live jazz at **Smalls** (p127) or the **Village Vanguard** (pictured; p128). End up at basement bar **Tippler** (p123) for craft beer or cocktails.

Need to Know

For detailed information, see Survival Guide (p237)

Currency
US dollar (US$)

Language
English

Visas
Nationals of 38 countries can enter the US without a visa, but must fill out an ESTA application.

Money
ATMs ubiquitous; credit cards accepted widely.

Mobile Phones
International travelers can use local SIM cards in an unlocked phone (or else buy a cheap US phone and load it with prepaid minutes).

Time
Eastern Standard Time (GMT/UTC minus five hours)

Tipping
Not optional in NYC. Restaurant servers 18–20%; bartenders $1 per beer or $2 per specialty cocktail; taxi drivers 10–15%; hotel cleaners $2–4 per day.

Daily Budget

Budget: Less than $250

Dorm bed: $40–70

Slice of pizza: around $4

Food-truck taco: from $3

Happy-hour glass of wine: $10

Bus or subway ride: less than $3

Midrange: $250–500

Double room in a midrange hotel: from $200

Empire State Building dual observatories ticket: $58

Midrange restaurant dinner for two: $150

Craft cocktail: $15–19

Discount Broadway tickets: around $80

Top end: More than $500

One night at opulent Greenwich Hotel: from $650

Upscale tasting menu: $90–315

One-hour massage at Great Jones Spa: $150

Metropolitan Opera orchestra seats: $85–445

Advance Planning

Two months before Reserve accommodation – prices increase closer to check-in. Snag tickets to Broadway blockbusters and request a free Big Apple Greeters tour.

One month before Most high-end restaurants release bookings four weeks ahead so reserve your table for that blow-out meal.

One week before Surf the web and scan blogs and Twitter for the latest restaurant and bar openings, music, comedy and art events.

Arriving in New York City

✈ John F Kennedy International Airport (JFK)

AirTrain ($5) links to the subway ($2.75); it's one hour into Manhattan. Express buses to Midtown cost $19. Taxis cost $52, excluding tolls, tip and rush-hour surcharge.

✈ LaGuardia Airport (LGA)

Take the Q70 express bus from the airport to the 74th St–Broadway subway station. Express buses to Midtown cost $16. Taxis range from $35 to $55, excluding tolls and tip.

✈ Newark Liberty International Airport (EWR)

Take the AirTrain ($5.50) to Newark Airport train station; board any train for New York's Penn Station ($13). Taxis range from $50 to $70 (plus around $15 toll and tip).

Getting Around

🚃 Subway

Cheap, efficient and operates 24/7. One ride is $2.75; uses MetroCard or OMNY system.

🚌 Bus

Convenient between Manhattan's eastern and western sides. $2.75 per ride; uses MetroCard.

🚖 Taxi

Hail on the street. Meters start at $2.50, increasing 50¢ per 0.2 miles. See www.nyc.gov/taxi.

⚓ Ferry

Makes waterside stops in Manhattan, Brooklyn and Queens. See www.ferry.nyc.

🚲 Bicycle

Citi Bike (www.citibikenyc.com; 24-hour pass $12) is very popular. BYO helmet.

Oculus transport hub (p47; designed by Santiago Calatrava), National September 11 Memorial & Museum

VLADIMIR MUCIBABIC/BABIC/SHUTTERSTOCK ©

New York Neighborhoods

Upper West Side & Central Park (p203)
Home to Lincoln Center and Central Park – the city's antidote to the endless stretches of concrete.

West Village, Chelsea & the Meatpacking District (p107)
Quaint streets and well-preserved brick townhouses lead to neighborhood cafes mixed with trendy nightlife options.

Financial District & Lower Manhattan (p39)
Home to the National September 11 Memorial & Museum, the Brooklyn Bridge and the Statue of Liberty.

Museum of Modern Art

Times Square

Empire State Building

The High Line

One World Observatory

National September 11 Memorial & Museum

Ellis Island

Brooklyn Bridge

Statue of Liberty

Brooklyn: Park Slope, Gowanus & Green-Wood Cemetery (p223)
Two of NYC's most popular residential areas and home to one of its best parks. Hidden treasure Green-Wood Cemetery is nearby.

Upper East Side (p181)
High-end boutiques and sophisticated mansions culminate in the architectural flourish of Museum Mile.

Central Park
Guggenheim Museum
Metropolitan Museum of Art
MoMA PS1

Midtown (p149)
This is the NYC you're thinking of: Times Square, Broadway theaters, canyons of skyscrapers and bustling crowds.

Union Square, Flatiron District & Gramercy (p135)
The tie that binds the colorful menagerie of surrounding areas. It's short on sights but big on buzz-worthy restaurants.

East Village & the Lower East Side (p85)
Old meets new on every block of this downtown duo – two of the city's hottest 'hoods for nightlife and cheap eats.

SoHo & Chinatown (p65)
Hidden temples and steaming dumpling houses dot Chinatown. Next door are SoHo's streamlined streets and high-end shopping.

Explore
New York City

Worth a Trip

New York City's Walking Tours

Aerial view over Central Park (p204) and Manhattan
HOWARD KINGSNORTH/GETTY IMAGES ©

Explore
Financial District & Lower Manhattan

Manhattan's southern tip is no longer strictly business. The Financial District houses some big-hitting sights, like the National September 11 Memorial & Museum and One World Observatory, and just offshore are Ellis Island and Lady Liberty herself. North of 'FiDi' are the warehouse conversions of prosperous Tribeca, with upmarket restaurants, shopping and art galleries.

The Short List

○ **Statue of Liberty (p40)** Climbing up inside America's most famous statue, peering out and seeing the world's greatest city spread out below.

○ **National September 11 Memorial & Museum (p46)** Reflecting on loss, hope and resilience at a beautifully transformed Ground Zero.

○ **One World Observatory (p48)** Zipping up to the top of the Western Hemisphere's tallest building for a knockout metropolitan panorama.

○ **Staten Island Ferry (p52)** Taking in sunset-blazing skyscrapers while crossing the harbor on one of NYC's fantastic – and free – floating icons.

○ **Ellis Island (p43)** Exploring American immigration at the USA's historically significant and personally poignant point of entry.

Getting There & Around

Ⓢ The Financial District is well serviced by subway lines; main hub Fulton St connects the A/C, J/Z, 2/3 and 4/5 lines. Take the 1 train to South Ferry for ferries to Staten Island or the Statue of Liberty and Ellis Island.

Neighborhood Map on p50

Lower Manhattan skyline GAGLIARDIPHOTOGRAPHY/SHUTTERSTOCK ©

Top Experience 📷
Visit the Statue of Liberty & Ellis Island

Lady Liberty has been gazing sternly toward 'unenlightened Europe' since 1886. Dubbed the 'Mother of Exiles,' she's often interpreted as a symbolic admonishment to an unjust old world. Emma Lazarus' 1883 poem 'The New Colossus' articulates this challenge: 'Give me your tired, your poor, your huddled masses yearning to breathe free, the wretched refuse of your teeming shore.'

◎ MAP P50, C8

www.nps.gov/stli

adult/child incl Ellis Island $18.50/9

🕑8:30am-6pm, hours vary by season

🚤to Liberty Island, ⑤1 to South Ferry, 4/5 to Bowling Green, then ferry

From the Suez to the City

It comes as a surprise to many that France's jumbo-size gift to America was not originally conceived with the US in mind. Indeed, when sculptor Frédéric-Auguste Bartholdi began planning the piece, his vision was for a colossal sculpture to guard the entrance to the Suez Canal in Egypt, one of France's greatest 19th-century engineering achievements. But the ambitious monument failed to attract serious funding from either France or Egypt, and Bartholdi's dream seemed destined for the scrap heap. A French politician and writer, Édouard de Laboulaye, proposed a gift to America as a symbol of the democratic values that underpinned both France and the US. Bartholdi tweaked his vision and turned his Suez flop into 'Liberty Enlightening the World' – an immortal gift to commemorate America's centennial of the Declaration of Independence.

Creating the Statue

Bartholdi spent almost 20 years turning his dream – to create the hollow copper colossus and mount it in New York Harbor – into reality. Hindered by serious financial problems, the statue's creation was helped by the fundraising efforts of newspaper publisher Joseph Pulitzer and poet Emma Lazarus, whose ode to Lady Liberty is now inscribed on the statue's pedestal, designed by American architect Richard Morris Hunt. Bartholdi's work on the statue was also delayed by structural challenges – a problem resolved by the metal-framework mastery of railway engineer Gustave Eiffel (yes, of the famous tower).

Finally completed in 1884 (a bit behind schedule for the centennial), it was shipped to NYC as 350 pieces packed into 214 crates, then reassembled over a span of four months and placed on the US-made granite pedestal.

★ Top Tips

o To see both the Statue of Liberty and Ellis Island, get a ferry before 2pm.

o Security at the ferry terminal is tight, with airport-style screening. Allow for 90-minute waits in high season.

o Don't believe any street sellers who tell you otherwise – official tickets are sold only through **Statue Cruises** (Map p50, C8; ☎877-523-9849; www.statuecruises.com; Battery Park, Lower Manhattan; adult/child from $18.50/9; ☉departures 8:30am-5pm, shorter hours winter). Buying tickets in advance online is strongly recommended.

✗ Take a Break

Skip the mediocre cafeteria fare on Liberty Island and pack a picnic lunch. Or visit early and return to Lower Manhattan for the gastronomic delights of French food emporium Le District (p55).

Its spectacular October 1886 dedication included New York's first ticker-tape parade and a flotilla of almost 300 vessels. The Lady was placed under the administration of the National Park Service in 1933; a restoration of her oxidized copper began in 1984, the same year she made it onto the UN's list of World Heritage Sites.

Liberty Today

Folks who reserve their tickets in advance are able to climb the (steep) 162 steps from the top of the pedestal level to Lady Liberty's crown, from where the city and harbor views are breathtaking. Be advised: crown access is extremely limited, and the only way in is to reserve your spot in advance; the further ahead you can do it, the better (a six-month lead time is allowed).

If you miss out on getting tickets to enter the crown, you may have better luck with tickets to the pedestal, which also offers commanding views. Like crown tickets, pedestal tickets are limited and should be reserved in advance, either online or by phone. Only crown- and pedestal-ticket holders have access to the **Statue of Liberty museum** in the pedestal.

If you don't have tickets to the crown or pedestal, don't fret. All ferry tickets to Liberty and Ellis Islands offer basic access to the grounds of Liberty Island, including guided ranger tours or self-guided audio tours.

Ellis Island Main Building

Ellis Island

America's most famous and historically important gateway, **Ellis Island** (212-363-3200, tickets 877-523-9849; www.nps.gov/elis) is where old-world despair met new-world promise. Between 1892 and 1924, over 12 million immigrants passed through this processing station, dreams in tow; an estimated 40% of Americans today have at least one ancestor who was processed here. The journey from Ellis Island led straight to the Lower East Side, where streets reflected these myriad origins with shop signs in Yiddish, Italian, German and Chinese.

An Irish Debut

Ellis Island's very first immigrant was 17-year-old Anna 'Annie' Moore. After a 12-day journey in steerage from County Cork, Ireland, Annie arrived on January 1, 1892, accompanied by her brothers Phillip and Anthony; the three were headed to America to join their parents, who had migrated to New York City four years earlier. She later married German immigrant Joseph Augustus Schayer and gave birth to at least 11 children, only five of whom survived. Annie died on December 6, 1924, and was laid to rest at Calvary Cemetery, Queens.

The Main Building

After the original wooden building burnt down in 1897, architects Edward Lippincott Tilton and William A Boring created a suitably impressive and imposing 'prologue' to America. The beaux-arts Main Building has majestic triple-arched entrances, decorative Flemish bond brickwork, and granite cornerstones and belvederes. Under the beautiful vaulted herringbone-tiled ceiling of the 338ft-long **Registry Room**, the newly arrived lined up to have their documents checked (polygamists, paupers, criminals and anarchists were turned back).

A Modern Restoration

After a $160 million restoration, the island's Main Building was reopened to the public in 1990 as the Ellis Island Immigration Museum. the museum delivers a poignant tribute to the immigrant experience: narratives from historians, immigrants themselves and other sources animate a fascinating collection of personal objects, official documents, photographs and film footage. Buy tickets online in advance (at www.statuecruises.com) to avoid the soul-crushingly long queues.

Top Experience 📷
Cross Brooklyn Bridge

One of NYC's most-photographed sights, and an engineering masterpiece, Brooklyn Bridge opened in 1883. With a then-unequalled span of 1596ft, it became the first land connection between Brooklyn and Manhattan, as well as the world's first steel suspension bridge. This timeless example of urban design has inspired poets, writers and painters – even today, it never fails to dazzle.

◉ MAP P50, F4

S 4/5/6 to Brooklyn Bridge-City Hall, J/Z to Chambers St, R/W to City Hall, 2/3 to Clark St, A/F to High St-Brooklyn Bridge Station

The Bridge's Heavy Toll

German-born engineer John Roebling designed the bridge, but after contracting tetanus when his foot was crushed by a ferry at Fulton Landing, he died before construction even began. His son, Washington Roebling, assumed responsibility for the project, which lasted 14 years. However, Roebling junior also became a victim, contracting 'the bends' from working underwater in a pressurized *caisson*. Bedridden within sight of the bridge for many years, he relied on his wife, Emily Warren Roebling, her-self a mathematician and engineer, to oversee construction in his stead. She also had to deal with budget overruns and unhappy politicians. Aside from the Roeblings, at least 27 workers died during the bridge's construction. And there was one final tragedy to come: in 1883, six days after the official opening, a massive crowd of pedestrians was bottlenecked at a stairway when rumours of a collapse, possibly started in jest, set off a stampede in which dozens were injured and 12 were crushed to death.

Crossing the Bridge

A stroll across the Brooklyn Bridge usually figures quite high on the 'must-do' list for NYC visitors. The pedestrian walkway affords wonderful views of Lower Manhattan, while ob-servation points under the support towers offer brass 'panorama' histories of the waterfront. It's about a mile across the bridge, which can take 20 to 40 minutes to walk, depending on how often you stop to admire the view.

The Manhattan entrance is directly off the eastern edge of City Hall Park; on the other side you'll find yourself on the border of two Brooklyn neighborhoods: leafy, residential Brooklyn Heights and hip shopping-and-dining destination Dumbo.

★ Top Tips

o Take care to stay on the pedestrian-signed side of the walkway – the other half is designated for cyclists, who use it for both commuting and leisure.

o To beat the crowds, come early in the morning (before 7am), when you'll have those views largely to yourself.

✗ Take a Break

For some post-walk fuel, choose from competing pizza joints Juliana's (p11) and **Grimaldi's** (☏718-858-4300; www.grimaldis-pizza.com; 1 Front St, cnr of Old Fulton St; pizzas $20-22; ⏱11:30am-10:45pm Mon-Thu, to 11:45pm Fri, noon-11:45pm Sat, to 10:45pm Sun; ⑤A/C to High St-Brooklyn Bridge), just under the bridge in Brook-lyn Heights.

Top Experience
Visit the National September 11 Memorial & Museum

The National September 11 Memorial & Museum is a dignified tribute to the victims of the worst terrorist attack to occur on American soil. Titled Reflecting Absence, the memorial's two massive reflecting pools (designed by Michael Arad and Peter Walker) feature the names of the thousands who lost their lives.

◎ **MAP P50, C5**

www.911memorial.org/museum

180 Greenwich St

memorial free, museum adult/child $26/15

⌚ 9am-8pm Sun-Thu, to 9pm Fri & Sat

S E to World Trade Center, 2/3 to Park Pl, R/W to Cortlandt St

Reflecting Pools

Surrounded by a plaza planted with 400 swamp white oak trees, the 9/11 Memorial's striking and deeply poignant reflecting pools (pictured) occupy the original footprints of the ill-fated Twin Towers. From their rim, a steady cascade of water pours 30ft down toward a central void. Bronze framing panels are inscribed with the names of those who died in the terrorist attacks of September 11, 2001, and in the World Trade Center car bombing on February 26, 1993.

Memorial Museum

The contemplative energy of the monument is further enhanced by the National September 11 Memorial Museum. Standing between the reflecting pools, the museum's glass entrance pavilion eerily evokes a toppled tower. Inside, an escalator leads down to the museum's subterranean main lobby. On the descent, visitors stand in the shadow of two steel tridents, originally embedded in the bedrock at the base of the North Tower. The moving *In Memoriam* gallery is lined with the photographs and names of those who perished, with details of their lives relayed through interactive touch screens.

A destroyed fire engine is testament to the inferno faced by those at the scene. The main exhibit's collection of videos, real-time audio recordings, images, objects and testimonies provide a rich, meditative exploration of the tragedy and the stories of grief, resilience and hope that followed. The last steel column removed during the clean-up is also on display, adorned with the messages and mementos of recovery workers, first-responders and loved ones of the victims.

★ Top Tips

o In the museum, look for the 'Angel of 9/11,' the eerie outline of a woman's face on a twisted girder.

o Outside, take a moment to appreciate Santiago Calatrava's huge white **Oculus**, inspired by a dove's wings.

o Last entry is two hours before closing time.

o Entry is free from 5pm to 8pm on Tuesday.

✗ Take a Break

o Escape the swarm of restaurants serving the lunching Wall St crowd and head to Tribeca for a variety of in-demand eateries, such as Locanda Verde (p55).

o A good alternative for less-expensive dining is Two Hands (p57).

Top Experience 📷
Crane Your Neck at One World Observatory

Filling what was a sore and glaring gap in the Lower Manhattan skyline, One World Trade Center symbolizes rebirth, determination and resilience. More than just another supertall skyscraper, it's a richly symbolic giant, well aware of the past yet firmly focused on the future. For lovers of New York, it's also the city's highest stop for dizzying, unforgettable urban views.

◉ MAP P50, B4

www.oneworld
observatory.com

285 Fulton St

adult/child/under-5s
$35/29/free

🕑 9am-9pm Sep-Apr,
from 8am May-Aug

S E to World Trade Center,
2/3 to Park Pl, A/C, J/Z,
4/5 to Fulton St

The Building

Leaping from the northwestern corner of the World Trade Center site, the 104-floor tower is architect David M Childs' redesign of Daniel Libeskind's original 2002 concept. The tapered giant is currently the tallest building in the Western Hemisphere – not to mention the sixth tallest in the world by pinnacle height. The tower soars skywards with chamfered edges, resulting in a series of isosceles triangles that, seen from the building's base, reach to infinity. Crowning the structure is a 408ft cable-stayed spire. Co-designed by sculptor Kenneth Snelson, it brings the building's total height to 1776ft, a symbolic reference to the year of American independence.

It's also one of the world's most sustainable buildings, winning LEED Gold certification for its various ecofriendly features. Almost half of the construction materials were made from postindustrial recycled content, and rainwater is harvested for cooling machinery and irrigating greenery. Natural light and low-consumption electrical and HVAC systems reduce electrical requirements.

From the Heights

The city's loftiest observation deck spans levels 100 to 102, reached by five Sky Pod elevators, among the fastest in the world. On level 100 is an epic 360-degree panorama guaranteed to keep you busy searching for landmarks, from the Brooklyn and Manhattan Bridges to Lady Liberty and the Woolworth, Empire State and Chrysler Buildings. If you need a hand, interactive mobile tablets programmed in eight languages are available for hire (included with the combo ticket for $10 more). As expected, the view is extraordinary, taking in all five boroughs and three adjoining states. Try to go on a clear day for the best experience.

★ Top Tips

o Prepurchase your tickets online (www.oneworldobservatory.com/tickets) to avoid the longest queues.

o When purchasing your ticket, you'll select a specific visiting time; head in by 9:15am for short waiting periods and thin crowds. Sunset is the busiest time.

o If you're really pressed for time (or just impatient), you can skip *all* the lines with a Priority Reserve ticket.

✕ Take a Break

There are dining options on level 101, but, being aimed at tourists, they're wildly overpriced. You're better off holding on to your appetite until you descend, then walking a block west to Brookfield Place and grabbing a bite at Hudson Eats (p58) or Le District (p55).

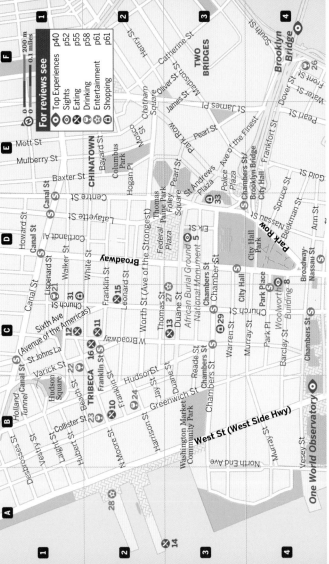

For reviews see

◉	Top Experiences	p40
◉	Sights	p52
✖	Eating	p55
◉	Drinking	p58
◉	Entertainment	p61
◉	Shopping	p61

200 m
0.1 miles

CHINATOWN

TWO BRIDGES

Brooklyn Bridge

TRIBECA

Broadway

West St (West Side Hwy)

One World Observatory

F

E

7

8

5

6

7

8

Pier 17

South Street

32 ①

Guilbert Beekman St

Pier 16

● Seaport Museum

30 ①

Cliff St

Fulton St

7 South Street

New York Water Taxi
Wall Street Landing

East River

Fulton St ⑤

John St

Platt St

TKTS Booth

Franklin D Roosevelt Dr

Pier 15

Dutch St

Maiden La

Fletcher St

17 ✕

**LOWER
MANHATTAN**

Cedar St

Front St

Pier 11

Dey St ⑤ Fulton St ⑤

Pine St

Gouverneur La

Cortlandt St ⑤

Liberty St

William St

Wall St ⑤

Water St

Old Slip

Nassau St

Broad St

Pier 6

Vietnam
Veterans
Plaza

Cedar St

Beaver St

19

S William St

Stone St

South St

Water St

Whitehall St

Ferry to Governors Island

Zuccotti
Park

Trinity 3 Wall St

Exchange Al

20

New St

Whitehall St

S William St

Pearl St

Staten Island Ferry

Broadway

Rector St ⑤

Cedar St

Thames St

Church St

Rector St

Greenwich St

● Trinity
Church

Morris
St

Broad St

Bowling
Green

National
Museum of the
American Indian

4 ①

Pearl St

Whitehall
Ferry
Terminal

State St

South ⑤
Ferry

1 ①

World Trade Center ⑤

**FINANCIAL
DISTRICT**

Carlisle St

Washington St

Edgar
St

Battery Pl

Battery ⑥
Park

State ⑥
St

Castle
Clinton

Statue ①
Cruises

Staten Island Ferry

9 ✕ 18

National September 11

Memorial & Museum

Memorial
Pools

Memorial
Pools

Liberty St

Albany St

Rector
Pl

W Thames St

South End Ave

Battery Pl

Robert F
Wagner Jr Park

Pier A

25 ①

**Statue of Liberty
& Ellis Island**

● ▲ ⑥

**BATTERY PARK
CITY**

North
Cove

South
Cove

2nd Pl

Museum of
Jewish Heritage

2 ①

Upper
New York Bay

Battery Park City Esplanade

West Side Hwy

Battery Pl

Hudson River

A

B

C

D

E

Sights

Staten Island Ferry

CRUISE

1 ◎ MAP P50, D8

Staten Islanders know these hulking orange ferries as commuter vehicles, while Manhattanites think of them as their secret, romantic vessels for a spring-day escape. Yet many tourists are also wise to the charms of the Staten Island Ferry, whose 25-minute, 5.2-mile journey between Lower Manhattan and the Staten Island neighborhood of St George is one of NYC's finest free adventures. (www.siferry.com; Whitehall Terminal, 4 Whitehall St, at South St, Lower Manhattan; admission free; ◎24hr; ⑤1 to South Ferry, R/W to Whitehall St, 4/5 to Bowling Green)

Museum of Jewish Heritage

MUSEUM

2 ◎ MAP P50, B7

This evocative waterfront museum explores all aspects of modern Jewish identity and culture, from religious traditions to artistic accomplishments. The museum's core exhibition covers three themed floors: *Jewish Life a Century Ago, Jewish Renewal* and *The War Against the Jews* – a detailed exploration of the Holocaust through thousands of personal artifacts, photographs, documentary films and survivor testimony. Also commemorating Holocaust victims is the external installation **Garden of Stones**, a narrow pathway of 18 boulders supporting living trees. (☎646-437-4202; www.mjhnyc.org; 36 Battery Pl, Financial District; adult/child $8/free, 4-9pm Wed & Thu free; ◎10am-9pm Sun-Thu, to 5pm Fri mid-Mar–mid-Nov, to 3pm Fri rest of year; ♿; ⑤4/5 to Bowling Green, R/W to Whitehall St)

Trinity Church

CHURCH

3 ◎ MAP P50, C6

New York City's tallest building upon consecration in 1846, Trinity Church features a 280ft-high bell tower and a richly colored stained-glass window over the altar. Famous residents of its serene cemetery include Founding Father and first secretary of the Treasury (and now Broadway superstar) Alexander Hamilton, while its excellent musical program includes organ-recital series Pipes at One (1pm Friday), and evening choral performances including new works co-commissioned by Trinity and an annual December rendition of Handel's *Messiah*. (☎212-602-0800; www.trinitywallstreet.org; 75 Broadway, at Wall St, Lower Manhattan; ◎7am-6pm, churchyard closes 6pm summer, dusk in winter; ⑤1, R/W to Rector St, 2/3, 4/5 to Wall St)

National Museum of the American Indian

MUSEUM

4 ◎ MAP P50, D7

An affiliate of the Smithsonian Institution, this elegant tribute to Native American culture occupies

Cass Gilbert's spectacular 1907 **Custom House**, one of NYC's finest beaux-arts buildings. Beyond a vast elliptical rotunda capped by a 140-ton skylight, sleek galleries play host to changing exhibitions featuring Native American art, culture, life and beliefs. The museum's permanent collection includes stunning decorative arts, textiles and ceremonial objects that document the diverse native cultures across the Americas, while the **imagiNATIONS Activity Center** explores their technologies. (☎212-514-3700; www.nmai.si.edu; 1 Bowling Green, Financial District; admission free; � 10am-5pm Fri-Wed, to 8pm Thu; 👬; ⑤4/5 to Bowling Green, R/W to Whitehall St)

African Burial Ground National Monument MEMORIAL

5 ◉ MAP P50, D3

In 1991, construction workers here uncovered more than 400 stacked wooden caskets, just 16ft to 28ft below street level. The boxes contained the remains of both enslaved and free African Americans from the 17th and 18th centuries (from 1697, nearby Trinity Church refused them burial in its graveyard). Today, a poignant **memorial site** and a **visitor center** with four rooms of educational displays honor the estimated 15,000 men, women and children buried in America's largest and oldest African cemetery. (☎212-637-2019; www.nps.gov/afbg; 290 Broadway, btwn Duane & Reade Sts, Lower

Staten Island Ferry

DROP OF LIGHT/SHUTTERSTOCK ©

Financial District & Lower Manhattan Sights

South Street Seaport

Before Hurricane Sandy flooded this enclave of cobbled streets, maritime warehouses and tourist-oriented shops in 2012, locals tended to leave this area to the tourists. Its nautical and historic importance was thought diluted by the manufactured 'Main Street' feel, street performers and poor-quality, often-mobbed restaurants. Revitalization and redevelopment have been slow, but recently momentum has picked up. A glossy new building on **Pier 17** (Map p50, F5; www.pier17ny.com; 89 South St, South Street Seaport, Lower Manhattan; Ⓢ 2/3, 4/5, A/C, J/Z to Fulton St) features some upmarket restaurants, an expansive river deck with breath-taking views and a rooftop bar and outdoor live-music venue; the development continues and supertall buildings might also be on the horizon. Like elsewhere in the city, the new and the novel are threatening historic preservation, but a few holdout bars and restaurants have maintained their atmospheric authenticity and are worth a look.

Manhattan; admission free; ⏱10am-4pm Tue-Sat; Ⓢ J/Z to Chambers St, R/W to City Hall, 4/5/6 to Brooklyn Bridge-City Hall)

Battery Park

PARK

 6 ⊙ MAP P50, C8

Skirting the southern edge of Manhattan, this 12-acre oasis lures with public artworks, meandering walkways and perennial gardens. Its memorials include tributes to those who died in the Korean War and Italian navigator Giovanni da Verrazzano. The first Dutch settlement on Manhattan was founded here in 1625, and the city's first battery was later erected in its defense. You'll also find the lovely **SeaGlass Carousel** (☎212-344-3491; www.seaglasscarousel.nyc; $5; ⏱10am-10pm), historic **Castle Clinton** (☎212-344-7220; www.nps.gov/cacl; admission free; ⏱7:45am-5pm) and the ferry service to Ellis Island and the Statue of Liberty. (www.nycgovparks.org; Broadway, at Battery Pl; ⏱6am-1am; Ⓢ 4/5 to Bowling Green, R/W to Whitehall St, 1 to South Ferry)

South Street Seaport Museum

MUSEUM

7 ⊙ MAP P50, E5

Dispersed amid the cobblestone streets of the seaport district, this 1967 museum consists of fascinating exhibitions relating to the city's maritime history, an 18th-century printing press and shop (p62), and a handful of mighty sailing ships to explore on Pier 16. Besides touring the moored 1885 *Wavertree* and the 1907 lightship *Ambrose*, in warmer months you can take a harbor cruise on the 1885 *Pioneer* and the 1930 wooden tugboat *WO Decker*. (📞212-748-8600; www. southstreetseaportmuseum.org; 12 Fulton St, btwn Water & Front Sts, Lower Manhattan; exhibitions & ships adult/child $20/free, printing press & shop free; ⏱ships & visitor center 11am-5pm Wed-Sun, print shop 11am-7pm Tue-Sun; 🚇; **S**2/3, 4/5, A/C, J/Z to Fulton St)

Woolworth Building

NOTABLE BUILDING

8 ◉ MAP P50, D4

The world's tallest building upon completion in 1913 (it was only surpassed in height by the Chrysler Building in 1930), Cass Gilbert's 60-story, 792ft-tall Woolworth Building is a neo-Gothic marvel, elegantly clad in masonry and terra-cotta. The breathtaking lobby – a spectacle of dazzling, Byzantine-like mosaics – is accessible only on prebooked guided tours, which also offer insight into the building's more curious original features, among them a dedicated subway entrance and a secret swimming pool. (📞203-966-9663; www.woolworthtours. com; 233 Broadway, at Park Pl, Lower Manhattan; 30/60/90min tours $20/30/45; **S**R/W to City Hall, 2/3 to Park Pl, 4/5/6 to Brooklyn Bridge-City Hall)

Eating

Le District

FOOD HALL $$$

9 🍴 MAP P50, B5

Paris on the Hudson reigns at this sprawling French food emporium selling everything from high-gloss pastries and pretty *tartines* to stinky cheese and steak-*frites*. Main restaurant **Beaubourg** does bistro classics such as *coq au vin*, but for a quick sit-down feed, head to the **Market District** counter for *frites* or the **Cafe District** for a savory crepe. (📞212-981-8588; www. ledistrict.com; Brookfield Place, 225 Liberty St, at West St, Lower Manhattan; market mains $12-30, Beaubourg dinner mains $19-36; ⏱Beaubourg 8am-10pm Mon, to 11pm Tue & Wed, to midnight Thu & Fri, 10am-midnight Sat, to 10pm Sun, other hours vary; 🛜; **S**E to World Trade Center, 2/3 to Park Pl, R/W to Cortlandt St, 4/5 to Fulton St, A/C to Chambers St)

Locanda Verde

ITALIAN $$$

10 🍴 MAP P50, B2

Curbside at the Greenwich Hotel is this Italian fine diner by Andrew Carmellini, where velvet curtains part onto a scene of loosened button-downs, black dresses and slick bar staff. It's a place to see and be seen, but the food – perhaps grilled swordfish with farro salad, *orecchiette* with duck sausage, or rigatoni with white-veal Bolognese – is still the main event. (📞212-925-3797; www.locandaverdenyc.com; 377 Greenwich St, at N Moore St, Tribeca;

mains lunch $24-36, dinner $27-58; ⊙7am-11pm Mon-Thu, to 11:30pm Fri, 8am-11:30pm Sat, to 11pm Sun; S 1 to Franklin St, A/C/E to Canal St)

Maman CAFE $

11 ⊗ MAP P50, C2

With faded white paint, skylight windows and dried lavender in jars, this beloved local cafe combines the air of a Provençal farmhouse with an industrial-hip downtown space. The French-inflected menu features a host of richly designed salads, omelettes and sandwiches, as well as luscious nectarine buttermilk waffles and a daily quiche. A front counter offers coffee and pastries to go. (www.maman nyc.com; 211 W Broadway, Tribeca; mains $13-16; ⊙8am-4pm Mon-Fri, 9am-4pm Sat & Sun; S 1 to Franklin St)

Bâtard EUROPEAN $$$

12 ⊗ MAP P50, C1

Austrian chef Markus Glocker heads this warm, Michelin-starred hot spot, where a pared-back interior puts the focus squarely on the food. Glocker's dishes are precise examples of classical French and Italian cooking: the prix-fixe menus hold rich delights such as striped bass with chanterelle mushrooms, or tagliatelle with roast lamb loin, olives and pecorino. (☎212-219-2777; www.batardtribeca.com; 239 W Broadway, btwn Walker & White Sts, Tribeca; 2/3/4 courses $65/89/99; ⊙5:30-10pm Mon-Wed, to 10:30pm Thu-Sat; S 1 to Franklin St, A/C/E to Canal St)

Tiny's & the Bar Upstairs AMERICAN $$$

13 ⊗ MAP P50, C3

The rustic interior of this 1810 Tribeca town house – antique wallpaper, salvaged wood paneling, original tin ceilings, pressed copper and marble bar tops, and handmade tiles – alone makes it worth a visit, but you won't regret staying for a meal or a cocktail. Food is modern American with French accents: perhaps seared duck with turnip and shallots or saffron mussels. (☎212-374-1135; www.tinysnyc.com; 135 W Broadway, btwn Thomas & Duane Sts, Tribeca; mains lunch $13-19, dinner $25-34; ⊙8am-midnight; S 1 to Franklin St, A, C to Chambers St)

Grand Banks SEAFOOD $$

14 ⊗ MAP P50, A3

Chef Kerry Heffernan's menu features sustainably harvested seafood at this restaurant on the *Sherman Zwicker*, a 1942 schooner moored on the Hudson, with the spotlight on Atlantic Ocean oysters. Alternatively, try the ceviche, lobster rolls or soft-shell crab. It's mobbed with dressy crowds after work and on weekends; come for a late-dinner sundowner and enjoy the stupendous sunset views. (☎212-660-6312; www.grandbanks. nyc; Pier 25, near N Moore St, Tribeca; oysters $3-4, mains $19-29; ⊙11am-12:30am Mon-Fri, from 10am Sat & Sun late Apr–Oct; S 1 to Franklin St; A/C/E to Canal St)

Two Hands   AUSTRALIAN $$

15 🍴 MAP P50, C2

An interior of whitewashed brick gives this modern 'Australian-style' cafe-restaurant an airy feel – and the local crowds love it. The menu offers light breakfast and lunch dishes such as a fully loaded acai bowl with berries and granola or a chicken sandwich with feta cream and olive tapenade. The coffee's top-notch, and there's happy hour from 2pm to 5pm. (www.twohandsnyc.com; 251 Church St, btwn Franklin & Leonard Sts, Tribeca; lunch & brunch mains $14-19; 🕗8am-5pm; 🖈; 🖸1 to Franklin St, N/Q/R/W, 6 to Canal St)

Gotan   CAFE $

16 🍴 MAP P50, C2

This buzzy, light-filled corner cafe is frequented by the downtown digerati, who make ample use of free wi-fi, thoughtfully placed power outlets and tabletop charging pads. The menu is light but filling, featuring sandwiches, salads and breakfast dishes with Mediterranean and Middle Eastern accents. Counter Culture coffee provides the beans; the skilled baristas do the rest. (📞212-431-5200; www.gotannyc.com; 130 Franklin St, btwn Varick St & W Broadway, Tribeca; sandwiches & salads $11-14; 🕗7am-5pm Mon-Fri, 8am-5pm Sat & Sun; 🛜🖈; 🖸1 to Franklin St)

Le District (p55)

Luchadores NYC

MEXICAN $

17 MAP P50, E5

On a nice day grab a seat in the tiny courtyard of this corner joint featuring fresh-made burritos, tacos and quesadillas made with short ribs, *carne asada* (charred beef), *pollo asado* (roasted chicken) or cajun shrimp. With a happy hour from 3pm to 6pm (nachos free with any two beers), it's a welcome alternative to less down-to-earth options around South Street Seaport. (📞 917-409-3033; 87 South St, at John St, Lower Manhattan; tacos $5-7, burritos $10-12; ⏰ noon-10pm; 🚇 2/3 to Wall St)

Hudson Eats

FOOD HALL $

18 MAP P50, B5

Sleekly renovated office-and-retail complex **Brookfield Place** is home to Hudson Eats, a shiny, upmarket food hall. Decked out with terrazzo floors, marble countertops and floor-to-ceiling windows with expansive views of Jersey City and the Hudson River, it has a string of respected, chef-driven eateries, including **Blue Ribbon Sushi**, **Fuku**, **Northern Tiger** and **Dos Toros Taqueria**. (📞 212-978-1698; www.bfplny.com/food; 225 Liberty St, at West St, Lower Manhattan; dishes from $7; ⏰ 8am-9pm Mon-Sat, to 7pm Sun; 📶; 🚇 E to World Trade Center, 2/3 to Park Pl, R/W to Cortlandt St, 4/5 to Fulton St, A/C to Chambers St)

Drinking

Dead Rabbit

BAR

19 MAP P50, D7

Named for a feared 19th-century Irish American gang, this three-story drinking den is regularly voted one of the world's best bars. Hit the sawdust-sprinkled Tap-room for specialty beers, historic punches and pop-ins (lightly soured ale spiked with different flavors). On the next floor there's the cozy Parlor, serving meticulously researched cocktails, and above that the reservation-only Occasional Room, 'for whiskey explorers.' (📞 646-422-7906; www.deadrabbitnyc.com; 30 Water St, btwn Broad St & Coenties Slip, Financial District; ⏰ Taproom 11am-4am Mon-Fri, 10am-3am Sat & Sun, Parlor 11am-3pm & 5pm-2am Mon-Sat, noon-midnight Sun; 🚇 R/W to Whitehall St, 1 to South Ferry)

Bluestone Lane

COFFEE

20 MAP P50, D6

The second installment in Bluestone Lane's booming US empire of Aussie-style coffee shops, this tiny outpost in the corner of an art deco office block is littered with Melbourne memorabilia. Alongside Wall St suits you'll find homesick antipodeans craving a decent, velvety flat white and a small selection of edibles, including the Australian cafe standard, smashed avocado on toast ($8).

(☎718-374-6858; www.bluestonelaneny.com; 30 Broad St, Financial District; ⊙7am-5pm Mon-Fri, 8am-4pm Sat & Sun; Ⓢ J/Z to Broad St, 2/3, 4/5 to Wall St)

La Colombe COFFEE

21 ⓔ MAP P50, C1

Coffee and a few baked treats is all you'll get at this roaster but, man, are they good. Join cool kids and clued-in Continentals for dark, intense espresso and signature offerings like draft latte, a naturally sweet iced caffe latte. Also on tap is La Colombe's cold-pressed Pure Black Coffee, steeped in oxygen-free stainless steel wine tanks for 16 hours. (☎212-343-1515; www.lacolombe.com; 319 Church St, at Lispenard St, Tribeca; ⊙7:30am-6:30pm Mon-Fri, from 8:30am Sat & Sun; Ⓢ A/C/E to Canal St)

Brandy Library COCKTAIL BAR

22 ⓔ MAP P50, C1

This brandy-hued bastion of brown spirits is the place to go for top-shelf cognac, whiskey and brandy. Settle into handsome club chairs facing floor-to-ceiling, bottle-lined shelves and sip your tipple of choice, paired with nibbles such as Gruyère-cheese puffs, hand-cut steak tartare and foie gras. Saturday nights are generally quieter than weeknights, making it a civilized spot for a weekend tête-à-tête. (☎212-226-5545; www.brandylibrary.com; 25 N Moore St, btwn

Varick & Hudson Sts, Tribeca; ⊙5pm-1am Sun-Wed, 4pm-2am Thu, 4pm-4am Fri & Sat; Ⓢ 1 to Franklin St)

Smith & Mills COCKTAIL BAR

23 ⓔ MAP P50, B2

Petite Smith & Mills ticks all the cool boxes: unmarked exterior, design-conscious industrial interior, and expertly crafted cocktails with a penchant for the classics. Space is limited, so head in early if you fancy kicking back on a plush banquette. A seasonal menu spans light snacks to a particularly notable burger bedecked with caramelized onions. (☎212-226-2515; www.smithandmills.com; 71 N Moore St, btwn Hudson & Greenwich Sts, Tribeca; ⊙11am-2am; Ⓢ 1 to Franklin St)

Terroir Tribeca WINE BAR

24 ⓔ MAP P50, B2

This amiable wine bar gratifies with its well-versed, well-priced wine list, including drops from the Old World and the New, among them natural wines and niche tipples from smaller producers. There's good knowledge behind the bar, a generous selection of wines by the glass and good French bistro food (mains $18 to $28). Offers early *and* late happy hours. (☎212-625-9463; www.wineisterroir.com; 24 Harrison St, btwn Greenwich & Hudson Sts, Tribeca; ⊙4pm-midnight Mon & Tue, to 1am Wed-Sat, to 11pm Sun; Ⓢ 1 to Franklin St)

Pier A Harbor House

BAR

25 MAP P50, C8

Built in 1886 as the New York City Board of Dock Commissioners' Headquarters, Pier A is a superspacious casual eating and drinking house right on New York Harbor. Go for a seat on the waterside deck in warm weather – picnic benches, sun umbrellas and the New York skyline create a brilliant spot for sipping craft beers or on-tap house cocktails. (☏212-785-0153; www.piera.com; 22 Battery Pl, Battery Park, Financial District; ⏱Harbor House 11am-midnight Sun-Wed, to 2am Thu-Sat, BlackTail 5pm-2am; 🛜; Ⓢ4/5 to Bowling Green, R/W to Whitehall St, 1 to South Ferry)

Cowgirl SeaHorse

BAR

26 MAP P50, F4

In an ocean of more serious bars and restaurants, Cowgirl SeaHorse is a party ship. Its ranch-meets-sea theme (wagon wheels and seahorses on the walls) and southern home cooking (blackened fish, oyster po'boy sliders, shrimp and grits etc) make it irresistibly fun. Live music on Monday, happy hour every day except Saturday and great frozen margaritas don't hurt, either. (☏212-608-7873; www.cowgirlsea horse.com; 259 Front St, at Dover St, Lower Manhattan; ⏱11am-2am Mon-Fri, 10am-1am Sat & Sun; ⓈA/C, J/Z, 2/3, 4/5 to Fulton St)

Pier A Harbor House

Entertainment

Flea Theater
THEATER

27 ⭐ MAP P50, C3

One of NYC's top off-off-Broadway venues, Flea is famous for staging innovative and timely new works. It houses three performance spaces, including the 'Siggy,' named for co-founder Sigourney Weaver. The year-round program includes music and dance productions, as well as Sunday shows for young audiences (aged two and up) and SERIALS, a rollicking late-night competition series of 10-minute plays. (📞 tickets 212-226-0051; www.theflea.org; 20 Thomas St, btwn Timble Pl & Broadway, Tribeca; tickets from $10; ♿; Ⓢ A/C, 1/2/3 to Chambers St, R/W to City Hall)

City Vineyard
LIVE MUSIC

28 ⭐ MAP P50, A2

This waterside bar-restaurant has an intimate, 233-seat cabaret-style theater that features live music nightly. The calendar tends toward emerging singer-songwriters, folk superstars and occasionally indie rock bands; past performers include notables such as Suzanne Vega, Squirrel Nut Zippers, Shawn Colvin, Robyn Hitchcock, Los Lobos, Aimee Mann, Billy Bragg and Yo La Tengo. (www.citywinery.com; Pier 26, 233 West St, near N Moore St, Tribeca; Ⓢ 1 to Franklin St; A/C/E to Canal St)

Downtown Discounts

Looking for discounted tickets to Broadway shows? Skip the long lines at the Times Square TKTS Booth for the much quieter **TKTS Booth** (Map p50, E5; www.tdf.org; cnr Front & John Sts, Lower Manhattan; ⏰ 11am-6pm Mon-Sat, to 4pm Sun; Ⓢ A/C, 2/3, 4/5, J/Z to Fulton St; R/W to Cortlandt St) at South Street Seaport. Queues usually move a little faster and you can also purchase tickets for next-day matinees (something you can't do at Times Square). The TKTS smartphone app offers real-time listings of what's on sale.

Shopping

Philip Williams Posters
VINTAGE

29 🔒 MAP P50, C3

You'll find more than 100,000 posters dating back to 1870 in this cavernous treasure trove, from oversized French advertisements for perfume and cognac to Eastern European film posters and decorative Chinese *nianhua* (New Year) posters. Prices range from $15 for small reproductions to thousands of dollars for rare, showpiece originals like a Cassandre. There's a second

HEATHER SHIMMIN/SHUTTERSTOCK ©

City Vineyard (p61)

entrance at 52 Warren St. (☏212-513-0313; www.postermuseum.com; 122 Chambers St, btwn Church St & W Broadway, Lower Manhattan; ⏰10am-7pm Mon-Sat; ⑤A/C, 1/2/3 to Chambers St)

Bowne & Co Stationers
GIFTS & SOUVENIRS

30 🔒 MAP P50, E5

Suitably set in cobbled South Street Seaport and affiliated with the attached South Street Seaport Museum (p54), this 18th-century veteran stocks reproduction-vintage New York posters and NYC-themed notepads, pencil cases, cards, stamps and even wrapping paper. At the **printing workshop** you can order custom-ized business cards or hone your

printing skills in monthly **classes** (see the museum website's Events page). (☏646-628-2707; 211 Water St, btwn Beekman & Fulton Sts, Lower Manhattan; ⏰11am-7pm; ⑤2/3, 4/5, A/C, J/Z to Fulton St)

Best Made Company
FASHION & ACCESSORIES

31 🔒 MAP P50, C1

Give your next camping trip a Manhattan makeover at this store/design-studio hybrid. Pick up handcrafted axes, leather duffel bags, sunglasses, enamel camping mugs and even designer dartboards and first-aid kits, many emblazoned with their signature 'X' logo. A small, smart collection of men's threads includes designer flannel shirts and pullovers, sweatshirts and rugged knitwear from Portland's Dehen Knitting Mills. (☎646-478-7092; www.bestmadeco.com; 36 White St, at Church St, Tribeca; ⏰noon-7pm Mon-Fri, 11am-7pm Sat, to 6pm Sun; ⏰A/C/E to Canal St; 1 to Franklin St)

Pasanella & Son

WINE

32 🔒 MAP P50, F5

Oenophiles adore this savvy wine peddler, with its 400-plus drops both inspired and affordable. The focus is on small producers, with a number of biodynamic and organic winemakers in the mix. It offers an impressive choice of American whiskeys and free wine-tastings of the week's new arrivals on Saturdays (from 5pm to 7pm). (☎212-233-8383; www.pasanella andson.com; 115 South St, btwn Peck Slip & Beekman St, Lower Manhattan; ⏰noon-9pm Mon-Sat, to 7pm Sun;

🚇A/C, J/Z, 2/3, 4/5 to Fulton St; R/W to Cortlandt St)

CityStore

GIFTS & SOUVENIRS

33 🔒 MAP P50, D3

Score all manner of officially produced New York City memorabilia here, from authentic-looking taxi medallions, sewer-hole-cover coasters and borough-themed T-shirts to NYPD baseball caps, subway-station signs and books about NYC. Curious, though less relevant for the average visitor, are the municipal building codes and other regulatory guides for sale. (☎212-386-0007; www.nyc.gov/citystore; North Plaza, Municipal Bldg, 1 Centre St, at Chambers St, Lower Manhattan; ⏰10am-5pm Mon-Fri; 🚇J/Z to Chambers St, 4/5/6 to Brooklyn Bridge-City Hall, R/W to City Hall)

Explore ✥

SoHo & Chinatown

Trendy neighborhoods SoHo (South of Houston), NoHo (North of Houston) and Nolita (North of Little Italy) are known for their boutiques, bars and eateries. Bustling Chinatown and a nostalgic sliver of Little Italy lure with idiosyncratic street life. Together, these areas offer a delicious, contradictory jumble of cast-iron architecture, strutting fashionistas, sacred temples and hook-hung salami.

The Short List

○ **Shopping (p80)** Maxing out the credit cards on SoHo's big-name fashion streets (as well as nearby Nolita and NoHo).

○ **Chinatown (p70)** Exploring bustling streets, slurping soup dumplings and haggling for designer knockoffs.

○ **Little Italy (p73)** Savoring a delicate tiramisu while listening in on grandfathers sipping grappa and speaking in the mother tongue.

○ **Merchant's House Museum (p70)** Exploring this time-jarred, possibly haunted museum, imagining NYC life in the 1800s.

○ **Peking Duck House (p76)** Digging into a tender, succulent Peking duck in the best spot to have it outside Beijing.

Getting There & Around

⑤ The subway lines dump off along various points of Canal St (J/Z, N/Q/R/W and 6). Once here, explore on foot.

🚌 ⊖ Avoid taking cabs or buses here – especially in Chinatown – as the traffic is full-on.

Neighborhood Map on p68

Chinatown (p70) MICHAL STIPEK/GETTY IMAGES ©

Walking Tour 🚶

An Artisanal Afternoon in Soho

Shopaholics across the world lust for SoHo and its sharp, trendy whirlwind of flagship stores, coveted labels and strutting fashionistas. Look beyond the giant global brands, however, and you'll discover that talented artisans and independent, one-off enterprises keep things local, unique and utterly inspiring.

Walk Facts

Start Café Integral
End McNally Jackson
Length 2mi; three hours

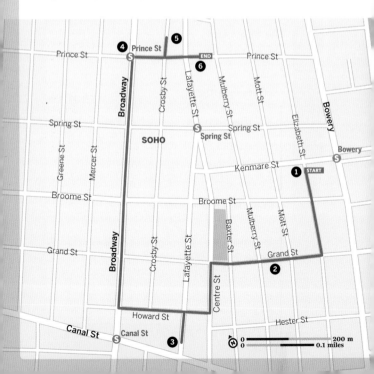

❶ Café Integral

Charge up with a cup of single-origin coffee and a tasty croissant from this airy **cafe** (☎646-801-5747; www.cafeintegral.com; 149 Elizabeth St, btwn Broome & Kenmare Sts, Nolita; ⏱7am-5pm Mon-Fri, from 8am Sat & Sun; Ⓢ N/Q/R, J/Z, 6 to Canal St) on Elizabeth St.

❷ Ferrara Cafe & Bakery

This **bakery** (☎212-226-6150; www.ferraranyc.com; 195 Grand St, btwn Mulberry & Mott Sts, Little Italy; pastries $7-9; ⏱9am-11pm Sun-Thu, to midnight Fri & Sat; Ⓢ J/Z, N/Q/R, 6 to Canal St; B/D to Grand St) has a huge selection of goodies, but don't pass up the chance to indulge in a world-class tiramisu ($8.95).

Ferrara Cafe & Bakery

MICHUSA/SHUTTERSTOCK ©

❸ Glossier Flagship

Get that dewy SoHo look with makeup and skincare products from the pink-laden, Insta-worthy showroom of this cult-favorite shop (p80).

❹ Sidewalk Art

The sidewalk engraving on the northwest corner of Prince St and Broadway is the work of Japanese-born sculptor Ken Hiratsuka, who has carved almost 40 sidewalks since moving to NYC in 1982. While this took about five hours of actual work, its completion took two years (1983–84), as Hiratsuka's illegal nighttime chiseling was often disrupted by pesky police patrols.

❺ MiN New York

Drop into this library-like **perfume apothecary** (☎212-206-6366; www.min.com; 117 Crosby St, btwn Jersey & Prince Sts, SoHo; ⏱11am-7pm Tue-Sat, noon-6pm Sun & Mon; Ⓢ B/D/F/M to Broadway-Lafayette St; N/R to Prince St) – with exclusive fragrances, bath and grooming products, and scented candles – and request a free 'fragrance flight.' You may go home smelling like a rose, a spa, the surf or the sea.

❻ McNally Jackson

This is one of the city's best-loved independent bookstores (p80), stocked with cognoscenti magazines and books, and an in-house cafe for quality downtime and conversation.

SoHo & Chinatown

For reviews see

◎	Sights	p70
✕	Eating	p73
◌	Drinking	p77
☆	Entertainment	p79
◍	Shopping	p80

Bowery

LITTLE ITALY

SOHO

CHINATOWN

Confucius Plaza

Chinatown

Columbus Park

St John's Park

New York City Fire Museum

Old Police Headquarters

Museum of Chinese in America

Drawing Center

Leslie-Lohman Museum of Gay & Lesbian Art

Broadway

200 m
0.1 miles

Sights

Chinatown

AREA

1  MAP P68, F8

A walk through Manhattan's most colorful, cramped neighborhood is never the same, no matter how many times you hit the pavement. Peek inside temples and exotic storefronts. Catch the whiff of ripe persimmons, hear the clacking of mah-jongg tiles on makeshift tables, see dangling duck roasts swinging in store windows and shop for anything from rice-paper lanterns and 'faux-lex' watches to tire irons and a pound of pressed nutmeg. (www.explorechinatown.com; south of Broome St & east of Broadway; S N/Q/R/W, J/Z, 6 to Canal St; B/D to Grand St; F to East Broadway)

Merchant's House Museum

MUSEUM

2  MAP P68, E1

Built in 1832 and purchased by merchant Seabury Tredwell three years later, this red-brick mansion remains the most authentic Federal house in town. It's as much about the city's mercantile past as it is a showcase of 19th-century high-end domestic furnishings, from the bronze gasoliers and marble mantelpieces to the elegant parlor chairs, attributed to noted furniture designer Duncan Phyfe. Even the multilevel call bells for the servants work to this day. (212-777-1089; www.merchants house.org; 29 E 4th St, btwn Lafayette St & Bowery, NoHo; adult/child $15/ free; noon-5pm Fri-Mon, to 8pm Thu,

Nom Wah Tea Parlor (p73)

GUILLAUME GAUDET/LONELY PLANET ©

Leslie-Lohman Museum of Gay & Lesbian Art

The world's first museum dedicated to LGBTIQ+ themes, the **Leslie-Lohman Museum of Gay & Lesbian Art** (Map p68, C6; ☎212-431-2609; www.leslielohman.org; 26 Wooster St, btwn Grand & Canal Sts, Little Italy; suggested donation $10; ⊗noon-6pm Wed & Fri-Sun, to 8pm Thu; ⑤A/C/E, N/Q/R, 1 to Canal St) stages six to eight annual exhibitions of both homegrown and international art. Offerings have included solo-artist retrospectives as well as themed shows; much of the work on display is from the museum's own collection, which consists of over 24,000 works. The space also hosts queer-centric lectures, readings, film screenings and performances; check the website for updates.

guided tours 2pm Thu-Mon & 6:30pm Thu; ⑤6 to Bleecker St; B/D/F/M to Broadway-Lafayette St)

New York City Fire Museum

MUSEUM

3 ◉ MAP P68, A5

In a grand old firehouse dating from 1904, this ode to firefighters includes a fantastic collection of historic equipment and artifacts. Eye up everything from horse-drawn firefighting carriages and early stovepipe firefighter hats to Chief, a four-legged firefighting hero from Brooklyn. Exhibits trace the development of the NYC firefighting system, and the museum's heavy equipment and friendly staff make this a great spot for kids. (☎212-691-1303; www.nycfiremuseum.org; 278 Spring St, btwn Varick & Hudson Sts, SoHo; adult/child $10/8; ⊗10am-5pm; ⑤C/E to Spring St)

Museum of Chinese in America

MUSEUM

4 ◉ MAP P68, E6

In this space designed by architect Maya Lin (designer of the famed Vietnam Memorial in Washington DC) is a multifaceted museum whose engaging permanent and temporary exhibitions shed light on Chinese American life, both past and present. Browse through interactive multimedia exhibits, maps, timelines, photos, letters, films and artifacts.The museum's anchor exhibit, *With a Single Step: Stories in the Making of America,* provides an often intimate glimpse into topics that include immigration, cultural identity and racial stereotyping. (MOCA; ☎212-619-4785; www.mocanyc.org; 215 Centre St, btwn Grand & Howard Sts, Chinatown; adult/child $12/8; 1st Thu of month free; ⊗11am-6pm Tue, Wed & Fri-Sun, to 9pm Thu; ⑤N/Q/R/W, J/Z, 6 to Canal St)

New York Earth Room

GALLERY

5 🔵 MAP P68, C3

Since 1980 the oddity of the New York Earth Room, the work of artist Walter De Maria, has been wooing the curious with something not easily found in the city: dirt (250 cu yd, or 280,000lb, of it, to be exact). Walking into the small space is a heady experience, as the scent will make you feel like you've entered a wet forest; the sight of such beautiful, pure earth in the midst of this crazy city is surprisingly moving. (📞212-989-5566; www.earthroom. org; 141 Wooster St, btwn Prince & W Houston Sts, SoHo; admission free; 🕓noon-3pm & 3:30-6pm Wed-Sun; Ⓢ N/R to Prince St)

Broken Kilometer

GALLERY

6 🔵 MAP P68, C5

Occupying a cavernous ground-floor space in SoHo is this 1979 installation by the late American artist Walter De Maria. The work consists of 500 solid brass rods, positioned in five parallel rows, with the space between the rods increasing by 5mm with each consecutive space, from front to back. The result: a playful subversion of spacial perception. The rods appear to be identically spaced, even though at the back they're almost 2ft apart. No photos allowed. (📞212-989-5566; www.diaart.org; 393 W Broadway, btwn Spring & Broome Sts, SoHo; admission free; 🕓noon-3pm & 3:30-6pm Wed-Sun, closed mid-Jun–mid-Sep; Ⓢ N/R to Prince St; C/E to Spring St)

Columbus Park

PARK

7 🔵 MAP P68, E8

Mahjong experts, slow-motion tai-chi practitioners and old aunties gossiping over homemade dumplings: it might feel like Shanghai, but this leafy oasis is core to NYC history. In the 19th century, this was part of the infamous Five Points neighborhood, the city's first tenement slums and the inspiration for Martin Scorsese's *Gangs of New York*. (Mulberry & Bayard Sts, Chinatown; Ⓢ J/Z, N/Q/R, 6 to Canal St)

Drawing Center

GALLERY

8 🔵 MAP P68, C6

America's only nonprofit institute focused solely on drawings, the Drawing Center uses work by masters as well as unknowns to juxtapose the medium's various styles. Historical exhibitions have included work by Michelangelo, James Ensor and Marcel Duchamp, while contemporary shows have showcased heavyweights such as Richard Serra, Ellsworth Kelly and Richard Tuttle. As to the themes themselves, expect anything from the whimsical to the politically controversial. (📞212-219-2166; www.drawingcenter.org; 35 Wooster St, btwn Grand & Broome Sts, SoHo; admission free; 🕓noon-6pm Wed & Fri-Sun, to 8pm Thu; Ⓢ A/C/E, 1, N/Q/R to Canal St)

Exploring Little Italy

In the last 50 years, New York's Little Italy has shrunk from a big, brash boot to an ultra-slim sandal. A mid-century exodus to the suburbs of Brooklyn and beyond would see this once-strong Italian neighborhood turn into a micro pastiche of its former self, with the most authentic Italian restaurants now found along Arthur Ave, up in the Bronx.

These days Little Italy is little more than **Mulberry Street** (SN/Q/R, J/Z, 6 to Canal St; B/D to Grand St), a kitsch strip of gingham-tablecloths, mandolin muzak and nostalgia for the old country. But a stroll around the area still offers up 19th-century tenement architecture, fresh pizza by the slice, gelato by the cone and some of the best tiramisu in town.

Come late September, Mulberry St turns into a raucous, 11-day block party for the **San Gennaro Festival** (www.facebook.com/san gennaronyc; ⊘Sep), a celebration honoring the patron saint of Naples. It's a loud, convivial affair, with food and carnival stalls, free entertainment and more big hair than Jersey Shore.

Eating

Nom Wah Tea Parlor CHINESE $

9 MAP P68, F8

Hidden down a narrow lane, 1920s Nom Wah Tea Parlor might look like an American diner, but it's actually the oldest dim sum place in town. Grab a seat at one of the red banquettes or counter stools and simply tick off what you want on the menu provided. Roast pork buns, Shanghainese soup dumplings, shrimp *siu mai*...it's all finger-licking good. (☑212-962-6047; www. nomwah.com; 13 Doyers St, Chinatown; dim sum from $4; ⊘10:30am-10pm Sun-Wed, to 11pm Fri & Sat; SJ/Z to Chambers St; 4/5/6 to Brooklyn Bridge-City Hall)

Chefs Club FUSION $$$

10 MAP P68, E3

In a building used in part for the show *Will & Grace*, Chefs Club sounds more like a discount warehouse than the spectacular dining spot it really is: visiting chefs prepare a menu for anywhere from three weeks to three months, offering their finest selections in menus that span the flavors of the globe. (☑212-941-1100; www.chefsclub.com; 275 Mulberry St, Nolita; prix-fixe menus $85-125; ⊘5:30-10:30pm Mon-Sat; SR/W to Prince St, B/D/F/M to Broadway-Lafayette St)

Dominique Ansel Bakery

SALVADOR MANIQUIZ/SHUTTERSTOCK ©

Tacombi Fonda Nolita

MEXICAN $

12  MAP P68, E3

Festively strung lights, foldaway chairs and Mexican men flipping tacos in an old VW Kombi: if you can't make it to the Yucatan shore, here's your Plan B. Casual, convivial and ever-popular, Tacombi serves up fine, fresh tacos, including a *barbacoa* (roasted black Angus beef). Wash down the goodness with a pitcher of sangria and start plotting that south-of-the-border getaway. (917-727-0179; www.tacombi.com; 267 Elizabeth St, btwn E Houston & Prince Sts, Nolita; tacos $4-9; 11am-11pm Sun-Wed, to midnight Thu-Sat; F to 2nd Ave; 6 to Bleecker St)

Dominique Ansel Bakery

BAKERY $

11  MAP P68, B4

One of NYC's best and most well-known patisseries has more to offer than just cronuts (its world-famous doughnut-croissant hybrid), including buttery *kouign-amman* (Breton cake), gleaming berry tarts, and the Paris-New York, a chocolate/caramel/peanut twist on the traditional Paris-Brest. If you insist on a cronut, head in by 7:30am on weekdays (earlier on weekends) to beat the 'sold out' sign. (212-219-2773; www.dominiqueansel. com; 189 Spring St, btwn Sullivan & Thompson Sts, SoHo; desserts $5-8; 8am-7pm Mon-Sat, from 9am Sun; C/E to Spring St)

Butcher's Daughter

VEGETARIAN $$

13  MAP P68, F5

The butcher's daughter certainly has rebelled, peddling nothing but fresh herbivorous fare in her whitewashed cafe. While healthy it is, boring it's not: everything from the soaked organic muesli to the spicy kale Caesar salad with almond Parmesan or the dinner-time Butcher's burger (vegetable and black-bean patty) is devilishly delish. (212-219-3434; www. thebutchersdaughter.com; 19 Kenmare St, at Elizabeth St, Nolita; salads & sandwiches $13-15, dinner mains $15-18; 8am-10pm; ; J to Bowery; 6 to Spring St)

Balthazar

FRENCH $$$

14  MAP P68, D5

Still the king of bistros after more than 20 years, bustling (OK, *loud*) Balthazar is never short of a mob. That's all thanks to three winning details: its location in SoHo's shopping-spree heartland; the uplifting Paris-meets-NYC ambience; and the something-for-everyone menu. Highlights include the outstanding raw bar, steak *frites,* Niçoise salad, as well as the roasted beet salad. (212-965-1414; www.balthazarny.com; 80 Spring St, btwn Broadway & Crosby St, SoHo; mains $22-45; 7:30am-midnight Sun-Thu, to 1am Fri, 8am-1am Sat; 6 to Spring St; N/R to Prince St)

Prince Street Pizza

PIZZA $

15 MAP P68, E4

It's a miracle the oven door hasn't come off at this classic standing-room-only slice joint, its brick walls hung with shots of celebrity fans like Rebel Wilson, Usher and Kate Hudson. The sauces, mozzarella and ricotta are made in-house and New Yorkers go wild for the pepperoni square. The pizza is decent, but not dazzling enough to justify the queues. (212-966-4100; 27 Prince St, btwn Mott & Elizabeth Sts, Nolita; pizza slices from $3.30; 11:45am-11pm Sun-Thu, to 2am Fri & Sat; R/W to Prince St; 6 to Spring St)

Butcher's Daughter

Eating in Chinatown

The most rewarding experience for Chinatown visitors is to access this wild and wonderful world through their taste buds. More than any other area of Manhattan, Chinatown's menus sport wonderfully low prices, uninflated by ambience, hype or reputation. But more than cheap eats, the neighborhood is rife with family recipes passed across generations and continents. Food displays and preparation remain unchanged and untempered by American norms; it's not unusual to walk by storefronts sporting a tangled array of lacquered animals – chickens, rabbit and duck, in particular – ready to be chopped up and served at a family banquet. Steaming street stalls clang down the sidewalk serving pork buns and other finger-friendly food. Wander down the back alleys for a Technicolor assortment of spices and herbs to perfect your own Eastern dishes.

Peking Duck House
CHINESE $$$

16 MAP P68, F8

Offering arguably the best Peking duck in the region, the eponymous restaurant has a variety of set menus that include the house specialty. The space is fancier than some Chinatown spots, making it great for a special occasion. Do have the duck: perfectly crispy skin and moist meat make the slices ideal for a pancake with scallion strips and sauce. (☏212-227-1810; www.pekingduckhousenyc.com; 28 Mott St, Chinatown; Peking duck per person $35-56; ⏲11:30am-10:30pm Sun-Thu, to 11:30pm Fri & Sat; Ⓢ J/Z to Chambers St; 6 to Canal St)

Buddha Bodai
CHINESE $

17 MAP P68, F8

Serves exquisite vegetarian and kosher cuisine with Cantonese flavors like a vegetarian 'duck' noodle soup, spinach rice rolls and vegetarian 'roast pork' buns. Since another restaurant with the same name and similar menu opened a few blocks away in 2015, this restaurant (which opened in 2004) is referred to as the 'Original Buddha Bodai'. Dim sum is served until 4pm. (☏212-566-8388; www.buddha-bodai.com; 5 Mott St, Chinatown; mains $9-22; ⏲11am-9:30pm Mon-Fri, from 10am Sat & Sun; ▧; Ⓢ J/Z to Chambers St; 4/5/6 to Brooklyn Bridge-City Hall)

Canal St Market
FOOD HALL $

18 MAP P68, D6

In the borderlands where Chinatown morphs into SoHo, this food and retail market unavoidably turns heads. The warehouse-like dining area is a world tour of food trends – Japanese shaved ice, ceviche, seasonal farm food etc. The shopping floor is the place to hunt for unusual indie gems such as vintage skateboards, K-pop clothing and locally made jewelry. (www.canalstreet.market; 265 Canal St, btwn Broadway & Lafayette St; food 10am-10pm Mon-Sat, to 6pm Sun; retail 11am-7pm Mon-Sat, to 6pm Sun; S 6, N/Q/R/W to Canal St)

Golden Steamer
CHINESE $

19 MAP P68, E6

Squeeze into this hole-in-the-wall for some of the fluffiest, tastiest *bao* (steamed buns) in Chinatown. Freshly made on-site, fillings include succulent roast pork, Chinese sausage, salted egg and the crowd favorite – pumpkin. For something a little sweeter, try the egg custard tart. Come early for the best choice. (212-226-1886; 143a Mott St, btwn Grand & Hester Sts, Chinatown; buns 80¢-$1.75, 3 for $2.50; 7am-7pm; S B/D to Grand St; N/Q/R, 6 to Canal St; J/Z to Bowery)

Rubirosa
PIZZA $$

20 MAP P68, E4

Rubirosa's infallible family recipe for its whisper-thin pie crust lures a steady stream of patrons from all over the city. Shovel slices from the bar stools or grab a table amid cozy surrounds and make room for savory appetizers and antipasti. Other options include bowls of pasta (the 'small' portion should fill most bellies). Gluten-free diners have their own menu. (212-965-0500; www.rubirosanyc.com; 235 Mulberry St, btwn Spring & Prince Sts, Nolita; pizzas $20-32, mains $13-34; 11:30am-11pm

DAN HALLMAN/LONELY PLANET ©

Apothéke

Sun-Wed, to midnight Thu-Sat; S N/R to Prince St; B/D/F/M to Broadway-Lafayette St; 6 to Spring St)

Drinking

Apothéke
COCKTAIL BAR

21 MAP P68, F8

It takes a little effort to track down this former opium-den-turned-apothecary bar on Doyers St (look for the 'chemist' sign with a beaker illustration hanging above the doorway). Inside, skilled barkeeps work like careful chemists, using local, seasonal produce from greenmarkets to concoct intense, flavorful 'prescriptions.' The pineapple-cilantro spiced Sitting Buddha is one of the best drinks on the menu. (212-406-0400; www.apothekenyc.com; 9 Doyers St,

Chinatown; ⏰6:30pm-2am Mon-Sat, from 8pm Sun; Ⓢ J/Z to Chambers St; 4/5/6 to Brooklyn Bridge-City Hall)

Ear Inn PUB

22 📍 MAP P68, A5

Want to see what SoHo was like before the trendsetters and fashionistas? Come to the creaking old Ear Inn, proudly billed as one of the oldest drinking establishments in NYC. The house it occupies was built in the late 18th century for James Brown, an African aide to George Washington. Drinks are cheap and the crowd's eclectic. (📞212-226-9060; www.earinn.com; 326 Spring St, btwn Washington & Greenwich Sts, SoHo; ⏰bar 11:30am-4am, kitchen to 2am; 📶; Ⓢ C/E to Spring St)

La Compagnie des Vins Surnaturels WINE BAR

23 📍 MAP P68, E5

A snug melange of Gallic-themed decor, svelte armchairs and tea lights, La Compagnie des Vins Surnaturels is an offshoot of a Paris bar by the same name. Head sommelier Theo Lieberman steers an impressive, French-heavy wine list, with some 600 drops and no shortage of arresting labels by the glass. A short, sophisticated menu includes housemade charcuterie and duck buns. (📞212-343-3660; www.compagnienyc.com; 249 Centre St, btwn Broome & Grand Sts, Nolita; ⏰5pm-1am Mon-Wed, to 2am Thu & Fri, 3pm-2am Sat, noon-1am Sun; Ⓢ6 to Spring St; R/W to Prince St)

Public Theater

©SUGI/SHUTTERSTOCK ©

Spring Lounge

BAR

24 🚇 MAP P68, E5

This neon-red rebel has never let anything get in the way of a good time. In Prohibition days, it peddled buckets of beer. In the '60s its basement was a gambling den. These days, it's best known for its kooky stuffed sharks, early-start regulars and come-one, come-all late-night revelry. Perfect last stop on a bar-hopping tour of the neighborhood. (☏212-965-1774; www.thespringlounge.com; 48 Spring St, at Mulberry St, Nolita; ⏰8am-4am Mon-Sat, from noon Sun; 🚇6 to Spring St; R/W to Prince St)

Jimmy

COCKTAIL BAR

25 🚇 MAP P68, B6

Lofted atop the James New York hotel in SoHo, Jimmy is a sky-high hangout with sweeping views of the city below. The summer months teem with tipsy patrons who spill out onto the open deck; in cooler weather, drinks are slung indoors from the centrally anchored bar guarded by floor-to-ceiling windows. An outdoor pool adds to the fun. (☏212-201-9118; www.jimmysoho.com; 15 Thompson St, at Grand St, SoHo; ⏰5pm-1am Mon-Wed, to 2am Thu & Fri, 3pm-2am Sat, 3pm-1am Sun; 🚇A/C/E, 1 to Canal St)

Joe's Pub

Part bar, part cabaret and performance venue, intimate **Joe's Pub** (Map p68, E1; ☏212-539-8778, tickets 212-967-7555; www.joespub.com; Public Theater, 425 Lafayette St, btwn Astor Pl & 4th St, NoHo; 🚇6 to Astor Pl; R/W to 8th St-NYU) serves up both emerging acts and top-shelf performers. Past entertainers have included Patti LuPone, Amy Schumer, the late Leonard Cohen and British singer Adele. Entrance is through the Public Theater.

Entertainment

Public Theater

LIVE PERFORMANCE

26 ⭐ MAP P68, E1

This legendary theater was founded as the Shakespeare Workshop back in 1954 and has launched some of New York's big hits, including *Hamilton* in 2015. Today, you'll find a lineup of innovative programming as well as reimagined classics, with Shakespeare in heavy rotation. Speaking of the bard, the Public also stages star-studded Shakespeare in the Park performances during the summer. (☏212-539-8500, tickets 212-967-7555; www.publictheater.org; 425 Lafayette St, btwn Astor Pl & 4th St, NoHo; 🚇6 to Astor Pl; R/W to 8th St-NYU)

Film Forum

This **nonprofit cinema** (Map p68, A3; 212-727-8110; www. filmforum.org; 209 W Houston St, btwn Varick St & Sixth Ave, SoHo; adult/child $15/9; noon-midnight; 1 to Houston St) shows an astounding array of independent films, revivals and career retrospectives from greats such as Orson Welles. Showings often include director talks or other film-themed discussions for hardcore cinephiles. In 2018, the cinema upgraded its theaters to improve the seating, leg room and sight lines, and expanded to add a fourth screen.

Shopping

Glossier Flagship   COSMETICS

27 MAP P68, D7

Initially established as an online beauty retailer, Glossier (franco-phonetically pronounced glo-see-eh) now beckons fans to its brick-and-mortar flagship, where the queue regularly runs beyond the Lafayette St storefront. Once inside, ascend red quartz stairs to the rosy, high-sheen showroom awash with Insta-worthy aesthetics like diffused light, polished concrete, pale-pink plaster and cushy banquette seating that resembles red lips. (www.glossier. com; 123 Lafayette St, SoHo; 11am-

9pm Mon-Sat, to 8pm Sun; 6; J/Z to Canal St)

Galeria Melissa   SHOES

28 MAP P68, D5

This Brazilian designer specializes in downpour-friendly plastic footwear. Recyclable, sustainable, stylish – women's and kids' shoes run the gamut from mod sandals to brogues, runners and, of course, boots. (212-775-1950; www.melissa. com.br/us/galerias/ny; 500 Broadway, btwn Broome & Spring Sts, SoHo; 10am-7pm Mon-Fri, to 8pm Sat, 11am-7pm Sun; ; 6 to Spring St, R/W to Prince St)

McNally Jackson   BOOKS

29 MAP P68, E4

Bustling indie MJ stocks an excellent selection of magazines and books, covering contemporary fiction, food writing, architecture and design, art and history. If you can score a seat, the in-store cafe is a fine spot to settle in with some reading material or to catch one of the frequent readings and book signings held here. (212-274-1160; www.mcnallyjackson.com; 52 Prince St, btwn Lafayette & Mulberry Sts, Nolita; 10am-10pm Mon-Sat, to 9pm Sun; R/W to Prince St; 6 to Spring St)

Resurrection   VINTAGE

30 MAP P68, E2

Resurrection gives new life to cutting-edge designs from past decades. Striking, mint-condition pieces cover the eras of mod, glam-rock and new-wave design, and design deities such as Marc Jacobs have dropped by for inspiration. Top picks include Halston dresses, Courrèges coats and Jack Boyd jewelry. (☎212-625-1374; www.resurrectionvintage.com; 45 Great Jones St, btwn Lafayette & Bowery Sts, NoHo; ☉10am-6pm Mon-Fri; Ⓢ6 to Spring St; N/R to Prince St)

3x1

FASHION & ACCESSORIES

31 Ⓐ MAP P68, C6

Design your most flattering pair of jeans at this bespoke denim factory/showroom, with three levels of service. Quick, on-the-spot 'ready-to-wear' lets you choose the hem for ready-to-wear denim (women's from $200, men's from $265); 'custom' has you choose the fabric and detailing for an existing fit ($625 to $1200); and 'full bespoke' ($1800) designs your perfect pair from scratch. (☎212-391-6969; www.3x1.us; 15 Mercer St, btwn Howard & Grand Sts, SoHo; ☉11am-7pm Mon-Sat, noon-6pm Sun; Ⓢ N/Q/R/W, J/Z, 6 to Canal St)

Opening Ceremony

FASHION & ACCESSORIES

32 Ⓐ MAP P68, D6

Opening Ceremony is famed for its A-list indie and streetwear labels. It showcases a changing roster of names from across the globe, both established and emerging, for men, women and unisex; complementing them are Opening Ceremony's

Glossier Flagship

own avant-garde creations. No matter who's hanging on the racks, you can always expect showstopping, 'where-did-you-get-that?!' threads that are refreshingly unexpected. (212-219-2688; www.openingceremony.com; 35 Howard St, btwn Broadway & Lafayette St, SoHo; 11am-8pm Mon-Sat, noon-7pm Sun; N/Q/R/W, J/Z, 6 wto Canal St)

Housing Works Bookstore

BOOKS

33 MAP P68, D3

Relaxed, earthy and featuring a great selection of secondhand books, vinyl, CDs and comics you can buy for a good cause (proceeds go to the city's HIV-positive homeless population), this creaky hideaway is a very local place to while away a few quiet afternoon hours browsing, sitting in the on-site cafe, or rummaging in its adjoining thrift store. (212-334-3324; www.housingworks.org/locations/bookstore-cafe; 126 Crosby St, btwn E Houston & Prince Sts, SoHo; 10am-9pm Mon-Thu, to 6pm Fri-Sun; B/D/F/M to Broadway-Lafayette St; N/R to Prince St)

Fong On

FOOD

34 MAP P68, F8

Shuttering after an 80-plus-year run, family-operated tofu purveyor Fong Inn Two recently got a reboot. Catering to both a new generation and devoted, longtime locals at the Eng family's original location, son Paul has recreated homemade tofu, soy milk, *bai tang gao* (a sweet, rice cake) *dau fu fa* (a syrupy tofu pudding) and more. (917-261-7222;

Housing Works Bookstore

ED ROONEY/ALAMY STOCK PHOTO ©

Shopping in SoHo & Chinatown

SoHo bursts at its fashionable seams with stores big and small. Hit Broadway for Main St chains, shoe shops and jean outlets, or the streets to the west for higher-end fashion and accessories. Over on Lafayette, shops cater to the DJ and skate crowds with indie labels and vintage thrown into the mix. Style fiends hyperventilate over SoHo's fashion-conscious streets but serious shopaholics should consult the city's in-the-know retail blogs before hitting SoHo and surrounds – there's always some sort of 'sample sale' or offer going on, or a new boutique showcasing fresh talent. Try thestylishcity. com, www.thecut.com and www.the12ishstyle.com.

If indie-chic is your thing, continue east to Nolita, home of tiny jewel-box boutiques selling unique threads, kicks and accessories. Mott St is best for browsing, followed by Mulberry and Elizabeth.

For medicinal herbs, exotic fruits, woks and Chinese teapots, scour the frenetic streets of Chinatown.

81 Division St, Chinatown; ⊙11am-7pm Tue-Sun; **S** F to East Broadway)

New York Shaving Company   HEALTH & WELLNESS

35 🔒 MAP P68, F4

This lovely shop was founded by John Scala, a Brooklyn-born Sicilian. Cabinets display grooming products, like beard creams, shaving gels and razor kits, as well as colognes. (⏍212-334-9495; www.nyshavingcompany.com; 202b Elizabeth St, btwn Prince & Spring Sts, Nolita; ⊙11am-8pm Mon-Fri, from 10am Sat, 11am-7pm Sun; **S** 6 to Spring St, J/Z to Bowery)

Rag & Bone   FASHION & ACCESSORIES

36 🔒 MAP P68, D4

Downtown label Rag & Bone is a hit with many of New York's sharpest dressers – both men and women. Pieces range from clean-cut shirts and blazers and graphic tees to monochromatic sweaters, featherlight strappy dresses, leather goods and Rag & Bone's highly prized jeans. Accessories include shoes, hats, bags and wallets. (⏍212-219-2204; www.rag-bone.com; 117-119 Mercer St, btwn Prince & Spring Sts, SoHo; ⊙11am-8pm Mon-Sat, to 7pm Sun; **S** R/W to Prince St)

Explore

East Village & the Lower East Side

Generations of immigrants began their American adventure in this low-rent landing place. Today, these areas buzz with bohemian energy, offering some of the city's finest bars and indie boutiques, though amid some vestigial grittiness. New development poses an inevitable threat, but there are still plenty of remnants of the 'authentic' Lower East Side.

The Short List

○ **Lower East Side Tenement Museum (p90)** *Witnessing the shockingly cramped conditions of 19th-century immigrants.*

○ **New Museum of Contemporary Art (p90)** *Appreciating the mind-bending iterations of art across myriad media.*

○ **St Marks Place (p91)** *Browsing knickknack shops and sake bars, then exploring the side streets.*

○ **Alphabet City (p91)** *Hitting up cocktail lounges and peeking into lush community gardens.*

○ **Essex Market (p97)** *Sampling international cuisines at this spacious new food hall and market.*

Getting There & Around

Ⓢ For the East Village, take the L to First or Third Aves, the 6 to Astor Pl or the F to Second Ave. For the Lower East Side, take the B/D to Grand St or the F or J/M/Z to Delancey-Essex Sts.

🚌 The M14, M21 and B39 buses run across 14th, Houston and Delancey Sts, respectively.

Neighborhood Map on p88

St Marks Place (p91) BEN BRYANT/SHUTTERSTOCK ©

Walking Tour 🥾

East Village Cultural Histories

The East Village has a long history as home to successive waves of communities from NYC's multicultural melting pot, remnants of which can still be seen on its streets.

Walk Facts

Start St Marks Pl
End Tompkins Square Park
Length 1 mile; 1¼ hours

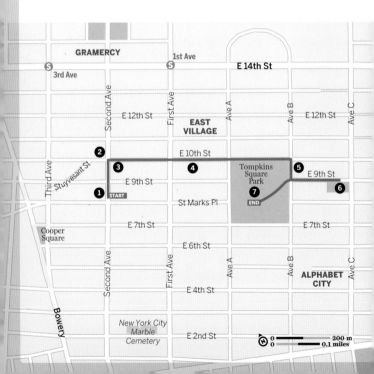

❶ German Library & Clinic

On Second Ave look for the ornate terra-cotta facades of a public library and a former medical clinic (now offices) at Nos 135 and 137; built in 1884, they served the sizable German immigrant population that lived here back when the neighborhood was nick-named 'Kleindeutschland' (Little Germany).

❷ St Mark's Church in-the-Bowery

In 1660 Dutch colonial governor Peter Stuyvesant built his family chapel on the site of this **church** (☎212-674-6377; www.stmarks bowery.org; 131 E 10th St, at Second Ave, East Village; ◷10am-6pm Mon-Fri; Ⓢ L to 3rd Ave, 6 to Astor Pl). Stuyvesant is buried in the crypt beneath), making this NYC's oldest religious site still in use.

❸ Yiddish Theater Memorial

Set into the pavement at the southeast corner of E 10th St and Second Ave are the names of actors and playwrights from the many Jewish theaters that thrived here pre-WWII (including crossover stars Molly Picon and Fyvush Finkel).

❹ Russian & Turkish Baths

Locals have been *shvitzing* in the saunas and steam rooms at these homey public baths (p93) since 1892.

❺ Charlie Parker's House

Head to Ave B between 9th and 10th Sts. No 151 was the home of legendary jazz saxophonist Charlie Parker in the 1950s.

❻ La Plaza Cultural

Take some time to explore the serene oasis of this community garden (p91), one of many that dot 'Loisada,' the strongly Hispanic eastern section of this neighborhood.

❼ Tompkins Square Park

This bustling green space (p92) that has offered respite to all of the neighborhood's various demographics over the years: the German, Jewish and other European immigrants of the 1800s and early 1900s; Alphabet City's post-war Puerto Rican populace; the revolutionaries, musicians and artists of the mid-20th century and today's young professionals and middle-class families.

East Village & the Lower East Side

ALPHABET CITY

Tompkins Square Park

Russian & Turkish Baths

EAST VILLAGE

St Marks Place

Cock

Nowhere

Cooper Square

Broadway

East Village & the Lower East Side

C5 Ave C

37 🔥

Attorney St

Attorney St

B5 Ave B

Clinton St

8 ❌

LOWER
EAST SIDE

Suffolk St

Stanton St

Rivington St

Norfolk St

Essex St

Essex
Market

Williamsburg Bridge

E5 Ave A

Stanton St

Norfolk St

Essex St

44 🏛

Delancey-
Essex Sts

Norfolk St

E **13** ❌

Grand St

For reviews see

🏛	Sights	p90
❌	Eating	p93
🍷	Drinking	p97
🎭	Entertainment	p101
🛍	Shopping	p103

200 m
0.1 miles

25 🔥 E 2nd St

36 ❌

11 ❌

Orchard St

Anastasia
Photo

6 🏛

Ludlow St

9 ❌

Delancey St

**Lower East Side
Tenement Museum** 🏛 **1**

29 🏛

16 ❌

First Ave

40 🏛

35 🏛

Allen St

Allen St

30 🏛

Broome St

5 🏛

Lesley ∙
Heller **34** 🛍

D

17 ❌

15 ❌

21 🏛

E 1st St

Forsyth St

Eldridge St

Forsyth St

20 🏛

New York City
Marble Cemetery

Second Ave

2nd Ave 🚇

Stanton St

Sperone
Westwater

Salon 94 Bowery

12 ❌

Rivington St

Chrystie St

Bowery 🚇

Sara D
Roosevelt
Park

Grand St 🚇

C

Forsyth St

Bowery

Bowery

46 🛍

Bowery

Hole

Bleecker St

E Houston St

Elizabeth St

**New Museum of
Contemporary Art 2** 🏛

Bowery

Rivington St

Grand St

LITTLE
ITALY

Broome St

B

NOHO

Bond St

Broadway

Bleecker St 🚇

Broadway-
Lafayette St 🚇

Jersey St

Prince St

NOLITA

Elizabeth St

Mott St

Spring St

Mulberry St

Kenmare St

Spring St 🚇

Centre St

Lafayette St

Grand St

Broadway

Prince St 🚇

SOHO

Spring St 🚇

A

Sights

Lower East Side Tenement Museum
MUSEUM

1 ◉ MAP P88, D7

This museum allows visitors to briefly inhabit the Lower East Side's heartbreaking, hardscrabble but unexpectedly inspiring heritage. Two remarkably preserved (and minimally restored) 19th-century tenements are the focus of various tours, including the impossibly cramped home and garment shop of the Levine family from Poland, and two immigrant dwellings from the Great Depressions of 1873 and 1929. Visits to the tenement building are available only as part of scheduled guided tours, with many departures each day.

(☎877-975-3786; www.tenement. org; 103 Orchard St, btwn Broome & Delancey Sts, Lower East Side; tours adult/student 6-17yr & senior $29/24; ⊙visitor center 10am-6:30pm Fri-Wed, to 8:30pm Thu; ♿; Ⓢ B/D to Grand St, F, J/M/Z to Delancey-Essex Sts)

New Museum of Contemporary Art
MUSEUM

2 ◉ MAP P88, C6

The New Museum of Contemporary Art is a sight to behold: a seven-story stack of ethereal, off-kilter white boxes (designed by Tokyo-based architects Kazuyo Sejima and Ryue Nishizawa of SANAA and New York firm Gensler) rearing above its medium-rise neighborhood. It was

New Museum of Contemporary Art

LEWIS TSE PUI LUNG/SHUTTERSTOCK ©

Alphabet City Community Gardens

After a stretch of arboreal abstinence in New York City, the community gardens of Alphabet City are breathtaking. A network of gardens was carved out of abandoned lots to provide the low-income and mainly Hispanic neighborhood (nicknamed 'Loisada,' for the local pronunciation of 'Lower East Side') with communal backyards. Trees and flowers were planted, sandboxes were built, found-art sculptures erected and domino games played – all within green spaces wedged between buildings or even claiming entire blocks. The **6th & B Garden** (www.6bgarden.org; E 6th St & Ave B; ⏰1-6pm Sat & Sun Apr-Oct; Ⓢ6 to Astor Pl; L to 1st Ave) is a well-organized space that hosts free music events, workshops and yoga sessions, while three dramatic weeping willows and a koi pond grace the twin plots of **La Plaza Cultural** (www.laplazacultural.com; 674 E 9th St, at Ave C; ⏰10am-7pm Sat & Sun Apr-Oct; Ⓢ F to 2nd Ave; L to 1st Ave). And while some were destroyed – in the face of much protest – to make way for the projects of developers, plenty of green spots have held their ground.

You can visit on weekends from April through October, when most gardens tend to be open to the public; many gardeners are activists within the community and are a good source of information about local politics. A map of all the area's gardens can be found on the website for **Loisada United Neighborhood Gardens** (www.lungsnyc.org).

a long-awaited breath of fresh air along what was a completely gritty Bowery strip when it arrived back in 2007 – since the museum's opening, many glossy new constructions have joined it, quickly transforming this once down-and-out area. (📞212-219-1222; www.newmuseum.org; 235 Bowery, btwn Stanton & Rivington Sts, Lower East Side; adult/child $18/free, 7-9pm Thu by donation; ⏰11am-6pm Tue, Wed & Fri-Sun, to 9pm Thu; ♿; Ⓢ F to 2nd Ave, R/W to Prince St, J/Z to Bowery, 6 to Spring St)

St Marks Place
STREET

3 ◎ MAP P88, C3

One of the most magical things about New York is that every street tells a story, from the action unfurling before your eyes to the dense history hidden behind colorful facades. St Marks Pl is one of the best strips of pavement in the city for storytelling, as almost every building on these hallowed blocks is rife with tales from a time when the East Village embodied creative bohemianism. (St Marks Pl, Ave A to Third Ave, East Village; Ⓢ6 to Astor Pl, L to 3rd Ave or 1st Ave, F to 2nd Ave)

Lower East Side Art Galleries

Though Chelsea may be the heavy hitter when it comes to the New York gallery scene, the Lower East Side has dozens of quality showplaces. One of the early pioneers, the **Sperone Westwater gallery** (Map p88, B6; 212-999-7337; www.speronewestwater.com; 257 Bowery, btwn E Houston & Stanton Sts; 10am-6pm Mon-Fri; F to 2nd Ave), which opened in 1975, represents art-world darlings, such as William Wegman and Richard Long, and its new home was designed by the famed Norman Foster, who's already made a splash in NYC with his designs for the Hearst Building and David Geffen Hall (formerly Avery Fisher Hall). Near the **New Museum of Contemporary Art** (p90) is the 4000-sq-ft **Hole** (Map p88, B5; 212-466-1100; www.theholenyc.com; 312 Bowery, at Bleecker St; noon-7pm Tue-Sun; 6 to Bleeker St; B/D/F/M to Broadway-Lafayette St) – known as much for its art as for its rowdy openings that gather both scenesters of the downtown art circuit and well-known faces, such as Courtney Love and Salman Rushdie.

Broome St between Chrystie and Bowery has galleries such as **Con Artist Collective** and **Jack Hanley** right next door to one another, while another buzzing strip of galleries runs down Orchard St between Rivington and Canal Sts, including **Lesley Heller** (Map p88, D8; 212-410-6120; www.lesleyheller.com; 54 Orchard St, btwn Grand & Hester Sts; 11am-6pm Wed-Sat, from noon Sun; B/D to Grand St; F to East Broadway).

Tompkins Square Park
PARK

4 MAP P88, E3

This 10.5-acre park dating from 1879 is like a friendly town square for locals, who gather for chess at concrete tables, picnics on the lawn, and spontaneous guitar or drum jams on various grassy knolls. It's also the site of basketball courts, a fun-to-watch dog run (a fenced-in area where humans can unleash their canines), a mini–public swimming pool for kids, frequent summer concerts and an always-lively playground. (www.nycgovparks.org; btwn E 7th & E 10th Sts & Aves A & B, East Village; 6am-midnight; ; 6 to Astor Pl)

Museum at Eldridge Street Synagogue
MUSEUM

5 MAP P88, D8

This landmark house of worship, built in 1887, was a center

of Jewish life before suffering a decline in the congregation in the late 1920s. After WWII, the main sanctuary was closed off and services relocated to the basement. The badly deteriorated synagogue was restored following a 20-year-long, $20-million restoration that was completed in 2007, and it now shines with its original splendor – it's a real stunner. Admission includes a guided tour, which departs hourly (last one is 4pm). (📞 212-219-0302; www.eldridgestreet.org; 12 Eldridge St, btwn Canal & Division Sts, Lower East Side; adult/child $14/8, Mon pay what you wish; 🕑 10am-5pm Sun-Thu, to 3pm Fri; 🚇 F to East Broadway, B/D to Grand St)

Anastasia Photo

GALLERY

6 ◉ MAP P88, D6

This small gallery specializes in documentary photography and photojournalism. Expect evocative, thought-provoking works covering subjects such as poverty in rural America, the ravages of war and disappearing cultures in Africa. Works are beautifully shot, and the staff member on hand can give a meaningful context to the images. (📞 212-677-9725; www.anastasia-photo.com; 143 Ludlow St, btwn Stanton & Rivington Sts, Lower East Side; 🕑 10am-6pm Tue-Sat; 🚇 F, J/M/Z to Delancey-Essex Sts)

Russian & Turkish Baths

BATHHOUSE

7 ◉ MAP P88, D2

Since 1892 this cramped, grungy downtown spa has been drawing a polyglot and eclectic mix: actors, students, Russian regulars and old-school locals, who strip down to their skivvies (or the roomy cotton shorts provided) and rotate between steam baths, an ice-cold plunge pool, a sauna and the sun deck. (📞 212-674-9250; www.russianturkishbaths.com; 268 E 10th St, btwn First Ave & Ave A, East Village; full-day visit $52; 🕑 noon-10pm Mon, Tue, Thu & Fri, from 10am Wed, from 9am Sun; 🚇 L to 1st Ave, 6 to Astor Pl)

Eating

Ivan Ramen

RAMEN $$

8 ⊗ MAP P88, E6

After creating two thriving ramen spots in Tokyo, Long Islander Ivan Orkin brought his talents back home. Few can agree about NYC's best ramen, but this intimate shop, where solo ramen-lovers sit at the bar watching their bowls take shape, is on every short list. The *tsukumen* (dipping-style) ramen with pickled collard greens and shoyu-glazed pork belly is unbeatable. (📞 646-678-3859; www.ivanramen.com; 25 Clinton St, btwn Stanton & E Houston Sts, Lower East Side; mains $15-21; 🕑 12:30-10pm

East Village & the Lower East Side Eating

Sun-Thu, to 11pm Fri & Sat; **S** F, J/M/Z to Delancey-Essex Sts, F to 2nd Ave)

Russ & Daughters Cafe

JEWISH $$

9 MAP P88, D7

Sit down and feast on shiny boiled bagels and perhaps the best lox (smoked salmon) in the city in all the comfort of an old-school diner, in this extension of the storied Jewish delicatessen Russ & Daughters (p103), just up Orchard St. Aside from thick, smoky fish, there are potato latkes, borscht, eggs plenty of ways, and even chopped liver, if you must. (212-475-4880; www.russand daughterscafe.com; 127 Orchard St, btwn Delancey & Rivington Sts, Lower East Side; mains $18-23; 9am-10pm Mon-Fri, from 8am Sat & Sun; **S** F, J/M/Z to Delancey-Essex Sts)

Veselka

UKRAINIAN $$

10 MAP P88, C3

This beloved vestige of the area's Ukrainian past has been serving up handmade pierogi (cheese, potato or meat dumplings), borscht and goulash since 1954. The cluttered spread of tables is available to loungers and carb-loaders all night long, though it's a great, warming pit stop any time of day, and a haunt for writers, actors and East Village characters. (212-228-9682; www.veselka.com; 144 Second Ave, at E 9th St, East Village; mains $13-19; 24hr; **S** 6 to Astor Pl, L to 3rd Ave)

Katz's Delicatessen

DELI $$

11 MAP P88, D5

Though visitors won't find many remnants of the classic, old-world Jewish Lower East Side dining scene, there are a few stellar holdouts – among them Katz's Delicatessen, where Meg Ryan faked her famous orgasm in the 1989 movie *When Harry Met Sally*. If you love classic deli grub like pastrami and salami on rye, it just might have the same effect on you. (212-254-2246; www.katzsdelicates sen.com; 205 E Houston St, at Ludlow St, Lower East Side; sandwiches $12-23.50; 8am-10:45pm Mon-Wed, to 2:45am Thu, from 8am Fri, 24hr Sat, to 10:45pm Sun; **S** F to 2nd Ave)

Freemans

AMERICAN $$$

12 MAP P88, C6

Tucked at the end of Freeman Alley, this charmingly located and somewhat labyrinthine place draws a mostly hipster crowd who gather around the wooden tables to sip overflowing cocktails and nibble on dishes like roast chicken or slow-poached halibut. Potted plants and taxidermied antlers lend an endearing rustic-cabin vibe – a charming escape from the bustle (when it isn't crowded inside). (212-420-0012; www.free mansrestaurant.com; Freeman Alley, off Rivington St, Lower East Side; mains lunch $16-34, dinner $27-38; 11am-11pm Mon-Thu, to 1am Fri, 10am-1am Sat, 10am-11pm Sun; **S** F to 2nd Ave)

Kossar's Bagels & Bialys

JEWISH $

13  MAP P88, E8

Since 1936 Kossar's has been serving up Jewish baked goods like bagels, chocolate and cinnamon babka (a bread-like cake) and bialys. What's a bialy you ask? Originating from Bialystok, Poland, it's a slightly flattened bread roll with a middle indent filled with roast onions or garlic – and it's delicious! Newer filling styles include olives and sun-dried tomatoes and pesto. (212-473-4810; www.kossars.com; 367 Grand St, Lower East Side; baked goods from $1.15; 6am-6pm; F/M, J/Z to Delancey-Essex Sts)

Dun-Well Doughnuts

PASTRIES $

14 MAP P88, D3

Brooklyn's finest artisanal vegan doughnuts have made their way over the East River to this pocket-sized shop on St Marks Pl. Baked daily from organic ingredients, the luscious treats come in flavors both classic (glazed, cinnamon, chocolate) and bespoke (matcha pecan, French toast, peanut butter and strawberry). Wash them down with a fresh-pulled espresso. (646-998-5462; www.dunwelldoughnuts.com; 102 St Marks Pl, btwn First Ave & Ave A, East Village; doughnuts from $2.50; 8am-9pm Mon-Thu, to 10pm Fri, 9am-10pm Sat, 9am-9pm Sun; 6 to Astor Pl)

East Village & the Lower East Side Eating

Freemans

Yonah Schimmel Knish Bakery

JEWISH $

15 MAP P88, C5

Step back in time at this bakery-cafe that's been selling old-fashioned Jewish knishes – a pocket of baked dough filled with mashed potatoes, buckwheat, cabbage, spinach, blueberries and sweet cheese or other fillings – since 1910. Other classic dishes (potato pancakes, apple strudel) are available, as are egg cream and lime rickey sodas. It doesn't get more authentic than this. (☏212-477-2858; www.knishery.com; 137 E Houston St, at Forsyth St, Lower East Side; knishes $4-5; ⏱10am-7pm Mon-Sun; ☝; ⑤F to Second Ave)

An Choi

VIETNAMESE $

16 MAP P88, D8

With faded communist party posters on the wall and a bar that looks like it was lifted out of the '70s, An Choi has cultivated a throwback style that denizens of the East Village love. It doesn't hurt that the food, simple Vietnamese dishes like pho (noodle soup) and banh mi (baguette) sandwiches, is tasty and not too expensive given the hipster credentials. (☏212-226-3700; http://anchoinyc.com; 85 Orchard St, btwn Broome & Grand Sts, Lower East Side; banh mi $11-15, mains $13-18; ⏱6pm-10:30pm Mon, from noon Tue-Thu, noon-11pm Fri & Sat, noon-10pm Sun; ⑤B/D to Grand St, F, J/M/Z to Delancey-Essex Sts)

Prune

AMERICAN $$

17 MAP P88, D5

Expect lines around the block on the weekend, when the hungover show up to cure their ills with Prune's brunches and excellent Bloody Marys (in a dozen varieties). The small room is always busy as diners pour in for grilled trout with mint-and-almond salsa, seared duck breast and rich sweetbreads. Reservations available for dinner and lunch only. (☏212-677-6221; www.prunerestaurant.com; 54 E 1st St, btwn First & Second Aves, East Village; dinner $19-28, brunch $15-19; ⏱noon-11pm Mon-Fri, 10am-3:30pm & 5:30-11pm Sat & Sun; ⑤F to 2nd Ave)

Luzzo's

PIZZA $$

18 MAP P88, D1

Fan-favorite Luzzo's occupies a thin, rustically designed sliver of real estate in the East Village, which is stuffed to the gills each evening as discerning diners feast on thin-crust pizzas, kissed with ripe tomatoes and cooked in a coal-fired stove. Cash only. (☏212-473-7447; www.luzzosgroup.com; 211 First Ave, btwn E 12th & 13th Sts, East Village; pizzas $18-20; ⏱noon-11pm; ⑤L to 1st Ave)

Cafe Mogador

MOROCCAN $$

19 MAP P88, D3

Mogador is a long-running East Village classic, serving fluffy piles of couscous, chargrilled lamb and *merguez* (a spicy lamb or beef sausage) with basmati rice and

Arabic salad, as well as satisfying platters of hummus with chickpeas, tomato and parsley. The standouts, however, are the tagines – fragrantly spiced, claypot-simmered chicken or lamb dishes in four different sauces. (☎ 212-677-2226; www.cafemogador.com; 101 St Marks Pl, btwn First Ave & Ave A, East Village; mains $17-24; ⏱ 9am-11:30pm Sun-Thu, to midnight Fri & Sat; ⓢ 6 to Astor Pl)

Drinking

Flower Shop   BAR

20 😊 MAP P88, D8

Take the stairs under the humming restaurant of the same name to discover an eclectically furnished basement bar of such meticulously retro sensibility that you'll feel you've stumbled into a mash-up of your dad's pool room and your grandparents' 'best' room. The randomly assembled photos and posters often raise a smile, while flowery banquettes and good cocktails encourage lingering. (☎ 212-257-4072; www.theflowershopnyc.com; 107 Eldridge St, btwn Grand & Broome Sts, Lower East Side; ⏱ 5pm-midnight Sun & Mon, to 2am Tue-Sat; ⓢ B/D to Grand St, J/Z to Bowery)

Bar Goto   COCKTAIL BAR

21 😊 MAP P88, C6

Maverick mixologist Kenta Goto has cocktail connoisseurs spellbound at his eponymous, intimate hot spot. Expect meticulous, elegant drinks that draw on Goto's

Essex Market

Founded in 1940 in a cramped building across Delancey St, the wide-ranging specialty food-and-dining hall **Essex Market** (Map p88, E7; www.essexmarket.nyc; 115 Delancey St, at Essex St, Lower East Side; ⏱ 8am-8pm Mon-Sat, 10am-8pm Sun; ♿; ⓢ F, J/M/Z to Delancey-Essex Sts) recently moved into expansive new digs. Browse fresh seafood, meats and artisanal cheeses before taking lunch upstairs to sunny, open-atrium seating. Vendors offer Scandinavian smoked fish, traditional Dominican food, Japanese bentos, Thai chicken, massive sandwiches, gourmet ice cream and much more.

Japanese heritage (the Umami Mary, with vodka, shiitake, dashi, miso, lemon, tomato and Clamato, is inspired), paired with authentic Japanese comfort bites, such as *okonomiyaki* (savory cabbage pancakes). (☎ 212-475-4411; www.bargoto.com; 245 Eldridge St, btwn E Houston & Stanton Sts, Lower East Side; ⏱ 5pm-midnight Tue-Thu & Sun, to 2am Fri & Sat; ⓢ F to 2nd Ave)

PDT   BAR

22 😊 MAP P88, D3

PDT ('Please Don't Tell') scores high on novelty. Pick up the receiver in the phone booth at the hot-dog shop Crif Dogs; once you're given the OK (reservations are recommended to avoid being turned away), the wall swings open and you step into an intimate, low-lit bar with the odd animal head on the wall and first-rate cocktails. (☎212-614-0386; www.pdtnyc.com; 113 St Marks Pl, btwn Ave A & First Ave, East Village; ◷6pm-2am Sun-Thu, to 4am Fri & Sat; ⑤6 to Astor Pl, L to 1st Ave)

Rue B
BAR

23 🚇 MAP P88, E2

There's live jazz (and the odd rockabilly group) nightly from 9pm to midnight ($10 cover) at this tiny, amber-lit drinking den on a bar-dappled stretch of Ave B. A celebratory crowd packs the small space – so mind the tight corners, lest the trombonist end up in your lap. Photos and posters of jazz greats and NYC icons enhance the ambience. (☎212-358-1700; www.rueb-nyc.com; 188 Ave B, btwn E 11th & E 12th Sts, East Village; ◷6pm-4am; ⑤L to 1st Ave)

Pouring Ribbons
COCKTAIL BAR

24 🚇 MAP P88, E1

Finding such a well-groomed and classy spot up a flight of stairs in Alphabet City is as refreshing as their drinks. Gimmicks and pretension are kept low; the flavors are exceptional. The encyclopedic cocktail menu could sate any ap-petite. Also, check out what could possibly be the largest collection

of Chartreuse in NYC. (☎917-656-6788; www.pouringribbons.com; 225 Ave B, 2nd fl, btwn E 13th & 14th Sts, East Village; ◷6pm-2am; ⑤L to 1st Ave)

Berlin
CLUB

25 🚇 MAP P88, D5

This brick-vaulted cavern beneath Ave A does its best to hide – access is through an unmarked door around the corner from the bar that seems to occupy Berlin's address, then steep stairs lead down into a dim, riotous indie lair. Once you're in, enjoy a night of rock, funk, disco, house and other party tunes in close proximity with your fellow revelers. (☎reservations 347-586-7247; www.berlinundera.com; 25 Ave A, btwn E 1st & E 2nd Sts, East Village; occasional cover $5; ◷8pm-2am Sun-Thu, to 4am Fri & Sat; ⑤F to 2nd Ave)

Angel's Share
BAR

26 🚇 MAP P88, B3

Show up early and snag a seat at this hidden gem, behind a Japanese restaurant on the same floor. It's quiet and elegant, with seriously talented mixologists serving up creative cocktails, plus a top-flight collection of whiskeys. You can't stay if you don't have a table or a seat at the bar, and they tend to go fast. (☎212-777-5415; 6 Stuyvesant St, 2nd fl, near Third Ave & E 9th St, East Village; ◷6pm-1:30am Sun-Wed, to 2am Thu, to 2:30am Fri & Sat; ⑤6 to Astor Pl)

Otto's Shrunken Head
BAR

27 MAP P88, E1

Sling yourself into one of the curved vinyl booths at this rockabilly tiki bar with a Mai Tai or Zombie served up in a classic tiki mug (yours to keep for an extra $6). The back room hosts nightly live music, comedy, drag shows and the like, while DJs spin up front, and there's never a cover. (212-228-2240; www.ottosshrunkenhead.com; 538 E 14th St, near Ave B, East Village; 2pm-4am; L to 1st Ave)

Phoenix
GAY & LESBIAN

28 MAP P88, D1

Literally risen from the ashes of its predecessor, The Bar (which burned down), The Phoenix is less 'divey' than it once was, but it's just as friendly. There's also happy hour from 2pm to 8pm, a pool table, karaoke and trivia nights. Check the website for a variety of theme nights. (212-477-9979; www.phoenixbarnyc.com; 447 E 13th St, btwn First Ave & Ave A, East Village; 2pm-4am; L to 1st Ave)

Proletariat
BAR

The cognoscenti of NYC's beer world pack this tiny shop-front bar just west of Tompkins Square Park, next to Dun-Well Doughnuts (see 14 Map p88. D3). Promising 'rare, new and unusual beers,' Proletariat delivers the goods with a changing lineup of brews you won't find elsewhere. Recent hits have included Brooklyn and New Jersey drafts from artisanal brewers. (www.proletariatny.com; 102 St Marks Pl, btwn Ave

Yonah Schimmel Knish Bakery (p96)

DANIEL M SILVA/SHUTTERSTOCK ©

Another Side of Gay NYC

If Chelsea is a muscly, over-achieving jock, then the Lower East Side is his wayward, punk, younger brother. Amid the frat dives and cocktail lounges you'll find many gay bars catering to guys who prefer flannels and scruff to tank tops and six-pack abs. **Nowhere** (Map p88, C1; 212-477-4744; www.nowherebarnyc.com; 322 E 14th St, btwn First & Second Aves; 3pm-4am; SL to 1st Ave) and **Phoenix** (p99) are great places to meet some new friendly faces, while the **Cock** (Map p88, C4; 93 Second Ave, btwn E 5th & E 6th Sts; 9pm-4am Mon & Tue, from 6pm Wed-Sun; SF/M to 2nd Ave) caters to a friskier crowd. The drinks are also typically much cheaper.

A & First Ave, East Village; 5pm-2am Mon-Thu, from 2pm Fri & Sat, 2pm-midnight Sun; SL to 1st Ave)

Ten Bells
BAR

29 MAP P88, D8

This charmingly tucked-away tapas bar has a grotto-like design, with flickering candles, dark tin ceilings, brick walls and a U-shaped bar that's an ideal setting for a conversation with a new friend. (212-228-4450; www.tenbellsnyc.com; 247 Broome St, btwn Ludlow & Orchard Sts, Lower East Side; 5pm-

2am Mon-Fri, from 3pm Sat & Sun; SF, J/M/Z to Delancey-Essex Sts)

Attaboy
COCKTAIL BAR

30 MAP P88, D7

One of those no-door-sign, speakeasy-vibe bars that are two-a-penny these days, this one is a notch above, serving knockout artisanal cocktails that will set you back $17 each. There is no menu, so let the expert bartenders guide you. (www.attaboy.us; 134 Eldridge St, btwn Delancey & Broome Sts, Lower East Side; 6pm-4am; SB/D to Grand St)

Abraço
CAFE

31 MAP P88, D3

Abraço is an East Village refuge in an open, ground-level space that serves up perfectly prepared espressos and lattes alongside housemade sweets. Find a table and sip your nicely balanced cappuccino while inhaling a slice of their dangerously addictive olive-oil cake. (www.abraconyc.com; 81 E 7th St, btwn First & Second Aves, East Village; 8am-10pm Tue-Sat, 9am-6pm Sun; SF to 2nd Ave; L to 1st Ave; 6 to Astor Pl)

Death & Co
COCKTAIL BAR

32 MAP P88, D3

Despite the morbid name, this award-winning cocktail bar is full of life. Relax in the dim, stylish interior and let the skilled bartenders shake, rattle and roll some of the most perfect cocktails in town (classics and new creations from $17). It's usually packed – if there's no room they'll take your number and call once there is. (☎212-388-0882; www.deathand company.com; 433 E 6th St, btwn First Ave & Ave A, East Village; ⏰6pm-2am Sun-Thu, to 3am Fri & Sat; Ⓢ F to 2nd Ave, L to 1st Ave)

Amor y Amargo   BAR

33 🍸 MAP P88, D3

'Love and Bitters' is a tiny but powerful specialist in crafty cocktails, showcasing its namesake selection of bitters. Ask the knowledgeable barkeeps for their advice on flavors. You won't be disappointed. (☎212-614-6818; www.amoryamargo ny.com; 443 E 6th St, btwn Ave A & First Ave, East Village; ⏰5pm-1am Sun-Thu,

to 3am Fri & Sat; Ⓢ F to 2nd Ave; L to 1st Ave; 6 to Astor Pl)

Entertainment

Metrograph   CINEMA

34 ⭐ MAP P88, D8

The Lower East Side hasn't gentrified this far yet, giving the owners of this true movie mecca the chance to acquire a building adequate for their vision. It has two screens, both a state-of-the-art digital projector and an old 35mm reel-to-reel. The expertly curated films often form series on subjects such as Japanese Studio Ghibli or provocateur Gasper Noé. (☎212-660-0312; www.metrograph. com; 7 Ludlow St, btwn Canal & Hester Sts, Lower East Side; tickets $15; ⏰11am-midnight Sun-Wed, to 2am Fri

Angel's Share (p98)

& Sat; 📶; **S** F to East Broadway, B/D to Grand St)

Rockwood Music Hall

LIVE MUSIC

35 ✪ MAP P88, D6

Opened by indie rocker Ken Rockwood, this breadbox-size concert space has three stages and a rapid-fire flow of bands and singer-songwriters. If cash is tight, try stage 1, which has free shows, with a maximum of one hour per band (die-hards can see five or more performances a night). Music kicks off at 3pm on weekends and 6pm on weeknights. (📞212-477-4155; www.rockwoodmusichall.com; 196 Allen St, btwn E Houston & Stanton Sts, Lower East Side; 🕐5:30pm-2am Mon-Fri, from 2:30pm Sat & Sun; **S** F to 2nd Ave)

Arlene's Grocery

LIVE MUSIC

36 ✪ MAP P88, D6

This Lower East Side institution (found in a former bodega) has been hosting a wide swath of nightly live music – but especially local rock, punk and alternative bands – since 1995. Everyone from Arcade Fire to The Strokes to Lady Gaga has played here. Upstairs is a separate bar where you can keep the night going after the show. (www.arlenesgrocery.net; 95 Stanton St, btwn Orchard & Ludlow Sts, Lower East Side; cover $8-10; 🕐bar 5pm-4am Sun-Thu, 2pm-4am Fri & Sat; **S** F to 2nd Ave)

Nuyorican Poets Café

LIVE PERFORMANCE

37 ✪ MAP P88, F5

Going strong since 1973, the legendary Nuyorican is home to poetry slams, hip-hop performances, plays, films, dance and music. It's living East Village history but also a vibrant, still-relevant nonprofit arts organization. Check the website for events and buy tickets online for the more-popular weekend shows. Or try out your lyrical skills at Monday's open-mic night (9pm; $8). (📞212-780-9386; www.nuyorican.org; 236 E 3rd St, btwn Aves B & C, East Village; tickets $5-15; **S** F to 2nd Ave)

Performance Space New York

THEATER

38 ✪ MAP P88, D2

Founded in 1980 as Performance Space 122, this cutting-edge theater once housed in an abandoned public school now boasts state-of-the-art performance spaces, artist studios, a new lobby and a roof deck. The bones of the former schoolhouse remain, as does its experimental-theater bona fides: Eric Bogosian, Meredith Monk, the late Spalding Gray and Elevator Repair Service have all performed here. (📞212-477-5829; www.performancespacenewyork.org; 150 First Ave, at E 9th St, East Village; **S** L to 1st Ave, 6 to Astor Pl)

La MaMa ETC
THEATER

39 ⭐ MAP P88, C4

A long-standing home for onstage experimentation (the ETC stands for Experimental Theater Club), La MaMa is now a three-theater complex with a cafe, an art gallery, and a separate studio building that features cutting-edge dramas, sketch comedy and readings of all kinds. There are $10 tickets available for each show, available (until they run out) by booking online. (☏ 212-352-3101; www.lamama.org; 74a E 4th St, btwn Bowery & Second Ave, East Village; tickets from $20; Ⓢ F to 2nd Ave)

Shopping

Russ & Daughters
FOOD

40 🅰 MAP P88, D5

Since 1914 this much-loved deli has served up Eastern European Jewish delicacies, such as caviar, herring, sturgeon and, of course, lox. Proudly owned by four generations of the Russ family, it's a great place to load up for a picnic or stock your fridge with breakfast goodies. Foodies, history buffs and interior designers will love it. (☏ 212-475-4800; www.russand daughters.com; 179 E Houston St, btwn Orchard & Allen Sts, Lower East Side; ⏰ 8am-6pm Fri-Wed, to 7pm Thu; Ⓢ F to 2nd Ave)

Arlene's Grocery

John Varvatos

and bracelets appear almost too precious...until a closer inspection reveals zombies, Godzilla robots, animal heads, dinosaurs and encircling claws – bringing a whole new level of miniaturized complexity to the realm of jewelry. (📞212-388-9045; www.verameat.com; 315 E 9th St, btwn First & Second Aves, East Village; 🕐noon-8pm; 🚇6 to Astor Pl; F/M to 2nd Ave)

No Relation Vintage   VINTAGE

43 🔒 MAP P88, D1

Among the many vintage shops of the East Village, No Relation is a winner for its wide-ranging collections that run the gamut from designer denim and leather jackets to vintage flannels, funky sneakers, plaid shirts, irreverent branded T-shirts, varsity jackets, clutches and more. Sharpen your elbows: hipster crowds flock here on weekends. (L Train Vintage; 📞212-228-5201; www.ltrainvintagenyc.com; 204 First Ave, btwn E 12th & 13th Sts, East Village; 🕐noon-8pm Sun-Thu, to 9pm Fri & Sat; 🚇L to 1st Ave)

Economy Candy   FOOD

44 🔒 MAP P88, E6

Bringing sweetness since 1937, this candy shop is stocked with floor-to-ceiling goods in package and bulk, and is home to some beautiful antique gum machines. You'll find everything from childhood favorites like jelly beans, lollipops, gum balls, Cadbury imports, gummy worms and rock candy, to more grown-up delicacies such as

Kiehl's   COSMETICS

41 🔒 MAP P88, B1

Making and selling skincare products since it opened in NYC as an apothecary in 1851, this Kiehl's flagship store has doubled its shop size and expanded into an international chain, but its personal touch remains – as do the coveted, generous sample sizes. (📞212-677-3171; 109 Third Ave, btwn 13th & 14th Sts, East Village; 🕐10am-9pm Mon-Sat, 11am-7pm Sun; 🚇L to 3rd Ave)

Verameat   JEWELRY

42 🔒 MAP P88, C2

Designer Vera Balyura creates exquisite little pieces with a dark sense of humor in this delightful small shop on 9th St. Tiny, artfully wrought pendants, rings, earrings halvah, green tea bonbons, hand-dipped chocolates, dried ginger and papaya. (☎212-254-1531; www.economycandy.com; 108 Rivington St, at Essex St, Lower East Side; ⏱9am-6pm Tue-Fri, 10am-6pm Sat-Mon; Ⓢ F, J/M/Z to Delancey-Essex Sts)

A-1 Records   MUSIC

45 🔒 MAP P88, D3

One of the last of the many record stores that once graced the East Village, A-1 has been around for over two decades. The cramped aisles, filled with a large selection of jazz, funk and soul, draw vinyl fans and DJs from far and wide. (☎212-473-2870; www.instagram.com/a1recordshop; 439 E 6th St, btwn First Ave & Ave A, East Village; ⏱1-9pm; Ⓢ F/M to 2nd Ave)

John Varvatos   FASHION & ACCESSORIES

46 🔒 MAP P88, B5

Occupying the former location of legendary punk club CBGB, this John Varvatos store goes to great lengths to acknowledge the site's rock-and-roll heritage, with records, high-end audio equipment and even electric guitars for sale alongside JV's denim, leather boots, belts and graphic tees. Sales associates dressed in Varvatos' downtown cool seem far removed from the Bowery's gritty past. (☎212-358-0315; www.johnvarvatos.com; 315 Bowery, btwn E 1st & E 2nd Sts, East Village; ⏱noon-8pm Mon-Fri, from 11am Sat, noon-6pm Sun; Ⓢ F/M to 2nd Ave, 6 to Bleecker St)

Explore

West Village, Chelsea & the Meatpacking District

The West Village's charming, twisty streets and well-preserved town houses offer intimate spaces for dining, drinking and wandering; hugging the river is the Meatpacking District, where Manhattan's young professionals flock to its many clubs and bars. North is Chelsea, home to art galleries and a vibrant gay scene. Meandering 30ft above all is the green-fringed, art-strewn High Line.

The Short List

○ **High Line (p108)** *Packing a picnic lunch from Chelsea Market for a uniquely pastoral moment above the city grid.*

○ **Chelsea Galleries (p110)** *Checking out the city's brightest art stars at top galleries.*

○ **Washington Square Park (p115)** *People-watching at this beloved Greenwich Village gathering spot.*

○ **Rubin Museum of Art (p115)** *Exploring fascinating exhibitions from the Himalayas and beyond.*

○ **Stonewall National Monument (p115)** *Reflecting on the night that sparked the LGBTIQ+ rights movement where it all began.*

Getting There & Around

[S] Sixth Ave, Seventh Ave and Eighth Ave have convenient subway stations, but options slim further west. Take the A/C/E or 1/2/3 lines to 14th St and walk from there, or to W 4th St-Washington Sq for the heart of the Village.

Neighborhood Map on p112

Washington Square Park (p115) MILA PARH/SHUTTERSTOCK ©

Top Experience 📸
Get a Bird's Eye View at the High Line

Snaking through the Meatpacking District at 30ft above street level, this 1.5-mile urban park is a fabulous example of industrial reuse. Once a freight line linking slaughterhouses to the Hudson River, it fell into disuse by the 1980s, only to be resurrected as a green, art-strewn ribbon running between the high-rises, hotels and art galleries flanking it.

◎ MAP P112, C4

www.thehighline.org

Gansevoort St

🕑 7am-11pm Jun-Sep, to 10pm Apr, May, Oct & Nov, to 7pm Dec-Mar

🚌 M14 crosstown along 14th St, M23 along 23rd St, **S** A/C/E, L to 8th Ave-14th St, 1, C/E to 23rd St, 7 to 34th St-Hudson Yards

From Rails to Real Estate

In the early 1900s the western area around the Meatpacking District and Chelsea was the largest industrial section of Manhattan. With street-level freight lines causing disruption and even fatalities – Tenth Ave was nicknamed 'Death Ave' – an elevated freight track was built, and the 'West Side Elevated Line' moved its first train in 1933. As the city developed, the line fell into disuse. Demolition was mooted, but in 1999 a plan was made to convert the rusting, weed-strewn metal viaduct into public green space. In 2009, phase one of the city's most beloved urban-renewal project opened with much ado, and it's been one of New York's star attractions ever since.

Visiting the High Line

Section 1 starts at Gansevoort St and runs parallel to Tenth Ave up to W 20th St. Full of sitting space in various forms – from giant chaises longues to bleacher-like benches – it quickly became the setting for various public works and activities. Over the next several years, the second and third sections opened, bringing the High Line up to 34th St, going up to and around the West Side Rail Yards in a U-like fashion. Here the path widens, offering open views of the Hudson, with rusting, weed-filled railroad tracks running alongside the walkway to evoke the sense of overgrown wilderness in the heart of the metropolis that existed prior to the park's creation. Finally, in 2019, the last remaining section of the original rail structure was completed. Known as the Spur, this stretch extends east to 10th Ave, with a large-scale art space known as the Plinth as its focal point.

Numerous stairways offer access to the park, including at Gansevoort, 14th, 16th, 17th, 20th, 23rd, 26th, 28th, 30th and 34th Sts. There are also elevators at Gansevoort, 14th, 16th, 23rd and 30th Sts.

★ Top Tips

o Beat the crowds by starting early at 30th St or 34th St, wandering south and exiting at 14th St for a bite at Chelsea Market before exploring the West Village. If your tummy's grumbling, tackle the High Line in the reverse direction, gelato in hand.

o The High Line also makes a convenient way to avoid walking through the convoluted streets of the Meatpacking District, especially if there's construction.

✖ Take a Break

o You'll find a wonderland of food vendors behind the brick walls of the Chelsea Market (p114), at the 14th St exit of the High Line.

o If you feel like treating yourself after a long walk, head to the Top of the Standard (p124) for a pricey cocktail with a million-dollar view.

Chelsea Galleries

Local knowledge comes in handy when navigating Chelsea's art spaces – the neighborhood's home to the densest concentration of galleries in NYC. Most lie in the 20s, between Tenth and Eleventh Aves, and open from Tuesday to Saturday (new openings are common on Thursday evening). Pick up Art Info's free Gallery Guide (with map) at most galleries, or visit www.chelseagalleries.nyc.

Walk Facts

Start Paula Cooper Gallery
End Artechouse
Length 1.3mi; three hours
Ⓢ 1, C/E to 23rd St

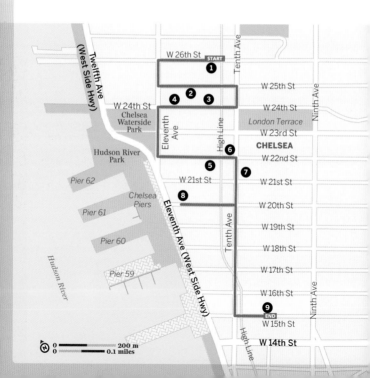

❶ Paula Cooper Gallery

Paula Cooper (📞212-255-1105; www.paulacoopergallery.com; 524 West 26th St, btwn Tenth & Eleventh Aves; ⏰10am-6pm Tue-Sat) focuses on conceptual and minimal art.

❷ Pace Gallery

Eight-story **Pace Gallery** (📞212-421-3292; www.pacegallery.com; 540 W 25th St, btwn Tenth & Eleventh Aves; ⏰10am-6pm Tue-Sat) showcases leading artists of recent years, including Loie Hollowell, Sol LeWitt and David Hockney.

❸ Gladstone Gallery

Famed curator Barbara Gladstone's **gallery** (📞212-206-9300; www.gladstonegallery.com; 515 W 24th St, btwn Tenth & Eleventh Aves, Chelsea; ⏰10am-6pm Mon-Sat) represents contemporaries such as Brits Anish Kapoor and Sarah Lucas.

❹ Gagosian

Global chain **Gagosian** (📞212-741-1111; www.gagosian.com; 555 W 24th St, at Eleventh Ave; ⏰10am-6pm Mon-Sat) rotates through exhibits of greats like Jeff Koons, Andy Warhol and Jean-Michel Basquiat.

❺ Matthew Marks Gallery

Chelsea pioneer **Matthew Marks** (📞212-243-0200; www.matthewmarks.com; 522 W 22nd St, btwn Tenth & Eleventh Aves; ⏰10am-6pm Tue-Sat) exhibits local artists, such as Nan Goldin and Terry Winters.

❻ Tía Pol

Great for a refueling pit stop, **Tía Pol** (📞212-675-8805; www.tiapol.com; 205 Tenth Ave, btwn 22nd & 23rd Sts; small plates $7-16; ⏰5:30-11pm Mon, from noon Tue-Thu, to midnight Fri, from 11am Sat, to 10:30pm Sun) is an intimate place for Basque and Spanish tapas.

❼ 192 Books

This delightful little **bookstore** (📞212-255-4022; www.192books.com; 192 Tenth Ave, btwn W 21st & W 22nd Sts; ⏰11am-7pm) offers literary works, artist monographs and children's books.

❽ David Zwirner

One of the major players in the art world, German curator **David Zwirner** (📞212-517-8677; www.davidzwirner.com; 537 W 20th St, btwn Tenth & Eleventh Aves; ⏰10am-6pm Tue-Sat) stages some of New York's most celebrated shows.

❾ Artechouse

Descend into **Artechouse** (www.artechouse.com/nyc; 439 W 15th St, Chelsea Market; adult/child $24/17; ⏰10am-10pm Sun-Thu, to 11pm Fri & Sat), an immersive center where art and technology converge in large-scale installations.

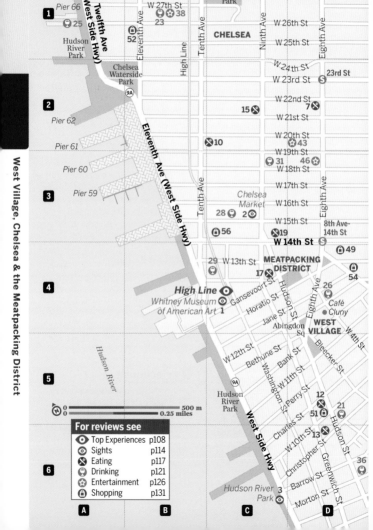

West Village, Chelsea & the Meatpacking District

A B C D

1

Pier 66

25

Hudson
River
Park

Twelfth Ave (West Side Hwy)

W 27th St
23 38

52

Chelsea
Waterside
Park

High Line

Eleventh Ave

Tenth Ave

Chelsea
Park

CHELSEA

W 26th St

W 25th St

W 24th St

W 23rd St

W 22nd St

W 21st St

W 20th St

W 19th St

W 18th St

Ninth Ave

Eighth Ave

23rd St

15

7

43

31   46

2

Pier 62

Pier 61

Pier 60

Pier 59

Eleventh Ave (West Side Hwy)

Tenth Ave

10

3

Chelsea
Market

W 17th St

W 16th St

W 15th St

W 14th St

28   2

56

19

8th Ave-
14th St

49

4

29

17

**MEATPACKING
DISTRICT**

W 13th St

Gansevoort St

Horatio St

Jane St

Abingdon
Sq

Hudson St

Eighth Ave

Greenwich Ave

26

Café
Cluny

**WEST
VILLAGE**

W 4th St

54

High Line

Whitney Museum
of American Art 1

W 12th St

Bethune St

Bank St

Washington St

Perry St

W 11th St

Charles St

W 10th St

Christopher St

Barrow St

Bleecker St

12

51

13

21

Hudson St

Greenwich St

Morton St

36

5

Hudson River

Hudson
River
Park

West Side Hwy

6

Hudson River
Park 3

0   500 m
0   0.25 miles

For reviews see

⊙	Top Experiences	p108
⊙	Sights	p114
⊗	Eating	p117
⊜	Drinking	p121
⊙	Entertainment	p126
⌂	Shopping	p131

A B C D

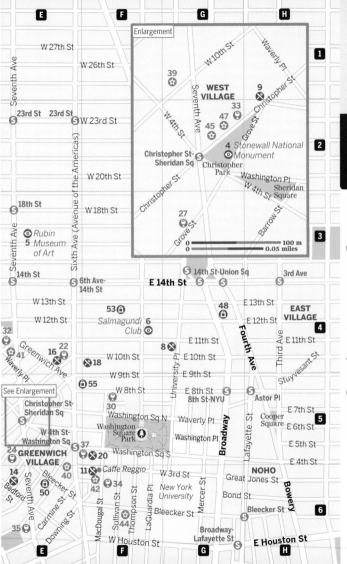

Enlargement

W 27th St

W 26th St

39

Seventh Ave

WEST VILLAGE

W 10th St

Waverly Pl

9

Christopher St

23rd St   23rd St   W 23rd St

33

47

Grove St

45

4 **Stonewall National Monument**

Christopher St-
Sheridan Sq

Christopher
Park

Washington Pl

W 4th St

Sheridan
Square

W 20th St

Christopher St

Barrow St

W 18th St

27

Grove St

18th St

**Rubin
5 Museum
of Art**

0   100 m
0   0.05 miles

Seventh Ave

Sixth Ave (Avenue of the Americas)

14th St

14th St-Union Sq

3rd Ave

6th Ave-
14th St

E 14th St

W 13th St

E 13th St

EAST VILLAGE

W 12th St

53

Salmagundi
Club 6

48

E 12th St

E 11th St

Third Ave

E 11th St

32

Greenwich Ave

16   22

8

W 10th St

E 10th St

Fourth Ave

41

18

W 9th St

E 9th St

Stuyvesant St

55

W 8th St

8th St-NYU

E 8th St

See Enlargement

Christopher St-
Sheridan Sq

30

Washington Sq N

Astor Pl

University Pl

Waverly Pl

Cooper
Square

E 7th St

W 4th St-
Washington Sq

37

Washington
Square
Park

Washington Pl

E 6th St

E 5th St

**GREENWICH
VILLAGE**

24

20

Washington Sq S

Broadway

Lafayette St

E 4th St

14

40

11   Caffe Reggio

W 3rd St

NOHO

50

42

34

Bedford St

Seventh Ave

Bleecker St

Sullivan St

New York
University

Great Jones St

Bowery

Bond St

35

Carmine St

Downing St

44

MacDougal St

Thompson St

LaGuardia Pl

Mercer St

Bleecker St

W Houston St

Broadway-
Lafayette St

Bleecker St

E Houston St

E   F   G   H

1

2

3

4

5

6

Sights

Whitney Museum of American Art
MUSEUM

1 ⊙ MAP P112, C4

After years of construction, the Whitney's downtown location opened to much fanfare in 2015. Anchoring the southern reaches of the High Line (p108), this stunning building – designed by Renzo Piano – provides 63,000 sq ft of space for the museum's unparalleled collection of American art. Inside the light-filled galleries you'll find works by all the greats, including Edward Hopper, Jasper Johns, Georgia O'Keeffe and Mark Rothko. Unlike at many museums, special emphasis is placed on the work of living artists. (📞212-570-3600; www.whitney.org; 99 Gansevoort St, at Washington St, Meatpacking District; adult/child $25/free, 7-10pm Fri pay-what-you-wish; ⏰10:30am-6pm Mon, Wed, Thu & Sun, to 10pm Fri & Sat; 🚇A/C/E, L to 8th Ave-14th St)

Chelsea Art Crawl

Join the fashionable, art-minded crowds at the latest gallery shows in Chelsea. Thursday night, when some galleries have openings (and free wine), is a good time to roam. In the Meatpacking District, the Whitney Museum of American Art and the High Line – with its integrated sculptures, murals, paintings and more – are beloved by locals and tourists alike.

Chelsea Market
MARKET

2 ⊙ MAP P112, C3

In a shining example of redevelopment and preservation, the Chelsea Market has transformed a former factory into a shopping concourse that caters to foodies. More than two dozen food vendors ply their temptations, including **Mokbar** (ramen with Korean accents); **Takumi** (mixing Japanese and Mexican ingredients); **Very Fresh Noodles** (hand-pulled northern Chinese noodles); **Bar Suzette** (crepes); **Num Pang** (Cambodian sandwiches); **Ninth St Espresso** (perfect lattes); **Doughnuttery** (piping hot mini-doughnuts); and **Fat Witch Bakery** (brownies and other decadent sugar hits). (📞212-652-2110; www.chelseamarket.com; 75 Ninth Ave, btwn W 15th & W 16th Sts, Chelsea; ⏰7am-2am Mon-Sat, 8am-10pm Sun; 🚇A/C/E, L to 8th Ave-14th St)

Hudson River Park
PARK

3 ⊙ MAP P112, C6

The High Line (p108) may be all the rage these days, but one block away from that famous elevated park stretches a 5-mile-long recreational space that has transformed the city over the past decade. Covering 550 acres (400 of which are on the water) and running from Battery Park

Washington Square Park

Once a potter's field and square for public executions, **Washington Square Park** (Map p112, F5; www.nycgovparks.org; Fifth Ave, at Washington Sq N, West Village; ⊙closes midnight; 👫; ⑤A/C/E, B/D/F/M to W 4th St-Washington Sq, R/W to 8th St-NYU) is now an enticing green space and the unofficial town square of Greenwich Village, hosting lounging NYU students, tuba-playing street performers, socialising canines, fearless squirrels, speed-chess pros, and barefoot children who splash about in the fountain on warm days. Locals have resisted changes to the shape and uses of the park, and its layout has remained largely the same since the 1800s. Check out the Washington Square Park Conservancy (www.washingtonsquareparkconservancy .org) for news and events.

The iconic Stanford White Arch (colloquially known as the Washington Square Arch) dominates the park with its 73ft of gleaming white Tuckahoe marble. Originally designed in wood to celebrate the centennial of George Washington's inauguration in 1889, it proved so popular that it was replaced with a stone version six years later.

at Manhattan's southern tip to 59th St in Midtown, Hudson River Park is Manhattan's wondrous backyard. The long riverside path is a great spot for cycling, running and strolling. (⊙212-627-2020; www.hudsonriverpark.org; ⊙6am-1am; 👫; 🚌M23 crosstown bus, ⑤1 to Christopher St, C/E to 23rd St)

Stonewall National Monument
NATIONAL PARK

4 ◉ MAP P112, G2

In 2016 President Barack Obama declared Christopher Park, a small fenced-in triangle with benches and some greenery in the heart of the West Village, a national park and on it the first national monument dedicated to LGBTIQ+

history. It's well worth stopping here to reflect on the Stonewall uprising of 1969, when LGBTIQ+ citizens fought back against discriminatory policing of their communities – many consider the event the birth of the modern LGBTIQ+ rights movement in the US. (www.nps.gov/ston; W 4th St, btwn Christopher & Grove Sts, West Village; ⊙9am-dusk; ⑤1 to Christopher St-Sheridan Sq, A/C/E, B/D/F/M to W 4th St-Washington Sq)

Rubin Museum of Art
GALLERY

5 ◉ MAP P112, E3

The Rubin is the first museum in the Western world to dedicate itself to the art of the Himalayas and surrounding regions. Its impressive collection spans 1500 years to the present day, and includes Chinese embroidered textiles, Nepalese gilt-copper bodhisattvas, Pakistani stone sculptures and intricate Bhutanese paintings, as well as ritual objects and dance masks from various Tibetan regions. Fascinating rotating exhibitions have included *Victorious Ones*, comprising sculptures and paintings of the Jinas, the 24 founding teachers of Jainism. (📞212-620-5000; www./rubin museum.org; 150 W 17th St, btwn Sixth & Seventh Aves, Chelsea; adult/child $19/free, 6-10pm Fri free; ⏱11am-5pm Mon & Thu, to 9pm Wed, to 10pm Fri, to 6pm Sat & Sun; 🚇1 to 18th St)

Salmagundi Club   GALLERY

6 ◉ MAP P112, F4

Far removed from the flashy Chelsea gallery scene, the Salmagundi Club features several gallery spaces focusing on representational American art set in a stunning historic brownstone on Fifth Ave below Union Sq. The club is one of the oldest art clubs in the US (founded in 1871) and still offers classes and exhibitions for its members. (📞212-255-7740; www.salmagundi.org; 47 Fifth Ave, btwn W 11th & 12th Sts, West Village; admission free; ⏱1-6pm Mon-Fri, to 5pm Sat & Sun; 🚇4/5/6, L, N/Q/R/W to 14th St-Union Sq)

Salmagundi Club

DW LABS INCORPORATED/SHUTTERSTOCK ©

Eating

Foragers Table
AMERICAN $$$

7 ✖ MAP P112, D2

The owners of this outstanding restaurant run a 28-acre Hudson Valley farm, from which much of the seasonal menu is sourced. It changes frequently, but recent temptations included pan-roasted duck breast with poached pears, mushroom pappardelle with sherry and toasted almonds, and cauliflower steak with sweet-potato tahini and sumac onions. (☏ 212-243-8888; www.foragers market.com/restaurant; 300 W 22nd St, at Eighth Ave, Chelsea; mains $20-39; ⏱ dinner 5:30-10pm Mon-Sat, to 9pm Sun, brunch 9am-3pm Sat & Sun; ✖; Ⓢ 1, C/E to 23rd St)

Nix
VEGETARIAN $$$

8 ✖ MAP P112, G4

At this modest yet Michelin-starred restaurant, chefs John Fraser and Garrett Eagleton transform vegetables into beautifully executed dishes that delight the senses. Start with tandoor bread with dips such as red pepper and walnut, then move to more complex plates such as burrata with Granny Smith apples or cauliflower tempura with steamed buns and pickles. (☏ 212-498-9393; www.nixny.com; 72 University Pl, btwn E 10th & E 11th Sts, West Village; mains $26-28; ⏱ 5:30-10:30pm Mon-Thu, 5-11pm Fri, 10:30am-2:30pm & 5-11pm Sat, 10:30am-2:30pm & 5-10:30pm

Sun; ✖; Ⓢ 4/5/6, N/Q/R/W, L to 14th St-Union Sq)

Jeffrey's Grocery
AMERICAN $$$

9 ✖ MAP P112, H1

This West Village classic is a lively eating and drinking spot that hits all the right notes. Seafood is the focus: there's an oyster bar and beautifully executed mains such as mussels with green curry, coconut milk and herbs, a panko skate sandwich and caviar toast. Meat dishes include hanger steak with fingerling potatoes and chimichurri sauce. (☏ 646-398-7630; www.jeffreysgrocery.com; 172 Waverly Pl, at Christopher St, West Village; mains $21-35; ⏱ 8am-11pm Mon-Wed, to 1am Thu-Fri, from 9:30am Sat, to 11pm Sun; Ⓢ 1 to Christopher St-Sheridan Sq)

Cookshop
AMERICAN $$

10 ✖ MAP P112, C2

A brilliant brunching pit stop before (or after) tackling the verdant High Line (p108) across the street, Cookshop is a lively place that knows its niche and nails it. Excellent service, eye-opening cocktails (good morning, Blushing Monk!), a perfectly baked bread basket, outdoor seating for warm days and inventive egg dishes make this a Chelsea favorite. (☏ 212-924-4440; www.cookshopny.com; 156 Tenth Ave, at W 20th St, Chelsea; mains brunch $14-18, lunch $16-25, dinner $23-34; ⏱ 8am-11:30pm Mon-Fri, from 10am Sat, to 10pm Sun; ✖; Ⓢ 1, C/E to 23rd St)

Mamoun's

WARREN EISENBERG/SHUTTERSTOCK ©

Mamoun's   MIDDLE EASTERN $

11 ✕ MAP P112, F6

This falafel and shawarma restaurant in lower Manhattan specializes in big, dripping platters and wraps that are served up quick and don't cost much. A NYC favorite, Mamoun's even has its own branded hot sauce. Be warned: it's not for anyone with a sensitive tongue. The West Village location is tiny, but there is some limited seating. (www.mamouns.com; 119 MacDougal St, btwn W 3rd St & Minetta Lane, West Village; sandwiches $4-7.50, plates $8-13; ⏲11am-5am; Ⓢ A/C/E, B/D/F/M to W 4th St-Washington Sq)

RedFarm   FUSION $$$

12 ✕ MAP P112, D5

Experience the unique, delectable artistry of Chinese-influenced cooking in this small, buzzing space. Diced tuna and eggplant bruschetta, crispy-skin smoked chicken with garlic, and pastrami egg rolls are among the many stunning, genre-defying dishes. Other hits include lobster sautéed with egg and chopped pork, Kowloon filet-mignon tarts, and crispy duck and crab dumplings. (☎212-792-9700; www.redfarmnyc.com; 529 Hudson St, btwn W 10th & Charles Sts, West Village; mains $20-58, dumplings $14-20; ⏲dinner 5-10:45pm Sun-Wed, to 11:30pm Thu-Sat, brunch 11am-2:30pm Sat & Sun; Ⓢ1 to Christopher St-Sheridan Sq, A/C/E, B/D/F/M to W 4th St-Washington Sq)

JeJu Noodle Bar   NOODLES $$

13 ✕ MAP P112, D6

With classic ramen continuing to rampage across the world's tables, perhaps it's time to explore its variations – such as the Korean *ramyun* served at this welcoming restaurant on Christopher St's quieter western stretch. Start with *toro ssam bap* (fatty tuna, toasted seaweed, *tobiko* rice and scrambled egg) before slurping down a *so ramyun* – brisket and noodles in veal broth. (☎646-666-0947; www.jejunoodlebar.com; 679 Greenwich St, at Christopher St, West Village;

noodles $18-19; ⏱5-10pm Sun-Wed, to 11pm Thu-Sat; 🚇M8 to Greenwich St-Christopher St, ⓢ1 to Christopher St-Sheridan Sq)

Sushi Nakazawa

SUSHI $$$

14 ❌ MAP P112, E6

The price is high, but the quality is phenomenal at this tiny sushi spot that opened to much acclaim in 2013. There are no cooked dishes and little in the way of individual choice. Instead the meal is a 20-course fixed-price affair created by chef Daisuke Nakazawa, who served under Jiro Ono, probably the world's finest sushi chef. (📞212-924-2212; www.sushinakazawa .com; 23 Commerce St, btwn Bedford St & Seventh Ave, West Village; prix-fixe menu $120 & $150; ⏱lunch 11:30am,

11:45am, 1:15pm & 1:30pm, dinner 5-10:15pm; ⓢ1 to Christopher St-Sheridan Sq)

Blossom

VEGAN $$

15 ❌ MAP P112, C2

Cozily occupying a historic Chelsea town house, this beacon to hungry vegans is a peaceful, romantic dining spot that offers imaginative, all-kosher tofu, seitan and vegetable creations, some raw. Brunch dishes like tofu Benedict and Florentine impersonate animal proteins deliciously, while superb dinner mains such as the spaghetti squash cake and mushroom risotto with saffron-cashew cream need no affectations. (📞212-627-1144; www.blossomnyc.com; 187 Ninth Ave, btwn 21st & 22nd Sts, Chelsea;

Gansevoort Market (p120)

West Village, Chelsea & the Meatpacking District Eating

mains lunch $14-24, dinner $22-25;
⏱noon-2:45pm & 5-9:30pm Mon-Thu,
to 10pm Fri & Sat, to 9pm Sun; 🖋; Ⓢ1,
C/E to 23rd St)

Rosemary's   ITALIAN $$$

16 ❌ MAP P112, E4

One of the West Village's hottest restaurants, Rosemary's
serves high-end Italian fare that
lives up to the hype. In a vaguely
farmhouse-like setting, diners tuck
into generous portions of housemade pastas, rich salads, and
cheese and cured meat boards.
Everything, from the beets with
bitter greens and hazelnuts to the
'Meiller Farm' pork with orange
mustard fruits, is incredible.
(📞212-647-1818; www.rosemarysnyc.
com; 18 Greenwich Ave, at W 10th St,
West Village; mains $26-28, lunch/
dinner prix-fixe menu $24/34; ⏱8am-
4pm & 5-11pm Mon-Thu, 8am-4pm &
5pm-midnight Fri, 10am-4pm & 5pm-
midnight Sat, 10am-4pm & 5-11pm Sun;
Ⓢ1 to Christopher St-Sheridan Sq)

Bagatelle   FRENCH $$$

17 ❌ MAP P112, C4

At Bagatelle, elegant bentwood
chairs, chandeliers, white linens
and (ultimately) the bill conspire
to give you the impression you're
eating somewhere top-drawer in
St-Tropez. Brunch, with a raw-
seafood bar and plenty of refined
egg dishes, is a favorite, but a
dinner of French classics is also
an occasion. (📞212-488-2110;
www.bagatellenyc.com; 1 Little W

12th St, btwn Ninth Ave & Hudson St,
Meatpacking District; mains $29-54;
⏱11:30am-midnight Sun-Wed, to 1am
Thu, to 2am Fri & Sat; ⓈA/C/E, L to
8th Ave-14th St)

Alta   TAPAS $$

18 ❌ MAP P112, F4

This gorgeous town house highlights the neighborhood's quaint-
ness, with plenty of exposed brick,
wood beams, flickering candles,
massive mirrors and romantic
fireplace glows. A small-plates
menu of encyclopedic propor-
tions cures indecision with the
likes of succulent lamb meatballs,
seared scallops with pistachio,
Japanese eggplant with époisses,
fried goat's cheese and braised
short rib. The wine list is outstanding, too. (📞212-505-7777; www.
altarestaurant.com; 64 W 10th St, btwn
Fifth & Sixth Aves, West Village; small
plates $13-26; ⏱5:30-9:30pm Sun &
Mon, to 10pm Tue-Thu, 5-10:45pm Fri
& Sat; ⓈA/C/E, B/D/F/M to W 4th
St-Washington Sq)

Gansevoort Market   MARKET $

19 ❌ MAP P112, C3

Inside a brick building in the heart
of the Meatpacking District is this
buzzing food emporium. A raw,
industrial space lit by skylights, it
features a bar and over a dozen
gourmet vendors slinging Korean
bibimbap, poke bowls, ceviche,
pizza, Japanese curry, ramen,
Belgian waffles and more. (📞646-
449-8400; www.gansevoortmarketnyc.

com; 353 W 14th St, btwn Eighth &
Ninth Aves, Meatpacking District; mains
$10-15; ⏰11am-9:30pm Mon-Thu, to
10:30pm Fri-Sun; 📶; 🚇A/C/E, L to
8th Ave-14th St)

Red Bamboo
VEGAN $

20 ❌ MAP P112, F5

Cajun soy 'shrimp', jerk-marinated
'chicken', 'cheesecake' so rich
you can barely finish? The soul-
and Asian-food temptations
Red Bamboo concocts make it a
must for vegans and vegetarians
eager to try something different.
Humble bare-wood furniture and
a plain, tiled dining room relax the
punters, while organic beers and
wines complete the essentials
for a night of culinary adventure.
(📞212-260-7049; www.redbamboo-
nyc.com; 140 W 4th St, btwn Sixth Ave
& MacDougal St, West Village; mains
$12-16; ⏰12:30-11pm Mon-Thu, to
11:30pm Fri, from noon Sat, to 11pm
Sun; 🍴; 🚇A/C/E, B/D/F/M to W 4th
St-Washington Sq)

Drinking

Employees Only
BAR

21 🍺 MAP P112, D5

This divine cocktail bar, tucked
behind a discreet green awning
on Hudson St, is a world-beater.
Ace mixologists shake up crazy
libations like the Ginger Smash,
and the wood-rich art deco space
makes everyone feel glamorous.
The kitchen plays its part, too,
producing delights such as bone-

Dining Out

With a bit of research and a
little cash in your pocket, you
can eat like royalty at every
meal in these neighborhoods.
The West Village is known for
its classy, cozy and intimate
spots, while the adjacent
Meatpacking District's dining
scene is generally more osten-
tatious, trend-driven
and pricey.

Chelsea strikes a balance
between the two, with a brash
assortment of eateries along
ever-popular Eighth Ave (a
must for see-and-be-seen
brunch), and more cafes lining
Ninth Ave further west.

marrow poppers and spicy shrimp
on polenta (mains $27 to $31).
(📞212-242-3021; www.employee-
sonlynyc.com; 510 Hudson St, btwn W
10th & Christopher Sts, West Village;
⏰6pm-12am; 🚇1 to Christopher
St-Sheridan Sq)

Happiest Hour
COCKTAIL BAR

22 🍺 MAP P112, E4

A supercool, tiki-licious cocktail
bar splashed with palm prints,
'60s pop and playful mixed drinks
that provide a chic take on the
fruity beach cocktail. The crowd
tends to be button-down after-
work types and online daters.
Beneath sits its serious sibling,
Slowly Shirley, an art deco–style

subterranean temple to beautifully crafted, thoroughly researched libations. (📞212-243-2827; www.happiesthournyc.com; 121 W 10th St, btwn Greenwich St & Sixth Ave, West Village; 🕐5pm-late Mon-Fri, from 2pm Sat & Sun; 🚇A/C/E, B/D/F/M to W 4th St-Washington Sq; 1 to Christopher St-Sheridan Sq)

Gallow Green

BAR

23 🚇 MAP P112, B1

Run by the creative team behind Sleep No More (p126) theater, Gallow Green is a rooftop bar festooned with vines, potted plants and fairy lights. It's a great add-on before or after experiencing the show, with waitstaff in period costume, a live band most nights and tasty rum-filled cocktails. You'll have to make a reservation. (📞212-564-1662; www.mckittrickhotel.com/gallow-green; 542 W 27th St, btwn Tenth & Eleventh Aves, Chelsea; 🕐5pm-midnight Mon-Wed, to 1am Thu & Fri, 11am-1am Sat, 11am-midnight Sun; 🚇1, C/E to 23rd St; 1 to 28th St)

Buvette

WINE BAR

24 🚇 MAP P112, E5

Buzzing with the animated conversation of locals, courting couples and theater types, this devotedly Francophile wine bar and restaurant makes a great rest stop amid a West Village backstreet wander. Enjoy a cocktail or a glass of wine, or settle in for a meal. Brunch

dishes such as croque monsieurs are replaced by tartines and small plates at dinner. (📞212-255-3590; www.ilovebuvette.com; 42 Grove St, btwn Bedford & Bleecker Sts, West Village; small plates $12-18; 🕐7am-2am; 🚇1 to Christopher St-Sheridan Sq, A/C/E, B/D/F/M to W 4th St-Washington Sq)

Pier 66 Maritime

BAR

25 🚇 MAP P112, A1

Salvaged from the bottom of the sea (or at least the Chesapeake Bay), the lightship *Frying Pan* and the two-tiered dockside bar where it's moored are fine go-to spots for a sundowner. On warm days the rustic open-air space brings in the crowds, who laze on deck chairs and drink ice-cold beers ($7/25 for a microbrew/pitcher). (📞212-989-6363; www.pier66maritime.com; Pier 66, at W 26th St, Chelsea; 🕐noon-midnight May-Sep & warm days Apr & Oct; 🚇1, C/E to 23rd St)

Cubbyhole

LGBTIQ+

26 🚇 MAP P112, D4

This West Village dive bills itself as 'lesbian, gay and straight friendly since 1994.' While the crowd's mostly ladies, it welcomes anyone looking for a drink in good company beneath a ceiling festooned with lanterns, toys and other ephemera. It's got a great jukebox, friendly bartenders and regulars who like to hang and chat. (📞212-243-9041; www.cubbyholebar.com;

281 W 12th St, at W 4th St, West Village; ⏱4pm-4am Mon-Fri, from 2pm Sat & Sun; Ⓢ A/C/E, L to 8th Ave-14th St)

Marie's Crisis

BAR

27 ⓜ MAP P112, G3

Ageing Broadway queens, wide-eyed out-of-town youngsters, giggly tourists and various other fans of musical theater assemble around the piano here and take turns belting out campy show tunes, often joined by the entire crowd – and the occasional celebrity. It's old-school fun, no matter how jaded you might be when you go in. Non-flash photography is allowed, but video is not. (📞212-243-9323; 59 Grove St, btwn Seventh Ave & Bleecker St, West Village; ⏱4pm-3am Sun-Thu, to 4am Fri & Sat; Ⓢ1 to

Christopher St-Sheridan Sq, A/C/E, B/D/F/M to W 4th St-Washington Sq)

Tippler

COCKTAIL BAR

28 ⓜ MAP P112, C3

Paying material homage to its once-industrial setting, this brick-and-wood cellar bar beneath Chelsea Market serves up properly blended cocktails ($15) and interesting craft beer. The decor makes use of materials from vintage sources – including an old NYC water tower and the nearby High Line – to create a warm and relaxing space. (📞917-261-7949; www.thetippler.com; 425 W 15th St, underneath Chelsea Market, Chelsea; ⏱4pm to 1am Sun-Thu, to 3am Fri & Sat; Ⓢ A/C/E, L to 8th Ave-14th St)

Buvette

West Village, Chelsea & the Meatpacking District Drinking

West Village Cafes

The West Village is the most desirable residential neighborhood in Manhattan, so do as the locals do and make the most of this quaint district stacked to the brim with cute cafes, such as Parisian-vibed **Café Cluny** (Map p112, D4; ☎212-255-6900; www.cafecluny. com; 284 W 12th St, cnr W 12th & W 4th Sts, West Village; mains lunch $18-34, dinner $25-40; ◷8am-10pm Mon, to 11pm Tue-Fri, from 9am Sat, to 10pm Sun; ⑤A/C/E, L 8th Ave-14th St) or Italian-eclectic **Caffe Reggio** (Map p112, F6; ☎212-475-9557; www.caffereggio.com; 119 MacDougal St, near W 3rd St, West Village; sandwiches around $12; ◷9am-3am Sun-Thu, to 4am Fri & Sat; ⑤A/C/E, B/D/F/M to W 4th St-Washington Sq). Grab a book and a latte and hunker down for a blissful afternoon of people-watching.

Top of the Standard BAR

29 🍴 MAP P112, C4

Afternoon tea and drinks morph into evening cocktails in this splendid perch atop the ever-so stylish Standard hotel. Small plates ($12 to $20), such as English-pea ravioli or Moroccan shrimp with pickled raisins and Greek yogurt, are on hand to address any pangs of hunger, while live jazz and fabulous views complete the picture of sophistication. (☎212-645-7600; www. standardhotels.com; 848 Washington St, at W 13th St, Meatpacking District; ◷4pm-midnight; ⑤A/C/E, L to 8th Ave-14th St)

Stumptown Coffee Roasters COFFEE

30 🍴 MAP P112, F5

This renowned Portland roaster is helping to reinvent the NYC coffee scene with its exquisitely made brews. It has an elegant interior with coffered ceiling and walnut bar, though its few tables are often overtaken by the laptop-toting crowd. (☎347-414-7802; www. stumptowncoffee.com; 30 W 8th St, at MacDougal St, West Village; ◷7am-8pm; ⑤A/C/E, B/D/F/M to W 4th St-Washington Sq)

Bathtub Gin COCKTAIL BAR

31 🍴 MAP P112, C3

Amid NYC's obsession with speakeasy-styled hangouts, Bathtub Gin manages to poke its head above the crowd with its super-secret front door hidden on the wall of the Stone Street Coffee Shop (look for the 'Stone Street Standard' sign). Once inside, chill seating, soft background beats and kindly staff make it a great place to enjoy bespoke cocktails with friends. (☎646-559-1671; www. bathtubginnyc.com; 132 Ninth Ave, btwn W 18th & W 19th Sts, Chelsea; ◷5pm-2am Mon-Wed, to 3am Thu, to 4am Fri, 4pm-4am Sat, 4pm-2am Sun;

S A/C/E, L to 8th Ave-14th St, 1, C/E to 23rd St, 1 to 18th St)

Vin Sur Vingt
WINE BAR

32 🚇 MAP P112, E4

A cozy spot just off Seventh Ave's bustle, Vin Sur Vingt is a slender wine bar with a strip of bar seating and a quaint row of two-seat tables, perfect for a first date. Warning: if you come for a pre-dinner drink, you'll inevitably be charmed into staying through dinner as you munch on the excellent selection of bar bites. (📞212-924-4442; www.vsvwinebars. com; 201 W 11th St, btwn Seventh Ave & Waverly Pl, West Village; 🕐4pm-1am Mon-Fri, to 2am Sat & Sun; **S**A/C/E, L to 8th Ave-14th St)

Stonewall Inn
LGBTIQ+

33 🚇 MAP P112, G2

Site of the 1969 Stonewall riots and one of the birthplaces of the gay-rights movement, Stonewall is a National Historic Monument and a de facto place of pilgrimage. Despite its international fame, it's a friendly, unpretentious spot that welcomes everyone under the LGBTIQ+ rainbow (and their allies) to nightly events such as 'I Love the '90s' karaoke and drag bingo. (📞212-488-2705; www.thestonewall innnyc.com; 53 Christopher St, at Christopher Park, West Village; 🕐2pm-4am Mon-Wed, from noon Thu-Sun; **S**1 to Christopher St-Sheridan Sq)

Stonewall Inn

West Village, Chelsea & the Meatpacking District Drinking

124 Old Rabbit Club

BAR

34 MAP P112, F6

You'll wanna pat yourself on the back when you find this well-concealed bar (hint: look for the tiny word 'Rabbit' over the door). Once you're inside the narrow, cavern-like space with its low-key vibe, grab a seat at the dimly lit bar and reward yourself with a quenching stout or one of the dozens of imported brews. (646-781-9646; www.rabbitclubnyc.com; 124 MacDougal St, at Minetta Lane, West Village; 6pm-2am Sun-Thu, to 4am Fri & Sat; S A/C/E, B/D/F/M to W 4th St-Washington Sq; 1 to Houston St)

Little Branch

COCKTAIL BAR

35 MAP P112, E6

If it weren't for the lines later in the evening, you'd never guess that a charming bar lay beyond this plain metal door set into a brick wall on a triangular corner. Walking downstairs to the basement den feels like a throwback to Prohibition: patrons clink glasses and sip artfully prepared cocktails, and there are jazz performances Sunday through Thursday. (212-929-4360; 22 Seventh Ave, at Leroy St, West Village; 7pm-2am Sun-Wed, to 3am Thu-Sat; S 1 to Houston St, A/C/E, B/D/F/M to W 4th St-Washington Sq)

Henrietta Hudson

LESBIAN

36 MAP P112, D6

All sorts of young women, many from neighboring New Jersey and Long Island, storm this 'Bar & Girl,' where theme nights bring in spirited DJs spinning hip-hop, house, rock and other genres. Happy hour is 4pm to 7pm daily. (212-924-3347; www.henriettahudson.com; 438 Hudson St, at Morton St, West Village; 4pm-2am Mon & Tue, to 4am Wed-Sun; S 1 to Houston St)

Vol de Nuit

PUB

37 MAP P112, F5

Even all the NYU students can't ruin this: a cozy Belgian beer bar with Delirium Tremens on tap and a few dozen bottle options, including Duvel and Lindemans Framboise (raspberry beer!). You can order *moules* (mussels) and *frites* (fries) to share at the front patio seats, the lounge, the communal wood tables or under the bar's dangling red lights. (212-982-3388; www.voldenuitbar.com; 148 W 4th St, btwn Sixth Ave & MacDougal St; 4pm-1am Sun-Thu, to 3am Fri & Sat; S A/C/E, B/D/F/M to W 4th St-Washington Sq)

Entertainment

Sleep No More

THEATER

38 MAP P112, B1

One of the most immersive theater experiences ever conceived, *Sleep No More* is a loose, noir retelling of *Macbeth* set inside a series of Chelsea warehouses that have been redesigned to look like the 1930s-era 'McKittrick Hotel' (a nod to Hitchcock's *Vertigo*); the jazz bar, Manderley, is another Hitchcock reference, this time to his adaptation of Daphne du Maurier's *Rebecca*. (📞box office 212-904-1880; www.sleepnomorenyc.com; 530 W 27th St, btwn Tenth & Eleventh Aves, Chelsea; tickets from $100; ⏱sessions begin 4-7pm; Ⓢ1, C/E to 23rd St)

Smalls
JAZZ

39 ⭐ MAP P112, G1

Living up to its name, this cramped but appealing basement jazz den offers a grab-bag collection of acts who take the stage nightly. Admission includes a come-and-go policy if you need to duck out for a bite, and there's an afternoon jam session on Saturday and Sunday that's not to be missed. (📞646-476-4346; www.smallslive.com; 183 W 10th St, btwn W 4th St & Seventh Ave S, West Village; cover $20; ⏱7pm-3:30am Mon-Fri, from 4pm Sat & Sun; Ⓢ1 to Christopher St-Sheridan Sq, A/C/E, B/D/F/M to W 4th St-Washington Sq)

IFC Center
CINEMA

40 ⭐ MAP P112, E6

This art-house cinema in NYU land has a solidly curated lineup of new indies, cult classics and foreign films. Catch shorts, documentaries, mini festivals, '80s revivals, director-focused series, weekend classics and frequent special series, such as cult favorites (*The Shining, Taxi Driver, Alien*) at midnight. (📞212-924-7771; www.ifccenter.com; 323 Sixth Ave, at W 3rd St, West Village; adult/child tickets

IFC Center

$16/13; 📶; Ⓢ A/C/E, B/D/F/M to W 4th St-Washington Sq)

Village Vanguard

JAZZ

41 ⭐ MAP P112, E4

Possibly NYC's most prestigious jazz club, the Vanguard has hosted literally every major star of the past 50 years. Starting in 1935 as a venue for beat poetry and folk music, it occasionally returns to its roots, but most of the time it's big, bold jazz all night long. The Vanguard Jazz Orchestra has been a Monday-night mainstay since 1966. (📞212-255-4037; www. villagevanguard.com; 178 Seventh Ave S, btwn W 11th & Perry Sts, West Village; cover around $35; ⏲7:30pm-12:30am; Ⓢ1/2/3 to 14th St, A/C/E, L to 8th Ave-14th St)

Comedy Cellar

COMEDY

42 ⭐ MAP P112, F6

This legendary, intimate comedy club beneath the Olive Tree cafe in the West Village features a cast of talented regulars (Colin Quinn, Judah Friedlander, Wanda Sykes), plus occasional high-profile drop-ins like Dave Chappelle, Jerry Seinfeld and Amy Schumer. Its success has spawned offspring – locations in Las Vegas and at the **Village Underground**, around the corner at 130 W 3rd St. (📞212-254-3480; www.comedycellar.com; 117 MacDougal St, btwn W 3rd St & Minetta Lane, West Village; cover $10-24; ⏲11am-3am; Ⓢ A/C/E, B/D/F/M to W 4th St-Washington Sq)

Atlantic Theater Company

THEATER

43 ⭐ MAP P112, D2

Founded by David Mamet and William H Macy in 1985, the Atlantic Theater is a pivotal anchor for the off-Broadway community, hosting many Tony Award and Drama Desk winners over the last three decades. (📞212-691-5919; www. atlantictheater.org; 336 W 20th St, btwn Eighth & Ninth Aves, Chelsea; Ⓢ1, C/E to 23rd St; 1 to 18th St)

(Le) Poisson Rouge

LIVE MUSIC

44 ⭐ MAP P112, F6

This high-concept art space hosts a highly eclectic lineup of live music, with the likes of Deerhunter, Gary Bartz and Yo La Tengo performing in past years. There's a lot of experimentation and cross-genre pollination between classical, folk, opera and more. (📞212-505-3474; www.lpr.com; 158 Bleecker St, btwn Sullivan & Thompson Sts, West Village; Ⓢ A/C/E, B/D/F/M to W 4th St-Washington Sq)

Duplex

CABARET

45 ⭐ MAP P112, G2

Cabaret, comedy and campy dance moves are par for the course at the legendary Duplex, on song since 1950. Pictures of Joan Rivers line the walls, and performers like to mimic her sassy form of self-deprecation while getting in a few jokes about audience members as well. It's a fun and un-pretentious place, but certainly not for the bashful. (☎212-255-5438; www.theduplex.com; 61 Christopher St, at Seventh Ave S, West Village; cover $10-25; ⊙4pm-4am; §1 to Christopher St-Sheridan Sq, A/C/E, B/D/F/M to W 4th St-Washington Sq)

Joyce Theater

DANCE

46 ⭐ MAP P112, D3

A favorite among dance junkies thanks to its excellent sight lines and offbeat offerings, this is an intimate venue, seating 472 in a renovated cinema. Its focus is on traditional modern companies, such as Martha Graham, Stephen Petronio Company and Parsons Dance, as well as global stars, such as Dance Brazil, Ballet Hispanico and MalPaso Dance Company.

(☎212-691-9740; www.joyce.org; 175 Eighth Ave, at W 19th St, Chelsea; §1 to 18th St; 1, C/E to 23rd St; A/C/E, L to 8th Ave-14th St)

55 Bar

LIVE MUSIC

47 ⭐ MAP P112, G2

Dating back to the Prohibition era, this friendly basement dive is great for low-key shows without high covers or dressing up. There are twice-nightly performances by quality artists-in-residence, some blues bands and Miles Davis' super '80s guitarist Mike Stern. There's a two-drink minimum. (☎212-929-9883; www.55bar.com; 55 Christopher St, at Seventh Ave, West Village; cover $15; ⊙1pm-4am; §1 to Christopher St-Sheridan Sq)

Comedy Cellar

A History of Queer New York

NYC – and the West Village in particular – is out and damn proud. It was here that the Stonewall Riots took place, that the modern gay-rights movement bloomed and that America's first Pride march hit the streets.

Before Stonewall

In the early 20th century a number of gay-owned businesses lined MacDougal St in Greenwich Village, among them the legendary Eve's Hangout at number 129, which was famous for two things: poetry readings and a door sign that read 'Men are admitted but not welcome.' The era's relative free-thinking was replaced with a new conservatism in the following decades: tougher policing aimed to eradicate queer visibility in the public sphere, forcing the scene underground in the 1940s and '50s. Though crackdowns on gay venues had always occurred, they became increasingly common.

The Stonewall Revolution

On June 28, 1969, police officers raided the Stonewall Inn (p125) – a gay-friendly watering hole in Greenwich Village – and patrons did the unthinkable: they revolted. Fed up with the harassment, they bombarded the officers with coins, bottles, bricks and chants of 'gay power' and 'we shall overcome.' Their collective anger and solidarity was a turning point, igniting intense and passionate debate about discrimination and forming the catalyst for the modern gay-rights movement, not just in New York, but across the US and the world.

Marriage & the New Millennium

The fight for complete equality took two massive steps forward in 2011. A federal law banning LGBTIQ+ military personnel from serving openly – the so-called 'Don't Ask, Don't Tell' policy – was repealed after years of intense lobbying. Persistence led to an even greater victory that year – the right to marry. The New York State Assembly passed the Marriage Equality Act and it was signed into law on the eve of NYC Gay Pride. State victory became a national one on June 26, 2015, when the US Supreme Court ruled that same-sex marriage is a legal right across the country, striking down the remaining marriage bans in 13 US states.

Shopping

Strand Book Store

BOOKS

48 🏠 MAP P112, G4

Beloved and legendary, the iconic Strand embodies downtown NYC's intellectual bona fides – a bibliophile's Oz, where generations of book lovers carrying the store's trademark tote bags happily lose themselves for hours. In operation since 1927, the Strand sells new, used and rare titles, spreading an incredible 18 miles of books (over 2.5 million of them) among three labyrinthine floors. (☏212-473-1452; www.strandbooks.com; 828 Broadway, at E 12th St, West Village; ◷9:30am-10:30pm; ⓢL, N/Q/R/W, 4/5/6 to 14th St-Union Sq)

Screaming Mimis

VINTAGE

49 🏠 MAP P112, D4

If you dig vintage, designer and rare threads, or flamboyant costumes, you may just scream too. This funtastic shop carries an excellent selection of yesteryear pieces, organized by decade, from the '40s to the '90s. From prim beaded wool cardigans to suede minidresses, fluoro furs, white leather go-go boots, accessories and jewelry, the stock is in great condition. (☏212-677-6464; www.screamingmimis.com; 240 W 14th St, btwn Seventh & Eighth Aves, Chelsea; ◷noon-8pm Mon-Sat, 1-7pm Sun; ⓢA/C/E, L to 8th Ave-14th St)

Murray's Cheese

FOOD & DRINKS

50 🏠 MAP P112, E6

Founded in 1940 by Spanish Civil War veteran Murray Greenberg, this is one of New York's best cheese shops. Former owner (now 'advisor') Rob Kaufelt is known for his talent for sniffing out the best curds from around the world: you'll find (and be able to taste) all manner of *fromage*, aged in cheese caves on site and in Queens. (☏212-243-3289; www.murrayscheese.com; 254 Bleecker St, btwn Morton & Leroy Sts, West Village; sandwiches $6-9; ◷8am-9pm Mon-Sat, 9am-8pm Sun; ⓢA/C/E, B/D/F/M to W 4th St-Washington Sq, 1 to Christopher St-Sheridan Sq)

Meadow

CHOCOLATE

51 🏠 MAP P112, D5

An import from Portland, this peaceful, pretty little shop is the place to go for single-origin chocolate, fine salt, honey and other pantry essentials. The owner selects exquisite chocolate from around the world (and has also written a 300-page book on salt). You may be offered hot, sticky chocolate (blended in-store), or popcorn generously sprinkled with truffle salt. (☏212-645-4633; www.themeadow.com; 523 Hudson St, btwn W 10th & Charles Sts, West Village; ◷11am-9pm Mon-Thu, to 10pm Fri & Sat, to 8pm Sun; ⓢ1 to Christopher St-Sheridan Sq)

West Village Wandering

Most of the West Village isn't served by any subway lines, and the L train goes only as far as Eighth Ave, so if you want to access the westernmost areas of Chelsea and the West Village by public transportation, try the M14 or the M8 bus. It's a shame, however, to use the bus or a taxi to get around the West Village – the charming cobblestone streets are perfect for a stroll. And it's perfectly acceptable to arm yourself with a map (or your smartphone) to get around the West Village's charming-but-challenging side streets – even some locals have a tricky time finding their way around here.

Printed Matter
BOOKS

52 MAP P112, B1

Printed Matter is a wondrous little shop dedicated to limited-edition artist monographs and strange little zines. Here you will find nothing carried by mainstream bookstores; instead, trim shelves hide call-to-arms manifestos, critical essays about comic books, flip books that reveal Jesus' face through barcodes and how-to guides written by prisoners. (☑212-925-0325; www.printedmatter.org; 231 Eleventh Ave, btwn 25th & 26th Sts, Chelsea; ⏱11am-7pm Sat & Mon-Wed, to 8pm Thu & Fri, noon-6pm Sun; Ⓢ7 to 34th St-Hudson Yards; 1 to 28th St)

Beacon's Closet
VINTAGE

53 MAP P112, F4

At Beacon's, which also has three locations in Brooklyn, you'll find a good selection of gently used clothing of a decidedly downtown/Brooklyn hipster aesthetic. Thrift shops are thin on the ground in this area, which makes this even more of a draw. Come midweek or be prepared to brave the crowds. (☑917-261-4863; www.beaconscloset.com; 10 W 13th St, btwn Fifth & Sixth Aves, West Village; ⏱11am-8pm; Ⓢ L, N/Q/R/W, 4/5/6 to 14th St-Union Sq)

Odin
CLOTHING

54 MAP P112, D4

Named after the mighty Norse god, Odin offers a bit of magic for men seeking a new look. The teeming boutique carries stylish labels such as Dickies Construct, Acne Studios and Second Layer, and gives rack space to up-and-coming designers. Stylin' extras include Albertus Swanepoel hats, Oliver Peoples sunglasses and Nikolai Rose jewelry. (☑212-243-4724; www.odinnewyork.com; 106 Greenwich Ave, btwn W 13th & W 12th Sts, West Village; ⏱noon-8pm Mon-Sat, to 7pm Sun; Ⓢ A/C/E, L to 8th Ave-14th St, 1/2/3 to 14th St)

CO Bigelow Chemists
COSMETICS

55 🔒 MAP P112, F5

The 'oldest apothecary in America' is a favorite among New Yorkers and a convenient spot to grab upscale lotions and face masks, organic soaps and bath bombs, and basic toiletries. It's a fun place to test high-end products before you grab a tube of toothpaste. (📞212-533-2700; www.bigelow chemists.com; 414 Sixth Ave, btwn 8th & 9th Sts, West Village; 🕐7:30am-9pm Mon-Fri, 8:30am-7pm Sat, 8:30am-5:30pm Sun; 🚇1 to Christopher St-Sheridan Sq; A/C/E, B/D/F/M to W 4th St-Washington Sq)

CO Bigelow Chemists

Jeffrey New York
FASHION & ACCESSORIES

56 🔒 MAP P112, C3

One of the pioneers in the Meatpacking District's makeover, Jeffrey sells several high-end designer clothing lines – Chanel, Gucci, Prada, Dior and company – as well as accessories and shoes. DJs spinning pop and indie add to the very hip vibe. (📞212-206-1272; www.jeffreynewyork.com; 449 W 14th St, btwn Ninth & Tenth Aves, Chelsea; 🕐10am-8pm Mon-Fri, to 7pm Sat, noon-6pm Sun; 🚇A/C/E, L to 8th Ave-14th St)

Explore

Union Square, Flatiron District & Gramercy

The bustling heart of this area, Union Square sees New Yorkers of all stripes meeting on park benches to catch up over lunch. The triangular Flatiron Building and the verdant respite of Madison Square Park sit to the north. Gramercy Park, with its namesake green space, offers a more subdued residential area to roam.

The Short List

○ **Flatiron Building (p139)** *Puzzling over the arresting triangularity of this architectural icon.*

○ **Union Square (p137)** *Watching the eclectic mix of locals pass through this bustling town square.*

○ **Union Square Greenmarket (p137)** *Inspecting fresh regional produce and sampling artisanal treats.*

○ **Raines Law Room (p143)** *Sipping flawless cocktails in upholstered-leather luxury from another era.*

○ **Eataly (p140)** *Savoring a culinary trip through Italy at this gigantic, venerated food hall and market.*

Getting There & Around

S Union Square is a transit hub: the 4/5/6 lines come from the Upper East Side, the L from Williamsburg and the N/Q/R lines from Queens and Brooklyn. Take the Q for an express link to Herald Square and Times Square.

🚌 The M14A and M14D lines run cross-town along 14th St, and the M23 on 23rd St.

Neighborhood Map on p136

Flatiron Building (p139) S-F/SHUTTERSTOCK ©

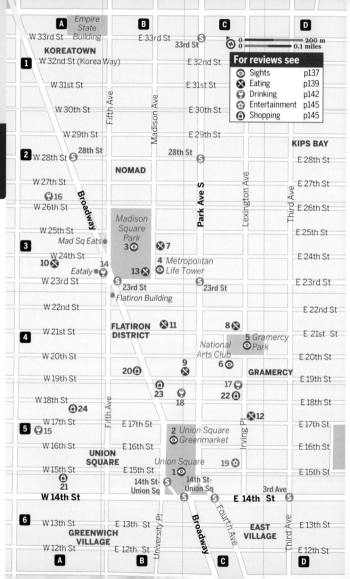

Union Square, Flatiron District & Gramercy

A

Empire State Building

W 33rd St

KOREATOWN

1 W 32nd St (Korea Way)

W 31st St

W 30th St

W 29th St

2 W 28th St Ⓢ 28th St

W 27th St

Ⓠ16
W 26th St

Broadway

W 25th St

Mad Sq Eats●

W 24th St

10Ⓧ 14

Eataly●

W 23rd St Ⓢ 23rd St
●Flatiron Building

W 22nd St

3

**FLATIRON
DISTRICT**

4 W 21st St

W 20th St

W 19th St

Fifth Ave

W 18th St

Ⓐ24

W 17th St

5 Ⓠ15

W 16th St

**UNION
SQUARE**

W 15th St

Ⓐ21

W 14th St

6 W 13th St

**GREENWICH
VILLAGE**

W 12th St

B

E 33rd St Ⓢ 33rd St

E 32nd St

E 31st St

E 30th St

Madison Ave

E 29th St

28th St Ⓢ 28th St

NOMAD

E 27th St

Park Ave S

Madison
Square
Park
3◉

Ⓧ7

4 Metropolitan
13Ⓧ ◉Life Tower

23rd St Ⓢ 23rd St

Ⓧ11

8Ⓧ

National
Arts Club
9
Ⓧ

20Ⓐ

6◉

23 Ⓐ
18 Ⓠ

Fifth Ave

2 Union Square
◉Greenmarket

E 17th St

Union Square
19 Ⓢ
1◉

14th St- Ⓢ
Union Sq

E 16th St

E 15th St

14th St-Ⓢ
Union Sq

E 13th St

University Pl

E 12th St

Broadway

C

▸ 0 ⊙ 200 m
0 0.1 miles

For reviews see

◉	Sights	p137
Ⓧ	Eating	p139
Ⓠ	Drinking	p142
☆	Entertainment	p145
Ⓐ	Shopping	p145

KIPS BAY

E 28th St

Lexington Ave

E 26th St

E 25th St

E 24th St

E 23rd St

E 22nd St

5 Gramercy
◉Park

E 21st St

GRAMERCY E 19th St

17 Ⓠ

22 Ⓐ E 18th St

Irving Pl

Ⓧ12 E 17th St

E 16th St

3rd Ave

E 14th St Ⓢ

Fourth Ave

**EAST
VILLAGE** E 13th St

E 12th St

D

Third Ave

E 28th St

E 25th St

E 22nd St

E 21st St

E 20th St

E 15th St

3rd Ave

Sights

Union Square

SQUARE

1  MAP P136, B5

Union Square is like the Noah's Ark of New York, rescuing at least two of every kind from the curling seas of concrete. In fact, one would be hard pressed to find a more eclectic cross-section of locals gathered in one public place: suited businessfolk gulping fresh air during their lunch breaks, dreadlocked loiterers tapping beats on their tablas, skateboarders flipping tricks on the southeastern stairs, old-timers poring over chess boards, and throngs of protesting masses chanting fervently for various causes. (www.unionsquarenyc.org; 17th St, btwn Broadway & Park Ave S, Union Square; ⑤4/5/6, N/Q/R, L to 14th St-Union Sq)

Union Square Greenmarket

MARKET

2 ⊙ MAP P136, B5

Don't be surprised if you spot some of New York's top chefs prodding the produce here: Union Square's green market is arguably the city's most famous. Whet your appetite trawling the stalls, which peddle anything and everything from upstate fruit and vegetables to artisanal breads, cheeses and cider. (☎212-788-7476; www.grownyc.org/unionsquaregreenmarket; E 17th St, btwn Broadway & Park Ave S, Union Square; ⊙8am-6pm Mon, Wed, Fri & Sat; ⑤4/5/6, N/Q/R/W, L to 14th St-Union Sq)

Union Square Greenmarket

Madison Square Park PARK

3 ⊙ MAP P136, B3

This park defined the northern reaches of Manhattan until the island's population exploded after the Civil War. These days it's a much-welcome oasis from Manhattan's relentless pace, with a popular children's playground, dog-run area and the Shake Shack (p143) burger joint. It's also one of the city's most cultured parks, with specially commissioned art installations and (in the warmer months) activities ranging from literary discussions to live-music gigs. See the website for more information. (📞212-520-7600; www. madisonsquarepark.org; E 23rd to 26th Sts, btwn Fifth & Madison Aves, Flatiron District; ⏰6am-11pm; 👫; ⑤R/W, F/M, 6 to 23rd St)

Metropolitan Life Tower HISTORIC BUILDING

4 ⊙ MAP P136, B3

Completed in 1909, this 700ft-high clock tower soaring above Madison Square Park's southeastern corner is the work of Napoleon LeBrun, a Philadelphia-born architect of French stock. Italophiles may feel a certain déjà vu gazing at the tower as LeBrun's inspiration was Venice's world-famous *campanile* (bell tower) in Piazza San Marco. Ironically, this New World version is now older than its muse: the original Venetian tower collapsed in 1902, with its replacement not completed until

1912. (1 Madison Ave, btwn E 23rd & E 24th Sts, Flatiron District; ⑤N/R, F/M, 6 to 23rd St)

Gramercy Park PARK

5 ⊙ MAP P136, C4

Romantic Gramercy Park was created by Samuel Ruggles in 1831 after he drained the area's swamp and laid out streets in an English style. You can't enter the private park (the only one in Manhattan), but peer through the gate and imagine tough-guy James Cagney enjoying it – the Hollywood actor once resided at 34 Gramercy Park E. At 15 Gramercy Park S stands the National Arts Club, whose members include Martin Scorsese, Uma Thurman and Ethan Hawke. (E 20th St, btwn Park & Third Aves, Gramercy; ⑤N/R, 6 to 23rd St)

National Arts Club ARTS CENTER

6 ⊙ MAP P136, C4

Founded in 1898 to promote public interest in the arts, the National Arts Club holds art exhibitions, with free admission to the public during weekdays; check the website for upcoming shows as well as evening events. Calvert Vaux – one of the creators of Central Park – designed the building itself, with a picture-lined front parlor adorned with a beautiful, vaulted stained-glass panel. The mansion was once home to Samuel J Tilden, a former New York governor and the failed 1876 presidential candidate. (📞212-475-3424; www.

The Flatiron Building

Designed by Daniel Burnham and built in 1902, the 20-story **Flatiron Building** (Map p136, B4; Broadway, cnr Fifth Ave & 23rd St, Flatiron District; S N/R, F/M, 6 to 23rd St) has a unique triangular footprint, with a traditional beaux-arts limestone and terra-cotta facade that gets more beautiful the longer you stare at it. Best viewed from the traffic island north of 23rd St, this singular structure dominated the plaza back in the dawning skyscraper era of the early 1900s, coinciding with the proliferation of mass-produced picture postcards. Even before its completion, images of the soon-to-be world's tallest tower (a title it would hold until 1909) circulated the globe, which helped make it an architectural icon. Actress Katharine Hepburn once quipped that *she'd* like to be admired as much as the grand old building.

For decades it was filled with small-business tenants, many in the publishing industry. Early tenant Frank Munsey published *Munsey's Magazine,* featuring the short stories of O Henry (best known for 'The Gift of the Magi'), the paintings of John Sloan and photographs of Alfred Stieglitz.

In recent years the ground floor of the building's 'prow' was transformed into a glassed-in art space. Past installations have included a life-size 3D-cutout replica of Edward Hopper's 1942 painting *Nighthawks,* its angular diner remarkably similar to the Flatiron's distinctive shape. Plans are underway to restore the building's former grandeur and turn it into a luxurious five-star hotel.

nationalartsclub.org; 15 Gramercy Park S, Gramercy; admission free; ⊙galleries 10am-5pm Mon-Fri; S N/R, 6 to 23rd St)

Eating

Eleven Madison Park

AMERICAN $$$

7 ✖ MAP P136, B3

Eleven Madison Park consistently bags a spot on top restaurant lists. Frankly, we're not surprised: this revamped poster child of modern, sustainable American cooking is also one of only five NYC restaurants sporting three Michelin stars. Insane attention to detail, intense creativity and whimsy are all trademarks of chef Daniel Humm's approach. (✆212-889-0905; www.elevenmadisonpark.com; 11 Madison Ave, btwn 24th & 25th Sts, Flatiron District; bar mains $35-50, tasting menu $175-335; ⊙5:30-10pm Mon-Wed, to 10:30pm Thu, noon-1pm & 5:30-10:30pm Fri-Sun; S R/W, 6 to 23rd St)

Feast at Eataly

Mario Batali's sprawling temple to Italian gastronomy, **Eataly** (Map p136, A3; 212-229-2560; www.eataly.com; 200 Fifth Ave, at W 23rd St, Flatiron District; 7am-11pm; ; R/W, F/M, 6 to 23rd St) is a veritable wonderland. Feast on everything from vibrant *crudo* (raw fish) and *fritto misto* (tempura-style vegetables) to steamy pasta and pizza at the emporium's string of sit-down eateries. Alternatively, guzzle espresso at the bar and enjoy a custom-filled cannoli before scouring the shelves for a DIY picnic hamper that *nonna* would approve of.

Maialino ITALIAN $$$

 8 MAP P136, C4

Fans reserve tables up to four weeks in advance at this Danny Meyer classic, but the best seats in the house are at the walk-in bar, with sociable, knowledgeable staffers. Wherever you're plonked, take your taste buds on a Roman holiday. Maialino's lip-smacking, rustic Italian fare is created using produce from the nearby Union Square Greenmarket (p137). (212-777-2410; www.maialinonyc. com; Gramercy Park Hotel, 2 Lexington Ave, at 21st St, Gramercy; mains $24-58; 7:30-10am, noon-2pm & 5:30-10:30pm Mon-Thu, to 11pm Fri, 10am-2pm & 5:30-11pm Sat, to 10:30pm Sun; 6, R/W to 23rd St)

Craft AMERICAN $$$

 9 MAP P136, C4

Humming, high-end Craft flies the flag for small, family-owned farms and food producers, their bounty transformed into pure, polished dishes. Whether nibbling on flawlessly charred braised octopus, juicy roasted quail or pumpkin *mezzaluna* pasta with sage, brown butter and Parmesan, expect every ingredient to sing with flavor. Book ahead Wednesday to Saturday or head in by 6pm or after 9:30pm. (212-780-0880; www.craftrestaurant. com; 43 E 19th St, btwn Broadway & Park Ave S, Union Square; mains $33-69; 5:30-10pm Mon-Thu, to 11pm Fri, 5-11pm Sat, to 9pm Sun; ; 4/5/6, N/Q/R/W, L to 14th St-Union Sq)

Tacombi Café El Presidente MEXICAN $

 10 MAP P136, A3

Channeling the cafes of Mexico City, pink-and-green Tacombi covers numerous bases, from juice and liquor bar to taco joint. Score a table, order a margarita and hop your way around a menu of Mexican street-food deliciousness. Top choices include *esquites* (grilled corn with *cotija* cheese and chipotle mayonnaise, served in a paper cup) and succulent carnitas tacos. (212-242-3491; www. tacombi.com; 30 W 24th St, btwn Fifth & Sixth Aves, Flatiron District; tacos $4-9; quesadillas $7-8; 11am-midnight

Mon-Sat, to 10:30pm Sun; 🖉; **S** F/M, R/W to 23rd St)

Clocktower BRITISH $$$

Brits do it best at Jason Atherton's clubby, new A-lister, hidden away inside the landmark Metropolitan Life Tower (See **4** 🎯 Map p136, B3). This is the latest venture for the Michelin-starred British chef, its wood-and-stucco dining rooms setting a handsome scene for high-end comfort grub like beet-cured heritage pork chop with heirloom carrots and black pudding and a 'macaroni 'n' cheese' with slow-cooked ox cheek. (🖉212-413-4300; www.theclocktowernyc.com; 5 Madison Ave, btwn 23rd & 24th Sts, Gramercy; dinner mains $27-47; ⏱7-10:30am, 11:30am-2:30pm & 5:30-10pm daily,

afternoon tea 3-5pm Fri-Sun; 🛜; **S** F/M, R/W, 6 to 23rd St)

Cosme MEXICAN $$$

11 ❌ MAP P136, B4

Mexican gets haute at this slinky, charcoal-hued restaurant, with innovative takes on south-of-the-border flavors from co-chefs Enrique Olvera and Daniela Soto-Innes. Subvert culinary stereotypes with the likes of delicate, invigorating scallops with avocado and jicama, a green mole with bok choy and purslane, herb guacamole or Cosme's cult-status duck carnitas. Book ahead or try your luck at the walk-in bar. (🖉212-913-9659; www.cosmenyc.com; 35 E 21st St, btwn Broadway & Park Ave S, Flatiron District; dinner dishes $19-29; ⏱noon-2:30pm & 5:30-11pm Mon-Thu,

Serra rooftop bar (p142) at Eataly

Mad Sq Eats

Each spring and fall, foodies flock to tiny General Worth Sq (wedged between Fifth Ave and Broadway, opposite Madison Square Park) for **Mad Sq Eats** (Map p136, B3; www.madisonsquarepark.org/mad-sq-food/mad-sq-eats; General Worth Sq, Flatiron District; ⏰spring & fall 11am-9pm; **S**R/W, F/M, 6 to 23rd St), a month-long culinary pop-up market. Its 30 or so vendors include some of the city's hottest eateries, cooking up anything from proper pizza to brisket tacos using top local produce.

to midnight Fri, 11:30am-2:30pm & 5:30pm-midnight Sat, to 11pm Sun; 🛜; **S**R/W, 6 to 23rd St)

Casa Mono TAPAS $$$

13 MAP P136, C5

Another success story from restaurateur Mario Batali and chef Andy Nusser, Casa Mono features a great, long bar where you can sit and watch your Michelin-starred tapas being prepared, or dine at tables for more discreet conversation. Either way, get set for flavor-slamming bites like creamy eggs with sea urchin, walnuts, lime and anchovy oil. (📞212-253-2773; www.casamononyc.com; 52 Irving Pl, btwn 17th & 18th Sts, Gramercy; small plates $13-22; ⏰noon-11pm Sun-Tue, to

midnight Wed-Sat; **S**4/5/6, N/Q/R/W, L to 14th St-Union Sq)

Shake Shack BURGERS $

13 MAP P136, B3

The flagship of chef Danny Meyer's gourmet burger chain (this is where it all started – in a hot-dog cart), Shake Shack whips up hyper-fresh burgers, hand-cut fries and a rotating line-up of frozen custards. Vegetarians can dip into the crisp portobello burger. Lines are long – but worth it – and you can eat while people-watching at tables and benches in the park. (📞646-889-6600; www.shakeshack.com; Madison Square Park, cnr E 23rd St & Madison Ave, Flatiron District; burgers $6-11; ⏰9am-11pm; **S**R/W, F/M, 6 to 23rd St)

Drinking

Serra ROOFTOP BAR

14 MAP P136, B3

The crown jewel of Italian food emporium Eataly (p140) is this covered rooftop garden tucked betwixt the Flatiron's corporate towers. The theme is refreshed each season, meaning you might find a Mediterranean beach escape one month and an alpine country retreat the next, but the setting is unfailingly impressive and food and drink always match up to the gourmet goodies below. (📞212-937-8910; www.eataly.com; 200 Fifth Ave, at W 23rd St, Flatiron District; ⏰11:30am-10pm Sun-Thu, to 11pm Fri & Sat; **S**F/M, R/W, 6 to 23rd St)

Shake Shack

Raines Law Room COCKTAIL BAR

15 MAP P136, A5

A sea of velvet drapes and over-stuffed leather lounge chairs, the perfect amount of exposed brick, expertly crafted cocktails using hard-to-find spirits – these folks are as serious as a mortgage payment when it comes to amplified atmosphere. There's no sign from the street; look for the '48' above the door and ring the bell to gain entry. (www.raineslawroom.com; 48 W 17th St, btwn Fifth & Sixth Aves, Flatiron District; ⏰5pm-2am Mon-Thu, to 3am Fri & Sat, to 1am Sun; Ⓢ F/M to 14th St, L to 6th Ave, 1 to 18th St)

Flatiron Room COCKTAIL BAR

16 MAP P136, A2

Vintage wallpaper, a glittering chandelier and hand-painted coffered ceilings make for a suitably elegant scene at this grown-up drinking den, its artfully lit cabinets graced with rare whiskeys. Fine cocktails pair nicely with high-end sharing plates, from deviled eggs with duck rillett to smoked oysters and charcuterie. Live music features most nights, including bluegrass and jazz. Reservations are highly recommended. (☎212-725-3860; www.theflatironroom.com; 37 W 26th St, btwn Sixth Ave & Broadway, Flatiron District; ⏰5pm-2am Mon-Sat, to midnight Sun; Ⓢ R/W to 28th St, F/M to 23rd St)

Art in Union Square

A walk around Union Square will reveal a string of whimsical, temporary sculptures. Of the permanent offerings is an imposing equestrian statue of George Washington (one of the first public pieces of art in New York City) and a statue of peacemaker Mahatma Gandhi.

Trumping both on the southeastern side of the square is a massive art installation that either earns confused stares or simply gets overlooked by passersby. A symbolic representation of the passage of time, *Metronome* has two parts: a digital clock with a puzzling display of numbers, and a wand-like apparatus with smoke puffing out of concentric rings.

We'll let you ponder the latter while we give you the skinny on what exactly the winking orange digits denote: the 14 numbers must be split into two groups of seven: the seven from the left tell the current time (hour, minute, second, tenth-of-a-second) and the seven from the right are meant to be read in reverse order; they represent the remaining amount of time in the day.

Irving Farm Roasters
CAFE

17 🟢 MAP P136, C5

From keyboard-tapping scribes to gossiping friends and academics, this bustling downstairs cafe is never short of a crowd. Hand-picked beans are lovingly roasted on a farm in the Hudson Valley (about 90 miles from NYC), and served alongside tasty edibles like Balthazar-baked croissants, granola, egg dishes, bagels and pressed sandwiches. (📞212-995-5252; www.irvingfarm.com; 71 Irving Pl, btwn 18th & 19th Sts, Gramercy; ⏰7am-8pm Mon-Fri, from 8am Sat & Sun; 🚇4/5/6, N/Q/R/W, L to 14th St-Union Sq)

Old Town Bar & Restaurant
BAR

18 🟢 MAP P136, B5

It still looks like 1892 in here, with the mahogany bar, original tile floors and tin ceilings – the Old Town is an old-world drinking-man's classic. It's frequently used as an old-school shooting location for movies and TV (and even Madonna's 'Bad Girl' video). Most people settle into one of the snug wooden booths for beers and a burger (from $12.50). (📞212-529-6732; www.oldtownbar.com; 45 E 18th St, btwn Broadway & Park Ave S, Union Square; ⏰11:30am-1am Mon-Fri, noon-1am Sat, 3pm-midnight Sun; 📶; 🚇4/5/6, N/Q/R/W, L to 14th St-Union Sq)

Entertainment

Irving Plaza

LIVE MUSIC

19 ⭐ MAP P136, C5

Rocking since 1978, Irving Plaza has seen them all: the Ramones, Bob Dylan, U2, Pearl Jam, you name it. These days it's a great in-between stage for quirkier rock and pop acts, from riot grrrls Sleater-Kinney to hard rockers Disturbed. There's a cozy floor around the stage, and good views from the mezzanine. (☏212-777-6817; www. irvingplaza.com; 17 Irving Pl, at 15th St, Union Square; S4/5/6, N/Q/R, L to 14th St-Union Sq)

Shopping

Fishs Eddy

HOMEWARES

20 🔒 MAP P136, B4

High-quality and irreverent design has made Fishs Eddy a staple in the homes of hip New Yorkers for years. Its store is a veritable land-slide of mugs, plates, dish towels, carafes and anything else that be-longs in a cupboard. Styles range from tasteful color blocking to delightfully outrageous patterns. The 'Brooklynese' line (*Cawfee, Shuguh, Sawlt* etc) makes for great souvenirs. (☏212-420-9020; www. fishseddy.com; 889 Broadway, at E 19th St, Union Square; ⏰10am-9pm Mon-Fri, to 8pm Sat & Sun; SR/W, 6 to 23rd St)

Old Town Bar & Restaurant

Where to Shop

From rare children's books and artisanal cheeses, to one of New York's best-loved farmers markets, this block of neighborhoods harbors retail gems. However, today there are as many big chain stores as independent boutiques – particularly around the edges of **Union Square** and up **Sixth Ave**. **Fourteenth St** (more west than east) is a shopping adventure all of its own, hawking everything from guitars and furniture to sportswear, wigs and tattoos. For midrange to more upscale chains like Zara, Banana Republic, Club Monaco, J Crew, Anthropologie and Intermix, strut north up **Fifth Ave**.

Rent the Runway   CLOTHING

21 🅐 MAP P136, A6

At the flagship store of this popular fashion-rental service anyone can pop in for an affordable fashion consultation ($30) for both planned and last-minute events. It's full of looks by high-end designers (Narciso Rodriguez, Badgley Mischka, Nicole Miller) available to rent. Perfect for those who pack light, but want to make a splash. (www.renttherunway.com; 30 W 15th St, btwn Fifth & Sixth Aves, Union Square; ⏰8am-9pm Mon-Fri, 9am-8pm Sat, to 7pm Sun; 🅂L, F/M to 14th St-6th Ave; 4/5/6, L, N/Q/R/W to 14th St-Union Sq)

Bedford Cheese Shop   FOOD

22 🅐 MAP P136, C5

Whether you're after local, raw-cow's-milk cheese washed in absinthe, or garlic-infused goat's-milk cheese from Australia, chances are you'll find it among the 200-strong selection at this outpost of Brooklyn's most-celebrated cheese vendor. Pair the cheesy goodness with artisanal charcuterie, deli treats and ready-to-eat sandwiches ($9 to $11.50), as well as a proud array of Made-in-Brooklyn edibles. (📞718-599-7588; www.bedfordcheeseshop.com; 67 Irving Pl, btwn E 18th & 19th Sts, Gramercy; ⏰8am-8pm Mon-Fri, 9am-8pm Sat, to 6pm Sun; 🅂4/5/6, N/Q/R/W, L to 14th St-Union Sq)

ABC Carpet & Home   HOMEWARES

23 🅐 MAP P136, B5

A hotspot for home designers and decorators brainstorming ideas, this beautifully curated, seven-level temple to good taste heaves with all sorts of furnishings, small and large. Shop for easy-to-pack knickknacks, boho textiles and jewelry, as well as statement furniture, designer lighting, ceramics and antique carpets. Come Christmas the shop is a joy to behold and it's a great place to buy decorations. (📞212-473-3000; www.abchome.com; 888 Broadway, at E 19th St, Flatiron District; ⏰10am-7pm

URBAN BY HABIT/SHUTTERSTOCK ©

Fishs Eddy (p145)

Mon-Sat, noon-6pm Sun; ⑤ 4/5/6, N/Q/R/W, L to 14th St-Union Sq)

Books of Wonder   BOOKS

24 🔒 MAP P136, A5

Devoted to children's and young-adult titles, this wonderful bookstore is a great place to take little ones on a rainy day, especially when a kids' author is giving a reading or a storyteller is on hand. There's an impressive range of NYC-themed picture books, plus a section dedicated to rare and vintage children's books and limited-edition children's-book artwork. (📞212-989-3270; www. booksofwonder.com; 18 W 18th St, btwn Fifth & Sixth Aves, Flatiron District; ⏰10am-7pm Mon-Sat, 11am-6pm Sun; 🚻; ⑤F/M to 14th St, L to 6th Ave)

Explore

Midtown

Central hub of the city, Midtown is the NYC of post-cards. More than 300,000 people a day jostle their way through its busy, cab-filled streets, home to icons like Times Square, Grand Central Terminal and the Empire State Building. Cultural knockouts include MoMA and the New York Public Library, with the food-packed, gay-friendly streets of Hell's Kitchen nearby.

The Short List

○ **Rockefeller Center (p160)** *Playing Spot the Land-mark at the jaw-dropping Top of the Rock observation deck, or taking a tour of NBC's historic TV studios.*

○ **Museum of Modern Art (p154)** *Hanging out with Picasso, Warhol and Rothko at a world-class museum.*

○ **Bryant Park (p159)** *Lunching alfresco, watching a movie under the stars or even just relaxing in this activity-filled Midtown oasis.*

○ **Jazz at Lincoln Center (p169)** *Gazing at the spec-tacular view while listening to world-class musicians hit their groove.*

○ **Broadway (p169)** *Adding a little sparkle to life with a toe-tapping, soul-lifting Broadway show.*

Getting There & Around

S Times Sq-42nd St, Grand Central-42nd St and 34th St-Herald Sq are Midtown's main interchange stations. A/C/E and 1/2/3 lines run north–south through Midtown West; 4/5/6 through Midtown East. The central B/D/F/M lines follow Sixth Ave, while N/Q/R/W follow Broadway. The 7, E and M lines offer some crosstown service.

Neighborhood Map on p156

Bryant Park (p159) GAGLIARDIPHOTOGRAPHY/SHUTTERSTOCK ©

Top Experience 📷
Stroll through Times Square

Love it or hate it, the intersection of Broadway and Seventh Ave – better known as Times Square – is New York City's heart. It's a restless, hypnotic torrent of glittering lights, giant billboards and raw urban energy that doesn't seem to have an off switch: it's nearly as busy in the wee hours as it is in the afternoon.

◉ MAP P156, D4

www.timessquarenyc.org

Broadway, at Seventh Ave

⑤ N/Q/R/W, S, 1/2/3, 7 to Times Sq-42nd St

Crossroads of the World

This is the New York of collective fantasies – the place where Al Jolson 'makes it' in the 1927 film *The Jazz Singer* and Alicia Keys and Jay-Z waxed lyrically about the concrete jungle.

But for several decades, the dream here was a sordid one. The economic crash of the early 1970s led to a mass exodus of corporations from Times Square. Billboard niches went dark, stores shut and once-grand hotels were converted into SRO (single-room occupancy) dives. While the adjoining Theater District survived, its respectable playhouses shared the streets with porn cinemas and strip clubs. That all changed with tough-talking former mayor Rudolph Giuliani who, in the 1990s, boosted police numbers and lured in a wave of 'respectable' retail chains, restaurants and attractions. By the new millennium, Times Square had gone from X-rated to G-rated, drawing almost 50 million visitors annually.

Today's Times Square

Almost as bright at 2am as it is at noon, and always jammed with people, Times Square proves that New York truly is the city that never sleeps. The massive billboards stretch half a skyscraper tall, and LED signs are lit for shows and performances. A mishmash of costumed characters on the square (from the cute, like Elmo, to the noble, like the Statue of Liberty, to the popular, like Marvel action heroes, to the just plain bizarre, like Naked Cowboy) mix with the jumble of humanity from every corner of the globe. Walk around and in minutes you'll hear more languages being spoken than you even knew existed. It's also an urban playground for public art and seasonal events, not forgetting the world's most famous spot to celebrate New Year's Eve.

★ **Top Tips**

In 2017, designated outdoor street-food areas launched in Times Square's pedestrian plazas (at the Broadway intersections with W 43rd and W 47th Sts). There's also a **tourist information booth** (212-484-1222; www.timessquarenyc.org; Broadway Plaza, at W 45th St; 8am-5pm).

✕ **Take a Break**

Times Square is so touristy and chaotic that if you want a proper meal, you're better off eating elsewhere. **Fournos Theophilos** (212-278-0015; www.fournos.com; 45 W 45th St, btwn Fifth & Sixth Aves; lunch $12; 7am-10pm Mon-Sat, from 8am Sun, closed 4-5pm;), a two-block walk east, is a quiet retreat for a delicious Greek lunch with baklava milkshakes.

Top Experience 📷
Catch the View at the Empire State Building

The Chrysler Building may be prettier, and One World Trade Center taller, but the queen bee of the New York skyline remains the Empire State Building. NYC's former tallest star has enjoyed close-ups in around a hundred films, from King Kong *to* Independence Day. *Heading up to the top is as quintessentially New York as pastrami, rye and pickles.*

◎ MAP P156, E5

www.empirestatebuilding.com

20 W 34th St

86th-fl observation deck adult/child $38/32, incl 102nd-fl deck $58/52

🕓 8am-2am, last elevators up 1:15am

Ⓢ 6 to 33rd St, B/D/F/M, N/Q/R/W to 34th St-Herald Sq

By the Numbers

The statistics are astounding: 10 million bricks, 60,000 tons of steel, 6400 windows and 328,000 sq ft of marble. Built on the original site of the Waldorf-Astoria Hotel, construction took a record-setting 410 days, using seven million hours of labor and costing a mere $41 million. It might sound like a lot, but it fell well below its $50 million budget (just as well, given it went up during the Great Depression). Coming in at 102 stories and 1454ft from top to bottom, the limestone tower opened for business on May 1, 1931. Generations later, Deborah Kerr's words to Cary Grant in *An Affair to Remember* still ring true: 'It's the nearest thing to heaven we have in New York.'

A Bird's-Eye View

Unless you're Ann Darrow (the unfortunate woman caught in King Kong's grip), heading to the top of the Empire State Building should leave you beaming. There are two observation decks. The open-air 86th-floor deck offers an alfresco experience, with telescopes (previously coin operated; now free) for close-up glimpses of the metropolis in action. Further up, at the top of the spire, the enclosed 102nd floor is New York's second-highest observation deck, trumped only by the observation deck at One World Trade Center. Needless to say, the views through the floor-to-ceiling windows over the city's five boroughs (and four neighboring states, weather permitting) are quite simply exquisite. The views from both decks are especially spectacular at sunset, when the city dons its nighttime cloak in dusk's afterglow.

★ Top Tips

o Getting here very early (eg 8am) or very late will help avoid delays, as will buying advance tickets online (for a $2 fee).

o On the 86th floor between 10pm and 1am from Thursday to Saturday, the twinkling sea of lights is accompanied by a live saxophone.

o Download the Empire State Building tour app (free with your ticket) or stream the audio version live using the on-site free wi-fi.

✖ Take a Break

o You're a short walk from Koreatown's abundant eating options, including peaceful Hangawi (p165).

o Or, stroll northward and lunch at the **Bryant Park Grill** (www.bryantparkgrillnyc.com; Bryant Park, 25 W 40th St, btwn Fifth & Sixth Aves; mains $20-49; ⏱11:30am-3:30pm & 5-11pm Apr-Dec, shorter hours Jan-Mar; 🍴; ⓢB/D/F/M to 42nd St-Bryant Park; 7 to 5th Ave).

Top Experience 📷

Explore Masterpieces at the Museum of Modern Art

MoMA boasts more A-listers than an Oscars after-party: Van Gogh, Matisse, Picasso, Warhol, Cassatt, Gaugin, Mondrian, Pollock and Bourgeois. Since its 1929 founding, the museum has amassed around 200,000 artworks, documenting the creativity of the late-19th century through to today.

◎ MAP P156, E2

📞 212-708-9400

www.moma.org

11 W 53rd St

adult/child $25/free, 5:30-9pm Fri free

🕐 10am-5:30pm Sat-Thu, to 9pm Fri & 1st Thu

Ⓢ E, M to 5th Ave-53rd St; F to 57th St

Highlights of the Collection

Works are rotated through the galleries every six months, so it's hard to say exactly what you'll find on display, but Van Gogh's phenomenally popular *The Starry Night* should be a sure bet – it's usually mobbed by a circle of star-struck fans wielding cameras. Other highlights of the collection include Picasso's *Les Demoiselles d'Avignon* and Henri Rousseau's *The Sleeping Gypsy,* not to mention iconic American works like Warhol's *Campbell's Soup Cans* and *Gold Marilyn Monroe,* Matisse's *Dance (I)* and Hopper's poignant *New York Movie.*

Abby Aldrich Rockefeller Sculpture Garden

With architect Yoshio Taniguchi's reconstruction of the museum in 2004 came the restoration of the Sculpture Garden to the original, larger vision of Philip Johnson's 1953 design, which he described as a 'sort of outdoor room.' On warm, sunny days, it feels like a soothing alfresco lounge, with works from greats such as Matisse, Giacometti, Calder and Picasso. It's open free of charge from 9:30am to 10:15am daily (except in inclement weather).

A Monumental Renovation

In 2019, MoMA underwent a months-long redesign by Diller Scofidio + Renfro, which added more than 40,000 sq ft of gallery space. The permanent collection has been curated as an overarching history of modern art, showcasing painting, sculpture, photography, film, architecture, industrial design and other disciplines, all set together in chronological segments on floor 5 (1880s–1940s), floor 4 (1940s–1970s) and floor 2 (1970s–present). Floor 3 features galleries for temporary exhibits, while the new 4th-floor Kravis Studio will be a dedicated showcase for performance and other experimental art.

★ **Top Tips**

⊙ To maximize your time and create a plan of attack, download the museum's free smartphone app from the website beforehand. It's available in several different languages.

⊙ Mondays and Tuesdays are the best (ie least-crowded) days to visit, except on public holidays. Friday evenings and weekends can be incredibly crowded and frustrating.

✕ **Take a Break**

⊙ For communal tables and a casual vibe, nosh on Italian-inspired fare at **Cafe 2** (dishes $12-14; ⊙11am-5:30pm Sat-Thu, to 7:30pm Fri).

⊙ For table service, opt for **Terrace Café** (small plates $8-21; ⊙11am-5:30pm Sat-Thu, to 7:30pm Fri), which features an outdoor terrace overlooking 53rd St.

A **B** **C** **D**

1

W 59th St

Columbus Ave

28

Columbus Circle

Central Park

Central Park South

21

57th St-7th Ave

57th St

W 58th St

W 57th St

Hearst Tower

Broadway

W 56th St

29

17

W 55th St

Eighth Ave

Seventh Ave

Sixth Ave (Avenue of the Americas)

W 54th St

7th Ave

Tenth Ave

W 53rd St

2

Dewitt Clinton Park

9A

Hudson River Park

Twelfth Ave (West Side Hwy)

W 52nd St

23

Ninth Ave

W 51st St

25

11

15

W 50th St

50th St

39

34

Worldwide Plaza

W 49th St

49th St

Eugene O'Neill Theatre

Eleventh Ave

W 48th St

THEATER DISTRICT

47th-50th Sts-Rockefeller Center

3

W 47th St

26

TKTS Booth

33

HELL'S KITCHEN

W 46th St

22

20

W 45th St

Richard Rodgers Theatre

27

31

W 44th St

35

Times Square

Bank of America Tower

W 43rd St

32

W 42nd St

42nd St-Port Authority

42nd St-Times Sq

42nd St-Bryant Park

4

W 41st St

W 41st St

Port Authority Bus Terminal

W 40th St

Lincoln Tunnel

W 39th St

Dyer St

W 38th St

38

GARMENT DISTRICT

Broadway

Sixth Ave (Avenue of the Americas)

W 37th St

Eighth Ave

W 36th St

Seventh Ave

W 35th St

HERALD SQUARE

5

34th St-Hudson Yards

34th St

W 34th St

34th St-Penn Station

Macy's

NYC Information Center

34th St-Herald Sq

W 33rd St

30

Penn Station

Eleventh Ave

Tenth Ave

Ninth Ave

W 31st St

W 31st St

0 — 500 m
0 — 0.25 miles

For reviews see

Top Experiences p150
Sights p158
Eating p163
Drinking p166
Entertainment p169
Shopping p173

6

W 30th St

W 30th St

W 29th St

W 29th St

W 28th St

Eighth Ave

Seventh Ave

W 28th St

A **B** **C** **D**

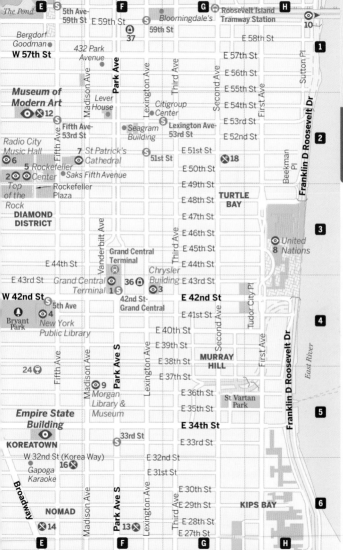

Midtown

The Pond

E **S** 5th Ave-59th St

Bergdorf Goodman
W 57th St

F E 59th St

S 59th St

Bloomingdale's

G ⊙ Roosevelt Island Tramway Station

H

⊙ 10

E 58th St

432 Park Avenue

S 37

E 57th St

1

E 56th St

Museum of Modern Art
⊙ ⊗ 12

Lever House

Citigroup Center

Madison Ave

Park Ave

Lexington Ave

Third Ave

Second Ave

First Ave

Sutton Pl

E 55th St

E 54th St

E 53rd St

⊙ Fifth Ave-53rd St

⊗ Lexington Ave-53rd St

E 52nd St

2

Seagram Building

Radio City Music Hall
⊙ 6

7 St Patrick's Cathedral
⊙

5 Rockefeller
2 ⊙ ⊙ Center
Saks Fifth Avenue

S 51st St

E 51st St

⊗ 18

E 50th St

Top of the Rock

Rockefeller Plaza

E 49th St

E 48th St

DIAMOND DISTRICT

E 47th St

TURTLE BAY

Beekman Pl

Franklin D Roosevelt Dr

East River

Vanderbilt Ave

E 46th St

Third Ave

E 45th St

3

⊙ United 8 Nations

E 44th St

E 44th St

Grand Central Terminal

E 43rd St

Chrysler Building

E 43rd St

E 42nd St

Tudor City Pl

E 43rd St

Grand Central Terminal ⊙ 1 **S**

36 **S**

⊙ 3

42nd St-Grand Central

4

W 42nd St

⊙ 5th Ave
⊙ 4

S

New York Public Library

E 41st St

E 40th St

Second Ave

First Ave

Q
Bryant Park

E 39th St

E 38th St

MURRAY HILL

E 37th St

24 ⊗

Fifth Ave

Madison Ave

⊙ 9

Park Ave S

Lexington Ave

E 36th St

E 35th St

St Vartan Park

5

Empire State Building
⊙

Morgan Library & Museum

E 34th St

KOREATOWN

S 33rd St

E 33rd St

W 32nd St (Korea Way)

16 ⊗

E 32nd St

E 31st St

Gapoga Karaoke

E 30th St

Third Ave

KIPS BAY

6

Broadway

NOMAD

⊗ 14

Madison Ave

Park Ave S

Lexington Ave

E 29th St

E 28th St

E 27th St

13 ⊗

Franklin D Roosevelt Dr

E

F

G

H

Sights

Grand Central Terminal
HISTORIC BUILDING

1 ◉ MAP P156, F4

Completed in 1913, Grand Central Terminal – commonly, if incorrectly, called Grand Central Station – is one of New York's most venerated beaux-arts beauties. Adorned with Tennessee-marble floors and Italian-marble ticket counters, its glorious main concourse is capped by a **vaulted ceiling** depicting the constellations, designed by French painter Paul César Helleu. When commuters complained that the sky is backwards – painted as if looking down from above, not up – it was asserted as intentional (possibly to avoid having to admit an error). (www.grandcentralterminal.com; 89 E 42nd St, at Park Ave; ◷5:30am-2am; ⑤S, 4/5/6, 7 to Grand Central-42nd St, ⊠Metro North to Grand Central)

Top of the Rock
VIEWPOINT

2 ◉ MAP P156, E2

Designed in homage to ocean liners and opened in 1933, this 70th-floor open-air observation deck sits atop 30 Rockefeller Plaza, the tallest skyscraper at the Rockefeller Center (p160). Top of the Rock beats the Empire State Building (p152) on several levels: it's less crowded, has wider observation decks (both outdoor and indoor) and offers a view of the Empire State Building itself. Before ascending, a fascinating 2nd-floor exhibition gives an insight into the

Grand Central Terminal

ANDERM/SHUTTERSTOCK ©

legendary philanthropist behind the art deco complex. (212-698-2000, toll free 877-692-7625; www.topoftherocknyc.com; 30 Rockefeller Plaza, entrance on W 50th St, btwn Fifth & Sixth Aves; adult/child $38/32, sunrise/sunset combo $56/45; 8am-midnight, last elevator at 11pm; S B/D/F/M to 47th-50th Sts-Rockefeller Center)

Chrysler Building
HISTORIC BUILDING

3 MAP P156, F4

Designed by William Van Alen and completed in 1930, the 77-floor Chrysler Building is the pinup for New York's purest art deco architecture, guarded by stylized eagles of chromium nickel and topped by a beautiful seven-tiered spire reminiscent of the rising sun. The building was constructed as the headquarters for Walter P Chrysler and his automobile empire. Unable to compete on the production line with bigger rivals Ford and General Motors, Chrysler trumped them on the skyline, and with one of Gotham's most beautiful lobbies. (405 Lexington Ave, at E 42nd St; lobby 7am-6:30pm Mon-Fri; S S, 4/5/6, 7 to Grand Central-42nd St)

New York Public Library
HISTORIC BUILDING

4 MAP P156, E4

Loyally guarded by 'Patience' and 'Fortitude' (the marble lions overlooking Fifth Ave), this beaux-arts show-off is one of NYC's best

Bryant Park

European coffee kiosks, al-fresco chess games, summer film screenings and winter ice skating: it's hard to believe that the leafy oasis of **Bryant Park** (Map p156, E4; 212-768-4242; www.bryantpark.org; 42nd St, btwn Fifth & Sixth Aves; 7am-midnight Mon-Fri, to 11pm Sat & Sun Jun-Sep, shorter hours Oct-May; S B/D/F/M to 42nd St-Bryant Park, 7 to 5th Ave) was a crime-ridden hellscape known as 'Needle Park' in the '70s. Nestled behind the beaux-arts **New York Public Library building**, it's a whimsical spot for a little time-out from the Midtown madness. Fancy taking a beginner Italian language, yoga or juggling class, joining a painting workshop or signing up for a birding tour? There's a daily smorgasbord of quirky activities.

free attractions. When dedicated in 1911, New York's flagship library ranked as the largest marble structure ever built in the US, and to this day its recently restored **Rose Main Reading Room** steals the breath away with its lavish coffered ceiling. And it's not just for show: anybody who's working can use it, making it surely the most glamorous coworking space in the world. (Stephen A Schwarzman Building; 917-275-6975; www.nypl.org;

Midtown Skyscrapers

Midtown's skyline is more than just the Empire State and Chrysler Buildings, with enough modernist and postmodernist beauties to satisfy the wildest of high-rise dreams. Here are six of Midtown's most notable.

Seagram Building (1956–58) 514ft (Map p156, F2; 100 E 53rd St, at Park Ave, Midtown East; [S] 6 to 51st St; E, M to Fifth Ave-53rd St)

Lever House (1950–52) 306ft (Map p156, F2; 390 Park Ave, btwn E 53rd & E 54th Sts, Midtown East; [S] E, M to 5th Ave-53rd St)

Citigroup Center (1974–77) 915ft (Map p156, F2; 601 Lexington Ave, at E 53rd St, Midtown East; [S] 6 to 51st St; E, M to Lexington Ave-53rd St)

Hearst Tower (2003–06) 597ft (Map p156, C1; 949 Eighth Ave, btwn 56th & 57th Sts, Midtown West; [S] A/C, B/D, 1 to 59th St-Columbus Circle)

Bank of America Tower (2004–09) 1200ft (One Bryant Park; Map p156, D4; www.durst.org; Sixth Ave, at W 42nd St; [S] B/D/F/M to 42nd St-Bryant Park)

432 Park Avenue (2011–15) 1396ft (Map p156, F1; www.432parkavenue.com; 432 Park Ave, btwn 56th & 57th Sts, Midtown East; [S] N/Q/R to Lexington Ave-59th St)

476 Fifth Ave, at W 42nd St; admission free; ⏱8am-8pm Mon & Thu, to 9pm Tue & Wed, to 6pm Fri, 10am-6pm Sat, 10am-5pm Sun, guided tours 11am & 2pm Mon-Sat, 2pm Sun; [S] B/D/F/M to 42nd St-Bryant Park, 7 to 5th Ave)

Rockefeller Center

HISTORIC BUILDING

5 ◎ MAP P156, E2

This 22-acre 'city within a city' debuted at the height of the Great Depression, with developer John D Rockefeller Jr footing the $100-million price tag. Taking nine years to build, it was America's first multiuse retail, entertainment and office space – a sprawl of 19 buildings (14 of which are the original moderne structures). The center was declared a National Landmark in 1987. Highlights include **NBC Studio Tours** (☎212-664-3700; www.thetouratnbcstudios.com; 30 Rockefeller Plaza, entrance at 1250 Sixth Ave; 1hr tours adult/child $33/29, children under 6yr not admitted; ⏱8:20am-2:20pm Mon-Thu, to 5pm Fri, to 6pm Sat & Sun, longer hours in summer) and the Top of the Rock (p158) observation deck. (☎212-588-8601; www.rockefellercenter.com; Fifth to Sixth Aves, btwn W 48th & 51st Sts; [S] B/D/F/M to 47th-50th Sts-Rockefeller Center)

Radio City Music Hall

HISTORIC BUILDING

6 ◉ MAP P156, E2

This spectacular moderne movie palace was the brainchild of vaudeville producer Samuel Lionel 'Roxy' Rothafel. Never one for understatement, Roxy launched his venue on December 23, 1932, with an over-the-top extravaganza that included camp dance troupe the Roxyettes (mercifully renamed the Rockettes). Guided tours (75 minutes) of the sumptuous interiors include the glorious auditorium, Witold Gordon's classically inspired mural *History of Cosmetics* in the Women's Downstairs Lounge, and the VIP Roxy Suite, where luminaries such as Elton John and Alfred Hitchcock have been entertained. (www.radiocity.com; 1260 Sixth Ave, at W 50th St; tours adult/child $31/27; ⊙tours 9:30am-5pm; 🚹; Ⓢ B/D/F/M to 47th-50th Sts-Rockefeller Center)

St Patrick's Cathedral

CATHEDRAL

7 ◉ MAP P156, E2

America's largest Catholic cathedral graces Fifth Ave with Gothic Revival splendor. Built at a cost of nearly $2 million during the Civil War (and spiffed up with a $200 million restoration in 2015), the building did not originally include the two front spires; those were added in 1888. Step inside to appreciate the Louis Tiffany–designed altar, gleaming

Radio City Music Hall

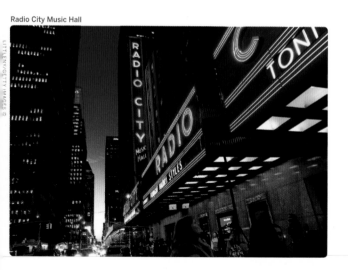

below a 7000-pipe church organ, and Charles Connick's stunning Rose Window above the Fifth Ave entrance. Occasional walk-in guided tours are available; check the website for details. (☎212-753-2261; www.saintpatrickscathedral.org; Fifth Ave, btwn E 50th & 51st Sts; ⏰6:30am-8:45pm; ⓢB/D/F/M to 47th-50th Sts-Rockefeller Center, E/M to 5th Ave-53rd St)

United Nations Building
HISTORIC BUILDING

8 ◎ MAP P156, H3

New York City is the home of the United Nations, a worldwide organization overseeing international law, security and human rights. The Le Corbusier–designed Secretariat building is off-limits, but guided tours cover the restored General Assembly Hall, Security Council Chamber, Trusteeship Council Chamber and Economic & Social Council (ECOSOC) Chamber, as well as exhibits about the UN's work and artworks donated by member states. Weekday tours must be booked online; kids under five years of age are not admitted. Photo ID is required. (☎212-963-4475; http://visit.un.org; visitors gate First Ave at 46th St, Midtown East; guided tour adult/child $22/12, grounds access Sat & Sun Mar-Dec free; ⏰1hr tours 9am-4:45pm Mon-Fri, visitor center also open 10am-4:45pm Sat & Sun; ⓢS, 4/5/6, 7 to Grand Central-42nd St)

Morgan Library & Museum
MUSEUM

9 ◎ MAP P156, F5

Incorporating the mansion once owned by steel magnate JP Morgan, this sumptuous cultural center houses a phenomenal array of manuscripts, tapestries and books (with no fewer than three Gutenberg Bibles). Adorned with Italian and Dutch Renaissance artworks, Morgan's personal study is only trumped by his personal library (East Room), an extraordinary, vaulted space with three stories of walnut bookcases, a 16th-century Dutch tapestry and zodiac-themed ceiling. The center's rotating exhibitions are often superb, as are its regular cultural events. Audioguides are free. (☎212-685-0008; www.themorgan.org; 225 Madison, at E 36th St, Midtown East; adult/child $22/free, 7-9pm Fri free; ⏰10:30am-5pm Tue-Thu, to 9pm Fri, 10am-6pm Sat, 11am-6pm Sun; ⓢ6 to 33rd St)

Roosevelt Island
AREA

10 ◎ MAP P156, H1

Floating in the East River between Manhattan's eastern edge and Queens, New York's anomalous, planned neighborhood sits on a tiny island no wider than a football field. At the southern tip of the island is architect Louis Kahn's striking **Four Freedoms Park** (☎212-204-8831; www.fdrfourfreedomspark.org; ⏰9am-7pm Wed-Mon Apr-Sep, to 5pm Wed-Mon Oct-Mar) memorial to Franklin D Roosevelt.

Zipping across the river via the four-minute **aerial tram** (📞212-832-4583; www.rioc.ny.gov/tramtransportation.htm; one-way $2.75; ⏰every 7-15 min 6am-2am Sun-Thu, to 3:30am Fri & Sat; 🚇N/Q/R, 4/5/6 to Lexington Ave-59th St) is a trip in itself and worth it for the stunning view of the East Side of Manhattan framed by the 59th St Bridge. (www.rihs.us; 🚇F to Roosevelt Island, 🚡from Roosevelt Island Tramway Station, 2nd Ave at E 60th St)

Eating

Totto Ramen JAPANESE $

11 ❌ MAP P156, C2

There might be two other Midtown branches but purists know that neither beats the tiny 20-seat original. Write your name and party size on the clipboard and wait your turn. Your reward: extraordinary ramen. Get the butter-soft *char siu* (pork), which sings in dishes like miso ramen (with fermented soybean paste, egg, scallion, bean sprouts, onion and homemade chili paste). (📞212-582-0052; www.tottoramen.com; 366 W 52nd St, btwn Eighth & Ninth Aves; ramen $14-18; ⏰noon-4:30pm & 5:30pm-midnight; 📷; 🚇C/E to 50th St)

Modern FRENCH $$$

12 ❌ MAP P156, E2

Shining two (Michelin) stars bright, the Modern delivers rich, confident creations like foie-gras tart and 'ants on a log' peanut-butter cake. Service is friendly and meals presented in a light-filled space reminiscent of MoMA's galleries, with giant windows overlooking the sculpture garden.

If you're on a writer's wage, you can opt for cheaper grub (3-course menu $75) in the adjacent Bar Room: also very popular, but a bit too dimly lit if you want to marvel at the food. The Modern has its own entrance on W 53rd St. Book a month ahead for the restaurant.*Sex and the City* fans may recall that Carrie announced her impending marriage to Mr Big here. (📞212-333-1220; www.themodernnyc.com; 9 W 53rd St, btwn Fifth & Sixth Aves; 3-/6-course lunch $138/188, 6-course dinner $188; ⏰restaurant 11:30am-2pm & 5-9:30pm Mon-Thu, to 10:30pm Fri & Sat, closed Sun, bar room 11:30am-10pm Mon-Wed, to 10:30pm Thu-Sat, to 2:30pm Sun; 📶; 🚇E, M to 5th Ave-53rd St)

O Ya SUSHI $$$

13 ❌ MAP P156, F6

With the cheapest nigiri pairs at close to $15, this is not a spot you'll come to every day. But if you're looking for a special night out and sushi's in the game plan, come here for exquisite flavors, fish so tender it melts like butter on the tongue, and preparations so artful you almost apologize for eating them. (📞212-204-0200; www.o-ya.restaurant; 120 E 28th St; nigiri $6-25; ⏰5:30-10pm Mon-Sat; 🚇4/6 to 28th St)

NoMad

AMERICAN $$$

14 MAP P156, E6

Sharing the same name as the 'it kid' hotel it inhabits, and run by the perfectionist restaurateurs behind Michelin-starred Eleven Madison Park (p139), NoMad has become a local culinary highlight. With a series of distinctly different spaces – including an elegant 'parlor' and a snacks-only 'library' – it serves indulgent delicacies like seared venison and suckling pig with a chicory-and-date confit. Book ahead. (☏ 212-796-1500; www. thenomadhotel.com; NoMad Hotel, 1170 Broadway, at W 28th St; mains $28-46; ⊗noon-2pm & 5:30-10:30pm Mon-Thu, to 11pm Fri, 11am-2:30pm & 5:30-11pm Sat, to 10pm Sun; ⑤N/R, 6 to 28th St; F/M to 23rd St)

Le Bernardin

SEAFOOD $$$

15 MAP P156, D2

The interiors may have been subtly sexed-up for a 'younger clientele' (the stunning storm-themed triptych is by Brooklyn artist Ran Ortner), but triple-Michelin-starred Le Bernardin remains a luxe, fine-dining holy grail. At the helm is French-born celebrity chef Eric Ripert, whose deceptively simple-looking seafood often borders on the transcendental. Life is short, and you only live (er, eat!) once. (☏212-554-1515; www.le-bernardin. com; 155 W 51st St, btwn Sixth & Seventh Aves; prix-fixe lunch/dinner $93/165, tasting menus $170-198; ⊗11:45am-2:30pm & 4:45-10:30pm Mon-Thu, to 11pm Fri, 4:45-11pm Sat; ⑤1 to 50th St; B/D, E to 7th Ave)

Totto Ramen (p163)

Hangawi

KOREAN $$

16 ✖ MAP P156, E6

Meat-free Korean is the draw at high-achieving Hangawi. Leave your shoes at the entrance and slip into a soothing, Zen-like space of meditative music, soft low seating and clean, complex dishes. Dishes include stuffed shiitake mushrooms, spicy kimchi-mushroom pancakes and a seductively smooth tofu claypot in ginger sauce. At lunchtime there's a four-course prix-fixe deal for $26. (✆212-213-0077; www.hangawi restaurant.com; 12 E 32nd St, btwn Fifth & Madison Aves; mains lunch $13-29, dinner $19-30; ⊙5:30-10:15pm Mon, noon-2:30pm & 5:30-10:15pm Tue-Thu, to 10:30pm Fri, 1-10:30pm Sat, 5-9:30pm Sun; ☑; ⓢB/D/F/M, N/Q/R/W to 34th St-Herald Sq)

Burger Joint

BURGERS $

17 ✖ MAP P156, D1

With only a small neon burger as your clue, this speakeasy-style burger hut lurks behind the lobby curtain in the Parker New York hotel. Though it might not be as secret as it once was (you'll see the queues), it still delivers the same winning formula of graffiti-strewn walls, retro booths and attitude-loaded staff slapping up beef 'n' patty brilliance. (✆212-708-7414; www.burgerjointny.com; 119 W 56th St, btwn Sixth & Seventh Aves; burgers $9-17; ⊙11am-11:30pm Sun-Thu, to midnight Fri & Sat; ☑; ⓢF to 57th St)

Great Northern Food Hall

FOOD HALL $

Ensconced in the beautiful beaux-arts Vanderbilt Hall, this airy food hall has upped the ante for food in Grand Central Terminal (see 1 ⓞ Map p156, F4). Pull up a stool beneath the glamorous chandelier and enjoy a glass of wine, Danish beer or artisan coffee. Gourmet bites on offer mesh Nordic flair with New York produce. Hours differ for individual kiosks. (www. greatnorthernfood.com; 89 E 42nd St, at Park Ave; sandwiches $7-12; ⊙7am-11pm Mon-Fri, 6am-8pm Sat & Sun; 🛜; ⓢS, 4/5/6, 7 to Grand Central-42nd St, ⍰Metro North to Grand Central-42nd St)

Smith

AMERICAN $$

18 ✖ MAP P156, G2

This bustling brasserie has an industrial-chic interior, sociable bar and well-executed grub. Much of the food is made from scratch, the seasonal menus a mix of nostalgic American and Italian inspiration (we're talking hot potato chips with blue-cheese fondue, spicy fried chicken served with kale slaw, and Sicilian baked eggs with artichokes, spinach and spicy tomato sauce). (✆212-644-2700; http://thesmithrestaurant.com; 956 Second Ave, at E 51st St, Midtown East; mains $22-33; ⊙7:30am-midnight Mon-Thu, to 1am Fri, 9am-1am Sat, 9am-midnight Sun; 🛜; ⓢ6, E/M to 51st St)

Mercado Little Spain

FOOD HALL $$

19 MAP P156, B6

Celebrity chef José Andrés has put his own spin on European food halls such as Eataly (p140) and Le District (p55) with Hudson Yards' buzzing new Mercado Little Spain. Explore the variety of Spanish cuisine via several sit-down restaurants and bars and a dozen kiosks serving Iberian specialties such as *jamón* (ham), paella, tapas, seafood, *pasteles* (pastries), an impressive selection of Spanish wines and much more. (646-495-1242; www.littlespain. com; 501 W 30th St, at Tenth Ave, Hudson Yards, Midtown; mains from $12; 7am-10pm Sun-Thu, to 11pm Fri & Sat; 7 to 34th St-Hudson Yards)

Margon

CUBAN $

20 MAP P156, D3

It's still 1973 at this ever-packed Cuban lunch counter, where orange Laminex tabletops and greasy goodness never went out of style. Go for gold with its legendary *cubano* sandwich (a pressed panino jammed with rich roast pork, salami, cheese, pickles, *mojo* sauce and mayo). It's obscenely good. (212-354-5013; 136 W 46th St, btwn Sixth & Seventh Aves; sandwiches $9-10, mains $11-14; 6am-5pm Mon-Fri, 7am-5pm Sat; B/D/F/M to 47th-50th Sts-Rockefeller Center)

Drinking

The Campbell

COCKTAIL BAR

In 1923 this hidden-away hall was the office of American financier John W Campbell. It later became a signalman's office, a jail and a gun storage before falling into obscurity. In 2017 it was restored to its original grandeur in Grand Central Terminal (see **1** Map p156, F4), complete with the stunning hand-painted ceiling and Campbell's original safe in the fireplace. Come for cocktails and you'll feel like you're waiting for Rockefeller or Carnegie to join you. (212-297-1781; www.thecampbellnyc.com; Grand Central Terminal, D Hall, 89 E 42nd St; noon-2am; S, 4/5/6, 7 to Grand Central-42nd St)

Robert

COCKTAIL BAR

21 MAP P156, C1

Perched on the 9th floor of the **Museum of Arts & Design** (MAD; 212-299-7777; www.madmuseum. org; adult/child $16/free, by donation 6-9pm Thu; 10am-6pm Tue, Wed, Fri-Sun, to 9pm Thu;), '60s-inspired Robert is technically a high-end, Modern American restaurant. While the food is satisfactory, we say visit late afternoon or post-dinner, find a sofa and gaze out over Central Park with a MAD Manhattan (bourbon, blood-orange vermouth and liqueured cherries). Check the website for live jazz sessions. (212-299-7730; www.robertnyc.com; /2 Columbus

Circle, btwn Eighth Ave & Broadway; ⏱11:30am-10pm Mon & Tue, to 11pm Wed-Fri, 10:30am-11pm Sat, to 10pm Sun; ⓈA/C, B/D, 1 to 59th St-Columbus Circle)

Bar Centrale

BAR

 22 MAP P156, C3

Set in an old brownstone building, this unmarked bar is a favorite hang out of Broadway actors, often seen here post-curtain debriefing and unwinding to sultry jazz. It's an intimate spot with a no-standing policy, so consider calling ahead (reservations are taken up to a week in advance). It's just up the stairs to the left of Joe Allen's. (☎212-581-3130; www.barcentralenyc.com; 324 W 46th St, btwn Eighth & Ninth Aves, Midtown West; ⏱5-11:30pm; ⓈA/C/E to 42nd St-Port Authority)

Industry

GAY

23 MAP P156, C2

What was once a parking garage is now one of the hottest gay bars in Hell's Kitchen – a slick, 4000-sq-ft watering hole with handsome lounge areas, a pool table and a stage for top-notch drag divas. Head in between 5pm and 9pm for the two-for-one drinks special or squeeze in later to party with the eye-candy party hordes. Cash only. (☎646-476-2747; www.industry-bar.com; 355 W 52nd St, btwn Eighth & Ninth Aves; ⏱5pm-4am; ⓈC/E, 1 to 50th St)

Midtown Drinking

Explore Koreatown

Centered on W 32nd St between Fifth Ave and the intersection of Sixth Ave and Broadway, this Seoul-ful jumble of Korean-owned restaurants, shops, salons and spas will satiate any kimchi pangs. Businesses are dense on the ground and often occupy 2nd floors, some migrating east of Fifth Ave and to 31st and 33rd Sts. Bars and karaoke spots are plentiful – try **Gagopa** (Map p156, E6; ☎212-967-5353; www.gagopakaraoke.com; 28 W 32nd St; rooms per hr from $36; ⏱6:30pm-4:30am Mon-Thu, 6pm-5:30am Fri & Sat, 7pm-4:30am Sun; ⓈB/D/F/M, N/Q/R/W to 34th Street-Herald Sq) if you're looking to sing the night away – and the block stays lively late into the night.

Top of the Strand

COCKTAIL BAR

24 MAP P156, E5

For that 'Oh my God, I'm in New York' feeling, head to the Marriott Vacation Club Pulse (formerly the Strand) hotel's rooftop bar, order a martini (extra dirty) and drop your jaw (discreetly). Sporting comfy cabana-style seating, a refreshingly mixed-age crowd and a retractable glass roof, its view of the Empire State Building is simply unforgettable. (☎646-368-6426; www.topofthestrand.com;

Marriott Vacation Club Pulse, 33 W 37th St, btwn Fifth & Sixth Aves, Midtown East; ⏱5pm-midnight Sun & Mon, to 1am Tue-Sat; 🛜; 🔲 B/D/F/M, N/Q/R to 34th St)

Therapy GAY

25 📍 MAP P156, C2

Multilevel Therapy was the first gay men's lounge/club to draw throngs to Hell's Kitchen, and it still pulls a crowd with its nightly shows (from live music to interviews with Broadway stars) and decent grub served Sunday to Friday (the quesadillas are especially popular). Drink monikers match the theme: 'Oral Fixation' and 'Freudian Sip,' to name a few. (📞212-397-1700; www.therapy-nyc.com; 348 W 52nd St, btwn Eighth & Ninth Aves, Midtown West;

⏱5pm-2am Sun-Thu, to 4am Fri & Sat; 🔲 C/E, 1 to 50th St)

Rum House COCKTAIL BAR

26 📍 MAP P156, C3

This slice of old New York is revered for its rums and whiskeys. Savor them straight up or mixed in impeccable cocktails like 'The Escape,' a potent piña-colada take. Adding to the magic is nightly live music, spanning solo piano tunes to jaunty jazz trios and sentimental divas. Bartenders here are careful with their craft; don't expect them to rush. (📞646-490-6924; www.therum housenyc.com; 228 W 47th St, btwn Broadway & Eighth Ave; ⏱noon-4am; 🔲 N/R/W to 49th St)

Carnegie Hall (p170)

DW LABS INCORPORATED/SHUTTERSTOCK ©

NYC Theater: Broadway & Beyond

In the early 20th century, clusters of theaters settled into the area around Times Square and began producing popular plays and suggestive comedies – a movement that had its roots in early vaudeville. By the 1920s, these messy works had evolved into on-stage spectacles like *Show Boat,* an all-out Oscar Hammerstein production about the lives of performers on a Mississippi steamboat. In 1943, Broadway had its first runaway hit – *Oklahoma!* – that remained on stage for a record 2212 performances.

Today, Broadway musicals are shown in one of 41 official Broadway theaters, lavish early 20th-century jewels that surround Times Square, and are a major component of cultural life in New York. If you're on a budget, look for off-Broadway productions. These tend to be more intimate, inexpensive and often just as good.

NYC bursts with theatrical offerings beyond Broadway, from Shakespeare to David Mamet to rising experimental playwrights including Young Jean Lee. In addition to Midtown staples such as **Playwrights Horizons** (p171) and **Second Stage Theatre** (p172), the **Lincoln Center theaters** and smaller companies like **Soho Rep** (Soho Repertory Theatre; ☏212-941-8632; www.sohorep.org; 46 Walker St, btwn Church St & Broadway, Tribeca; ⑤A/C/E to Canal St, 1 to Franklin St) are important hubs for works by modern and contemporary playwrights.

Rudy's Bar & Grill   BAR

27 🚇 MAP P156, B3

The big pantless pig in a red jacket out front marks Hell's Kitchen's best divey hangout, with cheap pitchers of Rudy's draft beers, half-circle vinyl booths covered in red duct tape and free hot dogs. A mix of folks come to flirt or watch muted Knicks games as classic rock plays. (☏646-707-0890; www.rudysbarnyc.com; 627 Ninth Ave, at W 44th St, Midtown West; ⏰8am-4am Mon-Sat, noon-4am Sun; 🛜; ⑤A/C/E to 42nd St-Port Authority Bus Terminal)

Entertainment

Jazz at Lincoln Center   JAZZ

28 ⭐ MAP P156, C1

Perched atop the Time Warner Center, Jazz at Lincoln Center comprises three state-of-the-art venues: midsized **Rose Theater**; panoramic, glass-backed **Appel Room**; and intimate, atmospheric **Dizzy's Club Coca-Cola**. It's the last of these that you're most likely to visit, given its nightly shows (cover charge $5 to $45). The talent here is often exceptional, as are

Broadway on a Budget

The discount **TKTS Booth** (Map p156, D3; www.tdf.org/tkts; Broadway, at W 47th St, Midtown; ⏱3-8pm Mon & Fri, 2-8pm Tue, 10am-2pm & 3-8pm Wed, Thu & Sat, 11am-7pm Sun; Ⓢ N/Q/R/W, S, 1/2/3, 7 to Times Sq-42nd St) in Times Square offers great deals, though rarely to the hottest shows. Many shows – including **Hamilton** (Richard Rodgers Theatre; Map p156, C3; 🎫tickets 877-250-2929; www.hamiltonmusical.com; 226 W 46th St, btwn Seventh & Eighth Aves; ⏱box office 10am-8pm Mon-Sat, noon-6pm Sun; Ⓢ N/R/W to 49th St) and **Book of Mormon** (Eugene O'Neill Theatre; Map p156, C3; 🎫tickets 877-250-2929; www.bookofmormonbroadway.com; 230 W 49th St, btwn Broadway & Eighth Ave; ⏱box office 10am-8pm Mon-Sat, noon-6pm Sun; Ⓢ N/R/W to 49th St, 1 to 50th St, C/E to 50th St) – run online lotteries for cheap tickets, though spots are limited and in high demand. Check the show websites to try your luck. Standing-room spots are sometimes offered cheaply if the show is sold out; enquire at the theater's box office.

the dazzling Central Park views. (🎫Dizzy's Club Coca-Cola reservations 212-258-9595, Rose Theater & Appel Room tickets 212-721-6500; www.jazz.

org; Time Warner Center, 10 Columbus Circle, Broadway at W 59th St; Ⓢ A/C, B/D, 1 to 59th St-Columbus Circle)

Carnegie Hall
LIVE MUSIC

29 ⭐ MAP P156, D1

The legendary Carnegie Hall may not be the world's biggest concert hall, nor its grandest, but it's definitely one of the most acoustically blessed. Opera, jazz and folk greats feature in the **Isaac Stern Auditorium**, with edgier jazz, pop, classical and world music in the popular **Zankel Hall**. Intimate **Weill Recital Hall** hosts chamber music, debut performances and panel discussions. (🎫212-247-7800; www.carnegiehall.org; 881 Seventh Ave, at W 57th St; tours adult/child $17/12; ⏱1hr tours 11:30am, 12:30pm, 2pm & 3pm Mon-Fri, 11:30am & 12:30pm Sat Sep-Jun; Ⓢ N/R/W to 57th St-7th Ave)

Madison Square Garden
LIVE PERFORMANCE

30 ⭐ MAP P156, C5

NYC's major performance venue – part of the massive complex housing **Penn Station** – hosts big-arena performers, from Kanye West to Madonna. It's also a sports arena, with **New York Knicks** (www.nba.com/knicks) and **New York Liberty** (https://liberty.wnba.com) basketball games and **New York Rangers** (www.nhl.com/rangers) hockey games, as well as boxing and events like the **Annual Westminster Kennel Club Dog Show** (www.westminsterkennelclub.org).

(MSG, 'the Garden'; www.thegarden. com; 4 Pennsylvania Plaza, Seventh Ave, btwn 31st & 33rd Sts; S A/C/E, 1/2/3 to 34th St-Penn Station)

Birdland

JAZZ

31 ⭐ MAP P156, C3

This bird's got a slick look, not to mention the legend – its name comes from bebop legend Charlie Parker (aka 'Bird'), who headlined at Birdland's former 52nd St location, along with Miles, Monk and just about everyone else (their photos are on the walls). The 44th St club is intimate; come for the electrifying Big Band session on Fridays at 5:30pm. (☏212-581-3080; www.birdlandjazz.com; 315 W 44th St, btwn Eighth & Ninth Aves; cover $30-50; ⏰5pm-1am; 🛜; S A/C/E to 42nd St-Port Authority Bus Terminal)

Playwrights Horizons

THEATER

32 ⭐ MAP P156, B4

An excellent place to catch what could be the next big thing, this veteran 'writers' theater' is dedicated to fostering contemporary American works. Notable past productions include Annie Baker's Pulitzer Prize–winning The Flick, Kenneth Lonergan's Lobby Hero, Bruce Norris' Tony Award–winning Clybourne Park, and Doug Wright's I Am My Own Wife and Grey Gardens. (☏212-564-1235; www. playwrightshorizons.org; 416 W 42nd St, btwn Ninth & Tenth Aves, Midtown West; S A/C/E to 42nd St-Port Authority Bus Terminal)

Roundabout Theatre Company

THEATER

33 ⭐ MAP P156, D3

The Harold and Miriam Steinberg Center for Theatre is a state-of-the-art, dual-theater venue where the Roundabout Theatre Company stages works by emerging and established playwrights, as well as revivals of classic plays and musicals. It also mounts productions at its flagship **American Airlines Theatre** on W 42nd St, the **Stephen Sondheim Theatre** on W 43rd St and **Studio 54** on W 54th St. (☏212-719-1300; www. roundabouttheatre.org; 111 W 46th St, btwn Sixth & Seventh Aves, Midtown West; S N/Q/R to 49th St; B/D/F/M to 47th-50th Sts)

Madison Square Garden

TV Show Tapings

Saturday Night Live (www.nbc.com/saturday-night-live) One of the most popular NYC-based shows – and difficult to get into. Try your luck for the fall lottery by emailing snltickets@nbcuni.com in August, or line up on the 48th St side of Rockefeller Plaza on the day of the show for the 7am distribution of standby tickets.

The Late Show with Stephen Colbert Tickets for this hugely popular late-night show are available online, but they commonly sell out on the day of their release. Check *The Late Show*'s official Twitter account (@colbertlateshow) and Facebook page for release date announcements, usually made one to two months in advance.

Last Week Tonight with John Oliver (www.lastweektickets.com) Tickets to this biting British comedian's news recap show are available online up to a month in advance of taping dates (Sundays at 6:30pm).

Full Frontal with Samantha Bee (www.samanthabee.com) Samantha Bee offers incisive and hilarious commentary on the politicos and scandal makers hogging the current news headlines. Her late-night shows are taped at 5:45pm on Wednesday. Go online to get tickets.

Caroline's on Broadway
COMEDY

34 ⭐ MAP P156, D2

You may recognize this big, bright, mainstream classic from comedy specials filmed here on location. It's a top spot to catch US comedy big guns and sitcom stars. Tickets for most shows are around $20. (☎212-757-4100; www.carolines.com; 1626 Broadway, at 50th St, Midtown West; ⑤N/R/W to 49th St; 1, C/E to 50th St)

Second Stage Theater
THEATER

35 ⭐ MAP P156, C3

This nonprofit theater company is famed for debuting the work of talented emerging writers as well as that of the country's more-established names. If you're after well-crafted contemporary American theater, this is a good place to find it. (Tony Kiser Theater; ☎tickets 212-246-4422; www.2st.com; 305 W 43rd St, at Eighth Ave, Midtown West; ⏰box office noon-6pm Sun-Fri, to 7pm Sat; ⑤A/C/E to 42nd St-Port Authority Bus Terminal)

Shopping

MoMA Museum & Design Stores
GIFTS & SOUVENIRS

The newly redesigned flagship store at the Museum of Modern Art (p154) is a fab spot for souvenir shopping. Besides gorgeous books (from art and architecture to culture critiques and kids' picture books), you'll find art posters and one-of-a-kind knickknacks. For furniture, homewares, jewelry, bags and artsy gifts, head to the **MoMA Design Store** (open 10am to 6:30pm daily) across the street. (☎212-708-9700; www.momastore.org; 11 W 53rd St, btwn Fifth & Sixth Aves; ⏰9:30am-6:30pm Sat-Thu, to 9pm Fri; Ⓢ E, M to 5th Ave-53rd St)

Grand Central Market
MARKET

36 🔒 MAP P156, F4

It's not all trains at Grand Central. The station also holds a 240ft corridor lined with perfectly coiffed fresh produce and artisanal treats. Stock up on anything from crusty bread and fruit tarts to sushi, chicken pot pies, Spanish quince paste, loose-leaf tea, antipasti and roasted coffee beans. There's even a Murray's Cheese stall, peddling milky wonders like cave-aged Gruyère. (www.grandcentralterminal.com/market; Grand Central Terminal, Lexington Ave, at 42nd St, Midtown East; ⏰7am-9pm Mon-Fri, 10am-7pm Sat, 11am-6pm Sun; Ⓢ S, 4/5/6, 7 to Grand Central-42nd St)

Grand Central Market

MICHAEL GODEK/GETTY IMAGES ©

High-End Fashion

One of the world's fashion capitals, NYC is ever setting trends for the rest of the country to follow. For checking out the latest designs hitting the streets, it's worth browsing some of the best-loved boutiques around town – regardless of whether you intend to spend. A few favorites include **Opening Ceremony** (p81-2), Issey Miyake, Marc Jacobs, **Rag & Bone** (p83), **John Varvatos** (p105) and By Robert James.

If time is limited, or you simply want to browse a plethora of labels in one go, then head to those heady conglomerations known worldwide as department stores. New York has a special blend of alluring draws – in particular you could lose an entire afternoon in **Saks Fifth Avenue** (Map p156, E2; ☏212-753-4000; www.saksfifthavenue. com; 611 Fifth Ave, at E 50th St; ⏰10am-8:30pm Mon-Sat, 11am-7pm Sun; ⓈB/D/F/M to 47th-50th Sts-Rockefeller Center, E, M to 5th Ave-53rd St), **Bergdorf Goodman** (Map p156, E1; ☏212-753-7300; www.bergdorf goodman.com; 754 Fifth Ave, btwn W 57th & 58th Sts; ⏰10am-8pm Mon-Sat, 11am-7pm Sun; ⓈN/R/W to 5th Ave-59th St, F to 57th St), **Macy's** (Map p156, D5; ☏212-695-4400; www.macys.com; 151 W 34th St, at Broadway, Midtown West; ⏰10am-10pm Mon-Sat, to 9pm Sun; ⓈB/D/F/M, N/Q/R/W to 34th St-Herald Sq; A/C/E to Penn Station) or **Bloomingdale's** (Map p156, F1; ☏212-705-2000; www.bloomingdales.com; 1000 Third Ave, at E 59th St; ⏰10am-8:30pm Mon-Sat, 11am-7pm Sun; 🛜; Ⓢ4/5/6 to 59th St; N/R/W to Lexington Ave-59th St).

Argosy

BOOKS

37 🏷 **MAP P156, F1**

Bookstores like this are becoming as rare as the books they contain, but since 1925 this six-story landmark has stocked fine antiquarian items such as books, old maps, art monographs and more. There's also an interesting booty of Hollywood, historical and literary memorabilia, from personal letters and signed books to autographed publicity stills. Prices range from costly to clearance. (☏212-753-4455; www.argosybooks.com; 116 E 59th St, btwn Park & Lexington Aves, Midtown East; ⏰10am-6pm Mon-Fri, to 5pm Sat; Ⓢ4/5/6 to 59th St; N/Q/R to Lexington Ave-59th St)

FAO Schwarz

TOYS

New Yorkers mourned the loss of this landmark toy store (c 1862) when it closed its famed flagship on Fifth Ave in 2015 (you might remember Tom Hanks playing a giant floor keyboard there in the movie *Big*). It was resurrected in this new location at Rockefeller Center (see 5 ◉ Map p156, E2) in 2018, looking jazzier than ever. Even the keyboard has made a comeback upstairs. (📞800-326-8638; www.faoschwarz.com; 30 Rockefeller Plaza; ⏱10am-8pm Mon-Thu, to 9pm Fri & Sat, to 7pm Sun; 🚻; Ⓢ B/D/F/M 47-50 Sts-Rockefeller Center)

Nepenthes New York
FASHION & ACCESSORIES

38 🔒 MAP P156, C4

Occupying an old sewing-machine shop in the Garment District, this cult Japanese collective stocks edgy menswear from the likes of Engineered Garments and Needles, known for their quirky detailing and artisanal production value, with a vintage-inspired Americana workwear feel. Accessories include bags and satchels, hats, gloves, eyewear and footwear. (📞212-643-9540; www.nepenthesny.com; 307 W 38th St, btwn Eighth & Ninth Aves; ⏱noon-7pm Mon-Sat, to 5pm Sun; Ⓢ A/C/E to 42nd St-Port Authority Bus Terminal)

Fine & Dandy
FASHION & ACCESSORIES

39 🔒 MAP P156, B2

This pocket-square-sized haberdashery specializes in retro fashion accessories for the dapper folk among us, with everything from proper bow ties, ascots, embroidered suspenders and cuff links to tie pins, straw boaters and newsboy caps, cigarette cases and watch fobs. (They even sell spats.) You've never seen so much tweed, tartan, paisley and argyle in one spot before. (📞212-247-4847; www.fineanddandyshop.com; 445 W 49th St, btwn Ninth & Tenth Aves, Midtown West; ⏱11:30am-7:30pm Mon-Sat, from 12:30pm Sun; Ⓢ C/E to 50th St)

New York Transit Museum Store
GIFTS & SOUVENIRS

For NYC souvenirs with a twist, stop by this shop next to the stationmaster's office in Grand Central Terminal (see 1 ◎ Map p156, F4), which carries a comprehensive supply of swag themed to NYC public transit: mugs, T-shirts and hats for your favorite subway line, jewelry made from old tokens, bags and pencil cases, toy trains and much more. (📞212-878-0106; www.nytransitmuseumstore.com; Grand Central Terminal, 89 E 42nd St, at Park Ave, Midtown East; ⏱8am-8pm Mon-Fri, 10am-6pm Sat & Sun; Ⓢ S, 4/5/6, 7 to Grand Central-42nd St)

Worth a Trip 🔭
MoMA PS1

The smaller, hipper sibling of Manhattan's Museum of Modern Art, MoMA PS1 hunts down razor-sharp art and serves it in an ex-school locale. Here you'll be peering at videos through floorboards and debating the meaning of nonstatic structures while staring through a hole in the wall. Nothing is predictable. Best of all, admission is free with your MoMA ticket within 14 days of your visit.

www.momaps1.org

22-25 Jackson Ave, Long Island City

suggested donation adult/child $10/free

🕑 noon-6pm Thu-Mon, Warm Up parties noon-9pm Sat Jul-early Sep

Ⓢ G, 7 to Court Sq, E/M to Court Sq-23rd St

Roots, Radicals & PS1 Classics

PS1 first hit the scene in the 1970s. This was the age of Dia, Artists' Space and the New Museum – new-gen projects showcasing the city's thriving experimental, multimedia art scene. In 1976, Alanna Heiss – a supporter of art in alternative spaces – took possession of an abandoned school building in Queens and invited artists like Richard Serra, James Turrell and Keith Sonnier to create site-specific works. The end result was PS1's inaugural exhibition, *Rooms.* Surviving remnants include Richard Artschwager's oval-shaped wall 'blps' and Alan Saret's light-channeling *The Hole at P.S.1, Fifth Solar Chthonic Wall Temple,* on the north wing's 3rd floor.

Summer 'Warm Up' Parties

On Saturday afternoons from July 4 through Labor Day, rock on at one of New York's coolest weekly music/culture events, Warm Up. It's a hit with everyone from verified hipsters to plugged-in music geeks, who spill into the MoMA PS1 courtyard to eat, drink and catch a stellar lineup of top bands, experimental music and DJs. Featured artists have included acid-house deity DJ Pierre and techno pioneer Juan Atkins.

Sunday Sessions

Another cultural treat is the Sunday Sessions, on Sundays November to April (timeframes vary yearly). Spanning lectures, film screenings, live music and performance art and beyond, the lineup has included experimental comedy, postindustrial noise jams and Latin art-house dance. One week you might catch a symphony debut, the next an architectural performance from Madrid. Upcoming events are listed on the MoMA PS1 website.

★ **Top Tips**

○ Check exhibitions online before heading out. Sometimes the museum has limited pieces on display.

○ Stock up on MoMA exhibition catalogs, coffee-table tomes, art and design mags and new media at the bookstore.

✕ **Take a Break**

Greek chef Mina Stone offers Greek comfort food in the museum's new restaurant, appropriately named **Mina's** (www.minas.nyc; mains $8-20; ◷noon-6pm Wed-Thu & Sat & Sun, to 8pm Fri).

★ **Getting There**

○ MoMA PS1 is 3 miles straight east of Times Square, in Queens.

○ Ⓢ Take the E or M to Court Sq-23rd St, or the 7 to Court Sq.

Walking Tour 🥾

Queens: Astoria

A short hop from Midtown Manhattan, Astoria is a charmingly diverse neighborhood of restaurant-lined boulevards, tree-lined side streets and indie shops and cafes. Come with an appetite, as eating and drinking is an essential part of the Astoria experience. The best time to visit is on weekends, when the neighborhood is at its liveliest.

Getting There

🚢 Hop aboard the NYC Ferry and disembark at Astoria. From the dock, it's a 7-minute walk south to Socrates Sculpture Park.

S Take the N or W to Broadway.

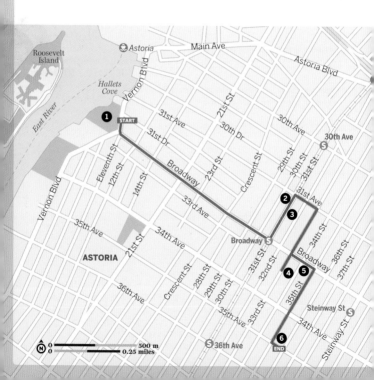

❶ Socrates Sculpture Park

Amid cutting-edge installations and wispy birch trees, this picturesque waterside **park** (www.socrates sculpturepark.org; 32-01 Vernon Blvd; admission free; ⏱9am-dusk) offers serene views across to Manhattan. It's hard to believe this abandoned landfill was once an illegal dump site. On summer weekends, there's often something afoot, including yoga and tai chi, markets and kayaking in Hallets Cove.

❷ King Souvlaki

Follow the plumes of smoke wafting along 31st St to this celebrated **food truck** (☎917-416-1189; www. kingsouvlakiofastoria.com; 31st St, at 31st Ave; sandwiches $7-10; ⏱9am-11pm Mon, to midnight Tue-Wed, to 5am Thu-Sat, 11am-11pm Sun), one of the best in Astoria. Come for the pita sandwiches stuffed with mouthwatering morsels of pork, chicken or beef, along with a side of feta-topped Greek fries.

❸ Astoria Bookshop

This much-loved indie **bookstore** (☎718-278-2665; www.astoriabook shop.com; 31-29 31st St, btwn 31st Ave & Broadway; ⏱11am-7pm) has ample shelf space dedicated to local authors – pick up a title about the Queens dining scene or the borough's ethnic diversity. A bulwark of the community, Astoria also hosts author readings, discussion groups and even writing workshops where you can hone your narrative skills.

❹ Lockwood

You'll find loads of gift ideas in this whimsical **store** (http://lockwood shop.com; 32-15 33rd St; ⏱11am-8pm), including plenty of intriguing Queens-related objects: vintage wall hangings, paper doll books of famous women, skull candles, scented candles, eye-catching flasks and so on. Lockwood has a shopping empire on this corner, with both a stationery shop and clothing store within earshot.

❺ Astoria Bier & Cheese

A neighborhood institution, this **deli and drinkery** (https://astoria bierandcheese.com/; 34-14 Broadway; ⏱noon-11pm Mon-Thu, to midnight Fri & Sat, to 10pm Sun) serves a wide variety of temptations, including gourmet grilled cheeses, mac 'n' cheese plates, avocado toast and fancy sandwiches stuffed with prosciutto and other goodness. The rotating selection of craft brews is an even bigger draw. There's outdoor seating in back – ideal for warm days.

❻ Sac's Place

Set inside the Kaufman Astoria Studios, **Sac's Place** (☎718-204-5002; www.sacsplace.com; 35-11 35th Ave; pizza from $10.50; ⏱11:30am-10pm Mon-Thu, to 11pm Fri & Sat) feels like a hidden spot with its side-door entrance inside a movie studio. Step inside and order one of Queen's signature pizzas – the pizzeria moved here from its Broadway location in 2019.

Explore ◈

Upper East Side

A manicured residential neighborhood beloved by NYC's upper crust, the Upper East Side is unsurprisingly home to some of the city's most expensive boutiques, which line Madison Ave. Architecturally magnificent Fifth Ave, running parallel to the leafy realms of Central Park, offers the 'Museum Mile' – one of the most cultured strips in New York.

The Short List

○ **Metropolitan Museum of Art (p182)** *Wandering amid the priceless treasures, from mesmerizing Egyptian artifacts to Renaissance masterpieces.*

○ **Guggenheim Museum (p186)** *Walking the spiral ramp of Frank Lloyd Wright's iconic architecture.*

○ **Neue Galerie (p190)** *Gazing at the lush, gilded paintings of Gustav Klimt, followed by a leisurely lunch at the museum's elegant cafe.*

○ **Frick Collection Concerts (p197)** *Listening to classical music on a Sunday evening, in a beaux-arts mansion surrounded by priceless artworks.*

○ **Bemelmans Bar (p195)** *Sipping cocktails at this elegant bar that hearkens back to the Jazz Age.*

Getting There & Around

Ⓢ The 4/5/6 trains travel along Lexington Ave; the Q runs up Second Ave to 72nd, 86th and 96th Sts.

🚌 M1, M2, M3 and M4 buses run down Fifth Ave and up Madison Ave. Crosstown buses at 66th, 72nd, 79th, 86th and 96th Sts head through Central Park to the Upper West Side.

Neighborhood Map on p188

Metropolitan Museum of Art (p182) POLUDZIBER/SHUTTERSTOCK ©

Top Experience 📷

Wander the Galleries of the Metropolitan Museum of Art

This sprawling, encyclopedic museum, founded in 1870, houses one of the world's largest and most important art collections, with more than two million individual objects, from Egyptian temples to American paintings. 'The Met' attracts over six million visitors a year to its 17 acres of galleries, making it the largest single-site attraction in NYC.

◎ MAP P188, A3

www.metmuseum.org

1000 Fifth Ave, at E 82nd St

3-day pass adult/senior/child $25/$17/free

⊘ 10am-5:30pm Sun-Thu, to 9pm Fri & Sat

⑤ 4/5/6, Q to 86th St, 6 to 77th St

Egyptian Art

The museum has an unrivaled collection of ancient Egyptian art, some of which dates back to the Paleolithic era. Located to the north of the Great Hall, the 39 Egyptian galleries open dramatically with one of the Met's prized pieces: the **Tomb of Perneb** (c 2300 BC), an Old Kingdom burial chamber crafted from limestone. From here, a web of rooms is cluttered with funerary stelae, carved reliefs and fragments of pyramids. Don't miss the intriguing models from the **Tomb of Meketre**, clay figurines meant to help in the afterlife, in Gallery 105. These eventually lead to the **Temple of Dendur** (Gallery 131), a sandstone temple to the goddess Isis given to the US by Egypt in 1965. It resides in a sunny atrium gallery with a reflecting pool – a must-see for the first-time visitor.

European Paintings

Want Renaissance? The Met's got it. On the museum's 2nd floor, the European Paintings galleries display a stunning collection of masterworks. This includes more than 1700 canvases from the roughly 500-year period starting in the 13th century, with works by every important painter from Duccio to Rembrandt. In fact, everything here is, literally, a masterpiece. At the time of writing, the skylights in these galleries were being replaced to improve the quality of light within. Once completed, hours spent viewing these many powerful works will be even more enjoyable.

Art of the Arab Lands

In the southeastern corner of the 2nd floor you'll find the Islamic galleries, with 15 incredible rooms showcasing the museum's extensive collection of art from the Middle East, and Central and South Asia. In addition to garments, secular decorative objects and manuscripts,

★ Top Tips

o Don't try to see everything – pick a few collections and really immerse yourself.

o Rent a self-guided audio tour in 10 languages (adult/ child $7/5) or access excerpts on the Met's free smartphone app.

o Docents offer guided tours of specific galleries (free with admission). Check the website or information desk for details.

✕ Take a Break

o The museum's casual **Petrie Court Café** (⏲11am-4:30pm) sells tasty salads, soups, pastas and hot sandwiches, plus wine and a good selection of tea – all served in an airy setting with floor-to-ceiling views of Central Park.

o For an inexpensive meal with old-fashioned New York character, head to nearby Lexington Candy Shop (p194) diner for a burger and an egg-cream soda.

you'll find a magnificent 14th-century *mihrab* (prayer niche) from Iran, lined with elaborately patterned blue, white and yellow tile work (Gallery 455). There's also a superb array of Ottoman textiles (Gallery 459), a medieval-style **Moroccan court** (Gallery 456) and the 18th-century **Damascus Room** (Gallery 461).

American Wing

In the northwestern corner, the two-floor American Wing showcases a wide variety of decorative and fine art from throughout US history. These include everything from colonial portraiture to Hudson River School art – not to mention Emanuel Leutze's massive canvas of *Washington Crossing the Delaware* (Gallery 760).

Greek & Roman Art

The 27 galleries devoted to classical antiquity are another Met doozy. From the Great Hall, a passageway takes you through a barrel-vaulted room flanked by the chiseled torsos of Greek figures. This spills right into one of the Met's loveliest spaces: the airy **Greek and Roman sculpture court** (Gallery 162), full of marble carvings of gods and historical figures. The statue of a bearded Hercules from 68–98 AD, with a lion's skin draped about him, is particularly awe-inspiring.

Modern & Contemporary Art

The rooms in the far southwestern corner of the 1st and 2nd floors feature art from the early 20th

American Wing

Exhibition of Greek art

century onward. All the rock stars of modern art are represented here. Notable names include Spanish masters Picasso (whose 'high' cubist *Still Life with a Bottle of Rum* hangs in Gallery 905), Dalí and Miró, as well as American painters Georgia O'Keeffe and Edward Hopper. Thomas Hart Benton's magnificent 1930s 10-panel mural *America Today* takes up an entire room in Gallery 909.

The Roof Garden

One of the best spots in the entire museum is the roof garden, which features rotating sculpture installations by contemporary and 20th-century artists. (Jeff Koons, Andy Goldsworthy and Imran Qureshi have all shown here.) Best of all are the views it offers of the city and Central Park. It's also home to the Cantor Roof Garden Bar (p196), an ideal spot for a drink – especially at sunset.

Top Experience 📷

Explore the Guggenheim Museum

A sculpture in its own right, this building by architect Frank Lloyd Wright almost overshadows the collection of 20th-century art inside. Even before it opened, the inverted ziggurat structure was derided by some critics but hailed by others, who welcomed it as a beloved architectural icon. Since its opening, this unusual structure has appeared on countless postcards, TV programs and in films.

◉ **MAP P188, A1**

www.guggenheim.org
1071 Fifth Ave, at E 89th St
adult/child $25/free,
cash-only pay-what-you-wish 5-8pm Sat

🕐 10am-5:30pm Wed-Fri, Sun & Mon, to 8pm Sat, to 9pm Tue

S 4/5/6, Q to 86th St

Abstract Roots

The Guggenheim came out of the collection of Solomon R Guggenheim, a New York mining magnate who began acquiring abstract art in his 60s at the behest of his art adviser, an eccentric German baroness named Hilla Rebay. In 1939, with Rebay serving as director, Guggenheim opened a temporary museum on 54th St titled the Museum of Non-Objective Painting. (Incredibly, it had grey velour walls, piped-in classical music and burning incense.) Four years later, the pair commissioned Wright to construct a permanent home for the collection.

Modernizing an Icon

A renovation in the early 1990s added an eight-story tower to the east, which seamlessly provided an extra 50,000 sq ft of exhibition space. These galleries feature rotating exhibitions from the permanent collection, while the ramps of the Rotunda are occupied by temporary exhibits.

The museum's holdings include works by Kandinsky, Picasso and Jackson Pollock. Over time, other key additions have included paintings by Monet, Van Gogh and Degas, sculpture by Constantin Brancusi, photographs by Robert Mapplethorpe, and key surrealist works donated by Guggenheim's niece Peggy.

Visiting the Museum

The museum's ascending ramp displays rotating exhibitions of modern and contemporary art. Though Wright intended visitors to go to the top and wind their way down, the cramped single elevator makes this difficult. Exhibitions, therefore, are installed from bottom to top. Fans of art and design should stop into the on-site **Guggenheim Store** to browse its excellent collection of books, posters, gifts and homewares.

★ Top Tips

o The ticket line can be brutal at any time of the year. Arrive early or save time by purchasing your tickets in advance on the website.

o If you have a smartphone, download the Guggenheim's free app, which has info on the building and the collections in five languages.

✕ Take a Break

o There are two good on-site food options, both incorporated into the original building. The Wright (p193), at ground level, is a classy modernist bistro serving seasonal dishes and classic cocktails.

o **Cafe 3** (sandwiches $13.50; ⏱10:30am-5pm Sun, Mon & Wed-Fri, to 7:30pm Tue & Sat), on the 3rd floor, offers windows to Central Park, coffee and light snacks (albeit overpriced).

Upper East Side

A

6 Jewish
7 Museum

Cooper-Hewitt
Smithsonian
5 Design Museum

Guggenheim
13 Museum

Jacqueline
Kennedy
Onassis
Reservoir

3 Neue
Galerie

La Boutique
Resale

11

27

Metropolitan
Museum
of Art

21

79th St
Transverse

Central
Park

14

Conservatory
Water

12

Met
2 Breuer

72nd St
Transverse

Frick
1 Collection

8 Temple
Emanu-El

65th St
Transverse

The Pond
Central
Park South

5th Ave-
59th St

B

25

86th St

Park Ave

Lexington Ave

29

17

77th St

19

28

UPPER
EAST
SIDE

Asia Society
& Museum

Madison Ave

Park Ave

68th St-
Hunter
College

Lexington Ave-
63rd St

E 61st St   Lexington Ave-
59th St

E 59th St

C

E 93rd St

E 92nd St

E 91st St   16

18

YORKVILLE

10

86th St   26

24

23

20

Second Ave

Third Ave

Lexington Ave

15

72nd St

Third Ave

Second Ave

E 90th St

E 89th St

E 88th St

E 87th St

E 86th St

E 85th St

E 84th St

E 83rd St

E 82nd St

E 81st St

E 80th St

E 79th St

E 78th St

E 77th St

E 76th St

E 75th St

E 74th St

E 73rd St

E 72nd St

4

30

E 71st St

E 70th St

E 69th St

E 68th St

E 67th St

E 65th St

E 64th St

E 62nd St

Roosevelt Island
Tramway Station

59th St

D

First Ave

York Ave

First Ave

22

9

York Ave

New York
Hospital-Cornell
Medical Center

Rockefeller
University

0   400 m
0   0.2 miles

For reviews see	
⊙ Top Experiences	p182
◎ Sights	p189
⊗ Eating	p192
⊕ Drinking	p195
✪ Entertainment	p197
⊕ Shopping	p198

A   **B**   **C**   **D**

Sights

Frick Collection
GALLERY

1 ◎ MAP P188, A4

This spectacular art collection sits in a mansion built by steel magnate Henry Clay Frick, one of the many such residences lining the section of Fifth Ave that was once called 'Millionaires' Row'. The museum has over a dozen splendid rooms displaying masterpieces by Titian, Vermeer, Gilbert Stuart, El Greco, Joshua Reynolds, Van Dyck and Rembrandt. Sculpture, ceramics, antique furniture and clocks are also on display. Fans of classical music will enjoy the piano and violin concerts (p197) on some Sunday evenings. (www.frick.org; 1 E 70th St, at Fifth Ave; adult/student $22/12, pay-what-you-wish 2-6pm Wed, free 6-9pm 1st Fri of month excl Jan & Sep; ⏰10am-6pm Tue-Sat, 11am-5pm Sun; ⑤6 to 68th St-Hunter College)

Met Breuer
MUSEUM

2 ◎ MAP P188, B4

The newest branch of the Metropolitan Museum of Art (p182) opened in the landmark former Whitney Museum building (designed by Marcel Breuer; there's an architecture tour you can listen to on the Met's website) in 2016. Exhibits are dedicated to 20th- and 21st-century art, with sculpture, photographs, video, design and paintings from the likes of American and international figures such as Edvard Munch, Claes Oldenburg and Robert Smithson. Your three-day admission includes

Upper East Side Sights

Frick Collection

(Almost) Free Museums

The Upper East Side is blessed with many of the finest museums in New York City, though visiting them all can be extremely pricey. But many museums here offer specific hours once per week where you can pay whatever admission price you wish, so plan to visit at those times to save some cash.

Some also offer completely free admission at specific times, such as the Neue Galerie (first Friday evening of each month) and the Asia Society & Museum (Friday evenings from September to June).

the main museum, and medieval exhibits at the Cloisters (p23). (🕿212-731-1675; www.metmuseum. org/visit/met-breuer; 945 Madison Ave, at E 75th St; 3-day pass adult/ senior/child $25/$17/free, pay-what-you-wish for NY State residents; 🕙10am-5:30pm Tue-Thu & Sun, to 9pm Fri & Sat; 🚇6 to 77th St, Q to 72nd St)

Neue Galerie   MUSEUM

3 ⊙ MAP P188, A2

This restored Carrère and Hastings mansion from 1914 is a resplendent showcase for Austrian and German art, featuring works by Paul Klee and Ernst Ludwig Kirchner, and incredible collections of Gustav Klimt and Egon Schiele. In pride of place on the 2nd floor is Klimt's golden 1907 *Portrait of Adele Bloch-Bauer I* – acquired for the museum by cosmetics magnate Ronald Lauder for a whopping $135 million. The fascinating story of the painting's history is told in the 2015 film *Woman in Gold*. (www.neuegalerie. org; 1048 Fifth Ave, at E 86th St; adult/ student $22/12, free 5-8pm 1st Fri of month; 🕙11am-6pm Thu-Mon; 🚇4/5/6, Q to 86th St)

Asia Society & Museum   MUSEUM

4 ⊙ MAP P188, B4

Founded in 1956 by John D Rockefeller III (an avid collector of Asian art), this cultural center hosts fascinating exhibits (Buddhist art of Myanmar, retrospectives of leading Chinese artists, contemporary Southeast Asian art), as well as Jain sculptures and Nepalese Buddhist paintings. Daily tours (free with admission) are offered at 2pm Tuesday through Sunday year-round and at 6:30pm Friday (excluding summer months). Note the museum is generally closed for three weeks or so in August and June for turning over exhibitors. (🕿212-288-6400; www.asiasociety. org; 725 Park Ave, cnr E 70th St; adult/ child $12/free, free 6-9pm Fri Sep-Jun; 🕙11am-6pm Tue-Sun, to 9pm Fri Sep-Jun; 🚇6 to 68th St-Hunter College; Q to 72nd St)

Cooper-Hewitt Smithsonian Design Museum

MUSEUM

5 ◉ MAP P188, A1

Part of the Smithsonian Institution in Washington DC, this is the only US museum dedicated to both historic and contemporary design. Housed in the 64-room mansion built by billionaire Andrew Carnegie in 1901, the 210,000-piece collection offers artful displays spanning 3000 years over three floors of the building. The beautiful garden is open to the public and accessible from 90th St or from inside the museum. Free tours are at 11:30am and 1:30pm on weekdays, and at 1pm and 3pm on weekends. (www.cooperhewitt. org; 2 E 91st St, at Fifth Ave; adult/child $18/free, pay-what-you-wish 6-9pm Sat; ◷10am-6pm Sun-Fri, to 9pm Sat; Ⓢ4/5/6 to 86th St)

Jewish Museum

MUSEUM

6 ◉ MAP P188, A1

This gem occupies a French-Gothic mansion from 1908, housing 30,000 items of Judaica including torah shields and Hannukah lamps, as well as sculpture, painting and decorative arts. Temporary exhibits are often excellent, featuring retrospectives on influential figures such as Art Spiegelman, Edith Halpert or Leonard Cohen, as well as world-class shows on luminaries like Chagall and Modigliani. (☏212-423-3200; www.thejewishmuseum.org; 1109 Fifth Ave, btwn E 92nd & 93rd Sts; adult/child $18/free, Sat free, pay-what-you-wish 5-8pm Thu; ◷11am-5:45pm Mon-Tue & Fri, 11am-8pm Thu, 10am-5:45pm Sat & Sun; ⬤; ⓈQ, 6 to 96th St)

Museum of the City of New York

MUSEUM

7 ◉ MAP P188, A1

Situated in a Georgian Colonial Revival–style building at the top end of Museum Mile, this local museum focuses on New York City's past, present and future. Don't miss the 28-minute film *Timescapes* (on the ground floor), which charts NYC's growth from a tiny trading post for Native Americans to a burgeoning metropolis. (www. mcny.org; 1220 Fifth Ave, btwn E 103rd & 104th Sts; suggested admission adult/child $20/free; ◷10am-6pm; Ⓢ6 to 103rd St)

Temple Emanu-El

SYNAGOGUE

8 ◉ MAP P188, A5

Founded in 1845 as the first Reform synagogue in New York, this temple, completed in 1929, is now one of the largest Jewish houses of worship in the world. An imposing Romanesque structure, it is more than 175ft long and 100ft tall, with a brilliant, hand-painted ceiling featuring gold details. It is best to call ahead before visiting because the synagogue regularly closes for funerals and other events. Services (6pm Fridays and

10:30am Saturdays) are open to all. (www.emanuelnyc.org; 1 E 65th St, at Fifth Ave; admission free; ⏰10am-4pm Sun-Thu, to 2pm Fri; Ⓢ6 to 68th St-Hunter College)

Eating

Tanoshi
SUSHI $$$

9 MAP P188, D4

It's not easy to snag one of the 22 stools at Tanoshi, a wildly popular, pocket-sized sushi spot. The setting may be humble, but the flavors are simply magnificent. Only sushi is on offer and only *omakase* (chef's selection) – which might include Hokkaido scallops, kelp-cured flake or mouthwatering *uni* (sea urchin). BYO beer, sake or whatnot. (www.tanoshisushinyc.com; 1372 York Ave, btwn E 73rd & 74th Sts; chef's sushi selection $95-100; ⏰seatings 6pm, 7:30pm & 9pm Tue-Sat; Ⓢ Q to 72nd St)

Café Sabarsky
AUSTRIAN $$

The lines can get long at this Neue Galerie (see 3 ◉ Map p188, A2) popular cafe evoking an opulent, turn-of-the-century Vienna coffeehouse. The Austrian specialties, courtesy of *Michelin*-starred chef Kurt Gutenbrunner, include crepes with smoked trout, goulash soup and roasted bratwurst – all beautifully presented. There's also a mouthwatering list of specialty sweets, including a divine Sacher torte – dark chocolate cake with apricot confiture. (www.neuegalerie.org/cafes/sabarsky; 1048 Fifth Ave, at E 86th St; mains $19-32; ⏰9am-6pm Mon & Wed, to 9pm Thu-Sun; Ⓢ4/5/6 to 86th St)

Papaya King
HOT DOGS $

10 MAP P188, C2

The *original* hot-dog-and-papaya-juice shop, from 1932, over 40 years before crosstown rival Gray's Papaya (p216) opened, Papaya King has lured many a New Yorker to its neon-lit corner for a cheap and tasty snack of hot dogs and fresh-squeezed papaya juice. (Why papaya? The informative wall signs will explain all.) Try the Homerun, with sauerkraut and New York onion relish. (www.papayaking.com; 179 E 86th St, at Third Ave; hot dogs $3-4.50; ⏰8am-midnight Sun-Thu, to 1am Fri & Sat; Ⓢ4/5/6, Q to 86th St)

William Greenberg Desserts
BAKERY $

11 MAP P188, B2

Stop in at this Manhattan institution for its signature New York–style black-and-white cookies – soft, cakey discs dipped in vanilla and chocolate glazes (grab a box of minis for the trip home). Classic egg-cream sodas come in three flavors; its brownies are divine, too. Take-out only. (☎212-861-1340; www.wmgreenbergdesserts.com; 1100 Madison Ave, btwn E 82nd & 83rd Sts; baked goods from $1.75; ⏰8am-6:30pm Mon-Fri, to 6pm Sat, 9:30am-4:30pm Sun; ♿; Ⓢ4/5/6 to 86th St)

Café Boulud

FRENCH $$$

12 ✖ MAP P188, B4

This long-standing *Michelin*-starred bistro by Daniel Boulud attracts a rather staid crowd with its globe-trotting French-Vietnamese cuisine. Seasonal menus include classics like bass 'en paupiette,' as well as fare such as duck with sour cherry and baby fennel. (📞212-772-2600; www.cafeboulud.com/nyc; 20 E 76th St, btwn Fifth & Madison Aves; breakfast $13-29, mains $39-52; ⏱7-10:30am, noon-2:30pm & 5:30-10:30pm Mon-Fri, 8-10:30am, 11:30am-2:30pm & 5:30-10:30pm Sat, 8-10:30am, 11:30am-3pm & 5-10pm Sun; 🖋; 🚇6 to 77th St)

Wright

AMERICAN $$

13 ✖ MAP P188, A1

The Wright restaurant at the Guggenheim (p186), serving such dishes as kohlrabi fritters, house-made pasta and seared salmon (the menu changes regularly), is somewhat overshadowed by its gleaming-white, modernist design aesthetic. Four intricately woven canvas collages by Sarah Crowner were installed in early 2017. On weekends it serves brunch. (📞212-423-3665; www.guggenheim.org; Guggenheim Museum, 1071 Fifth Ave, at E 89th St; mains $20-27; ⏱11:30am-3:30pm Mon-Fri, from 11am Sat & Sun; 🛜; 🚇4/5/6, Q to 86th St)

Cooper-Hewitt Smithsonian Design Museum (p191)

OSUGI/SHUTTERSTOCK ©

Cheaper Eats

The Upper East Side is the epitome of old-school opulence, especially the area that covers the blocks from 60th to 86th Sts between Park and Fifth Aves. If you're looking for eating and drinking spots that are easier on the wallet, head east of Lexington Ave. Third, Second and First Aves are lined with less pricey neighborhood venues.

Sant Ambroeus   ITALIAN $$

14 ✖ MAP P188, B3

Behind a demure facade lies this dressy Milanese bistro and cafe that oozes old-world charm. The long granite counter up front dispenses rich cappuccinos, pastries and mini panini (grilled with the likes of cotto ham and San Daniele prosciutto DOP); the elegant dining room behind dishes up northern Italian specialties, such as breaded veal chop, risotto and tagliatelle al ragù. (☏212-570-2211; www.santambroeus.com; 1000 Madison Ave, btwn E 77th & 78th Sts; panini $7-9, mains $21-69; ⊙7am-11pm Mon-Fri, from 8am Sat & Sun; ✶; ⑤6 to 77th St)

Candle Cafe   VEGAN $$

15 ✖ MAP P188, C4

The moneyed yoga set piles into this minimalist vegan cafe serving a long list of sandwiches, salads, comfort food and market-driven specials. The specialty here is the housemade seitan. There is a juice bar, a gluten-free menu and organic cocktails. (☏212-472-0970; www.candlecafe.com; 1307 Third Ave, btwn E 74th & 75th Sts; mains $16-22; ⊙11:30am-10pm Mon-Fri, from 11am Sat, 11am-9:30pm Sun; ✶; ⑤Q to 72nd St)

Drunken Munkey   INDIAN $$

16 ✖ MAP P188, C1

This lively lounge channels colonial-era Bombay with vintage wallpaper, cricket-ball door handles and jauntily attired waitstaff. The monkey chandeliers may be pure whimsy, but the craft cocktails (favoring gin, not surprisingly) and tasty curries are serious business. Expect a good level of spice in Anglo-Indian dishes like masala Bombay lamb chops and Goan pork vindaloo. Book ahead. (☏646-998-4600; www.drunken munkeynyc.com; 338 E 92nd St, btwn First & Second Aves; mains $18-34; ⊙4:30pm-2am Mon-Tue & Fri, to 3am Wed-Thu, 11:30am-3am Sat, 11am-2am Sun; 🛜; ⑤Q, 6 to 96th St)

Lexington Candy Shop   DINER $

17 ✖ MAP P188, B2

Founded in 1925, this picture-perfect diner is a bygone slice of NYC. Sadly it's more a tourist attraction than neighborhood favorite these days. Slip into a booth or sit at the long counter for reliable standards like burgers, tuna melts and milkshakes – plus egg creams (soda, milk and flavored syrup) made fresh from the old-fashioned soda fountain. (☏212-288-0057; www.lexington candyshop.net; 1226 Lexington Ave, at E 83rd St; mains $9.50-19; ⏱7am-7pm Mon-Fri, from 8am Sat, 8am-6pm Sun; ⓢ4/5/6, Q to 86th St)

Drinking

UES NYC
COCKTAIL BAR

18 🚇 MAP P188, C1

Scooping delicious ice cream by day, this candy-colored parlor lets rip as a speakeasy by night. Cocktails ($15 to $25) are named after Upper East Side landmarks, such as 'Meet me at the Met' and '2nd Avenue Subway.' Beware: there's a dress code, so no sneakers, flip-flops, ripped jeans or T-shirts. (☏646-559-5889; www. theuesnyc.com; 1707 Second Ave, btwn E 88th & 89th Sts; ⏱5pm-late Mon-Sat; ⓢQ to 86th St)

Bemelmans Bar
LOUNGE

19 🚇 MAP P188, B3

Sink into a chocolate-leather banquette and take in the glorious, old-school elegance at this atmospheric bar – the sort of place where the waiters wear white jackets and serve martinis, a pianist tinkles on a baby grand and the ceiling is 24-carat gold leaf. The walls are covered in charming murals by the bar's namesake Ludwig Bemelmans, famed creator of the

Madeline books. (☏212-744-1600; www.thecarlyle.com; Carlyle Hotel, 35 E 76th St, at Madison Ave; ⏱noon-1:30am; 🛜; ⓢ6 to 77th St)

Flora Bar
BAR

Forget that this is essentially a museum bar in the Met Breuer (see 2 🚇 Map p188, B4); Flora is a sophisticated drinking lounge that shows off the building's architectural extravagance. Park yourself at the marble bar or curl into a deep modernist armchair to marvel at the double-story concrete cathedral and gigantic glass wall that leads to a sunken garden: an oasis beneath Madison Ave. (☏646-558-5383; www. florabarnyc.com; Met Breuer, 945 Madison Ave, lower fl, at E 75th St; ⏱bar 11:30am-3:30pm & 5:30-10pm, cafe 10am-5:30pm Tue-Sun; 🛜; ⓢ6 to 77th St, Q to 72nd St)

Irving Farm Roasters
COFFEE

20 🚇 MAP P188, C3

This pioneering New York artisanal coffeehouse serves full-bodied espressos and single-origin pour-overs, along with a small yet tasty cafe menu. This is the largest of its 10 Manhattan locations, with a roomy seating area at the back. Its policy is 'no wi-fi' – bring a book. (☏646-861-2949; www. irvingfarm.com; 1424 Third Ave, at E 81st St; ⏱7am-7pm Mon-Fri, from 8am Sat & Sun; ⓢ6 to 77th St, 4/5/6 to 86th St)

Cantor Roof Garden Bar

ROOFTOP BAR

21 🚇 MAP P188, A3

The sort of setting you can't get enough of (even if you are a jaded local). Located atop the Met, this rooftop bar sits right above Central Park's tree canopy, allowing for splendid views of the park and the city skyline all around. Sunset is when you'll find fools in love... then again, it could all be those martinis. (www.metmuseum.org/visit/dining; Metropolitan Museum of Art, 1000 Fifth Ave, 5th fl, at E 82nd St; ⏰11am-4:30pm Sun-Thu, to 8:15pm Fri & Sat mid-Apr–Oct; 🛜; 🚇4/5/6 to 86th St)

Pony Bar

CRAFT BEER

22 🚇 MAP P188, D4

The best craft-beer destination in Upper Manhattan, Pony Bar pours exclusively American craft (including cask-conditioned ales) with a near total devotion to New York State breweries. You'll find 20 rotating taps and a whole lot of rustic hardwoods (the bar, the seating, the barrels, the canoe...). If you're in pursuit of a locally devout hoptopia in the UES, look no further. (www.theponybar.com; 1444 First Ave, btwn E 75th & 76th Sts; ⏰3pm-4am Mon-Tue & Thu-Fri, to 1:30am Wed, noon-4am Sat & Sun; 🚇Q/R to 72nd St)

Bemelmans Bar (p195)

Caledonia BAR

23 MAP P188, C2

The name of this unpretentious, dimly lit bar is a dead giveaway: it's devoted to Scotch whisky, with over a hundred single malts to choose from (be they Highlands, Islands, Islay, Lowlands or Speyside), as well as some blends and even a few from the US, Ireland and Japan. (www.caledoniabar.com; 1609 Second Ave, btwn E 83rd & 84th Sts; 5pm-2am Mon-Thu, 4pm-4am Fri & Sat, 4pm-1am Sun, happy hour to 7pm Mon-Fri; Q, 4/5/6 to 86th St)

Ethyl's Alcohol & Food BAR

24 MAP P188, C2

This funky, divey 1970s-themed bar harks back to the gritty, artsy NYC of yore, before famed punk club CBGB became a fashion boutique. (The $14 cocktails make it decidedly modern.) There's '60s/'70s music nightly from bands or DJs, plus go-go dancers and occasional burlesque shows, and a famed *Fi-Dolla* ($5) burger. (www.ethylsnyc.com; 1629 2nd Ave, btwn E 84th & 85th Sts; 5pm-2am Mon-Wed, to 4am Thu, 4pm-4am Fri & Sat, 4pm-2am Sun; Q/R to 86th St)

Entertainment

Frick Collection Concerts CLASSICAL MUSIC

Every two to four weeks, the opulent Frick Collection (see 1 Map p188, A4) hosts a Sunday 5pm concert that brings in world-renowned performers, such as cellist Yehuda

Top Shopping for Less

Madison Ave isn't for amateurs. Some of the globe's glitziest shops line the stretch from 60th St to 72nd St, with flagship boutiques from the world's top designers, including Gucci, Prada and Cartier. A handful of consignment stores offer preloved designer deals; for gently worn top brands such as Louboutin, Fendi, and Dior try **Michael's** (p198) or **La Boutique Resale** (Map p188, B2; 212-517-8099; www.laboutiqueresale.com; 1132 Madison Ave, btwn E 84th & 85th Sts, 2nd fl; 10am-7pm Mon-Sat, 10:30am-6:30pm Sun; 4/5/6 to 86th St).

Hanani and violinist Thomas Zehetmair: check the website for the schedule. (212-547-0715; www.frick.org/programs/concerts; 1 E 70th St, at Fifth Ave; $45; 6 to 68th St-Hunter College)

92nd Street Y ARTS CENTER

25 MAP P188, B1

In addition to its wide spectrum of concerts, dance performances, literary readings and family-friendly events, this nonprofit cultural center hosts an excellent lecture and conversation series. Playwright Edward Albee, cellist Yo-Yo Ma, comedian Steve Martin and novelist Salman Rushdie have all taken the stage here. (212-415-5500;

The Second Avenue Subway

Nearly a century in the making (and an NYC in-joke for decades), the Second Avenue Subway finally opened to the public on January 1, 2017... well, the first phase of it, anyway. Two new miles of track – which took 10 years to build and cost $4.5 billion – connect an extended Q line to the F train at 63rd St and Lexington Ave, then continue up Second Ave for stops at 72nd, 86th and 96th Sts. With an airy feel and broad, open platforms, the three gleaming new stations feature permanent tile and mosaic installations by artists Chuck Close, Jean Shin, Vik Muniz and Sarah Sze. All the trouble seems to have been worth it: the new line is carrying 176,000 people per day, and Second Ave (especially between 82nd and 86th Sts) has now become a hotbed of worthwhile bars and restaurants whose appeal reaches beyond the folks in the neighborhood.

East Harlem residents are still waiting for Phase Two (due for completion by 2029), which will offer new stations at 103rd and 116th Sts and a connection with the 4/5/6 and the Metro-North Railroad at 125th St. Pity the downtown crowd, though: proposed Phases Three and Four, which will extend south to Houston St and then Hanover Sq, haven't even been funded yet.

www.92y.org; 1395 Lexington Ave, at E 92nd St; ⏱box office 30min prior to ticketed events; 🛗; Ⓢ Q, 6 to 96th St)

Shopping

Schaller & Weber   FOOD & DRINK

26 🔒 MAP P188, C2

This award-winning charcuterie and delicatessen is a holdover from when the Yorkville neighborhood was a largely German enclave. It sells over 15 varieties of sausage made at its factory in Pennsylvania – such German classics as *bauernwurst* and *weisswurst,* chicken bratwurst, cheddar-stuffed brat', Irish bangers, Polish kielbasa and more – alongside imported European goodies: cheese, pickles, condiments, chocolate, wine and beer. (www.schallerweber.com; 1654 Second Ave, cnr E 86th St; ⏱10am-8pm Mon-Sat, noon-6pm Sun; Ⓢ Q, 4/5/6 to 86th St)

Michael's   CLOTHING

27 🔒 MAP P188, B2

In operation since the 1950s and as of 2018 in a new street-facing location, this vaunted Upper East Side resale store features high-end labels, including Chanel, Gucci, Prada and Jimmy Choo. Almost everything on display is less than two years old. It's pricey but cheaper than shopping the flagship boutiques on Madison Ave.

(212-737-7273; www.michaelscon signment.com; 1125 Madison Ave, btwn E 84th & 85th Sts; 10am-6:30pm Mon-Sat, to 8pm Thu, noon-6pm Sun, closed Sun Jul & Aug; S 6 to 77th St)

Diptyque

PERFUME

28 MAP P188, B4

Come out smelling like a rose – or wisteria, jasmine, cypress or sandalwood – at this olfactory oasis. Parisian company Diptyque has been creating signature scents since 1961, using innovative combinations of plants, woods and flowers. (212-879-3330; www. diptyqueparis.com; 971 Madison Ave, cnr E 76th St; 10am-7pm Mon-Sat, noon-6pm Sun; S 6 to 77th St)

Mary Arnold Toys

TOYS

29 MAP P188, B3

Several generations of Upper East Siders have spent large chunks of their childhood browsing the stuffed shelves of this personable local toy store, opened in 1931. Its range is extensive – stuffed animals, action figures, science kits, board games, arts and crafts, educational toys – even Lomo cameras for budding retro photo-graphers. (212-744-8510; www. maryarnoldtoys.com; 1178 Lexington Ave, btwn E 80th & 81st Sts; 9am-6pm Mon-Fri, from 10am Sat, 10am-5pm Sun; S 4/5/6 to 86th St)

Second Avenue Subway at 72nd Street

Shakespeare & Co

BOOKS

30 MAP P188, B5

No relation to the Paris seller, this popular bookstore is one of NYC's great indie options. There's a wide array of contemporary fiction and nonfiction, and art and local history books, plus a small but unique collection of periodicals, while an Espresso book machine churns out print-on-demand titles. A small cafe serves coffee, tea and light meals. (212-772-3400; www. shakeandco.com; 939 Lexington Ave, at E 69th St; 7:30am-8pm Mon-Fri, 8am-7pm Sat, 9am-6pm Sun; ; S 6 to 68th St-Hunter College)

Walking Tour 🥾

Harlem Soul

Harlem: the neighborhood where Billie Holiday crooned; where Ralph Ellison penned Invisible Man, *his epic novel on truth and intolerance; where acclaimed artist Romare Bearden pieced together his first collages. Simultaneously vibrant and effusive, brooding and melancholy, Harlem is the deepest recess of New York's soul.*

Getting There

S 1 line to Cathedral Pkwy (110th St)

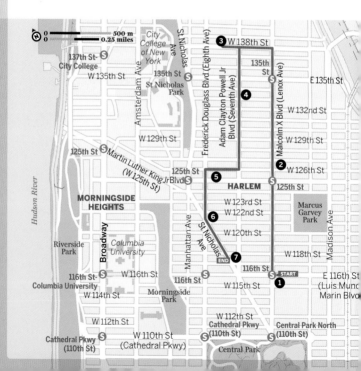

❶ Malcolm Shabazz Harlem Market

Trawl this low-key, semi-enclosed **market** (52 W 116th St, btwn Malcolm X Blvd & Fifth Ave; admission free; ⏱10am-8pm; 👫; **S**2/3 to 116th St) for African jewelry, textiles, drums, leather goods and oils.

❷ Sylvia's

This soul-food Southern **restaurant** (📞212-996-0660; www.sylvias restaurant.com; 328 Malcolm X Blvd, btwn 126th & 127th Sts; mains $15-28; ⏱8am-10:30pm Mon-Sat, 11am-8pm Sun; **S**2/3 to 125th St) has drawn locals, celebrities and even a few presidents with authentic home-style cooking since the 1960s.

❸ Strivers' Row

The blocks of 138th and 139th Sts are graced with these 1890s **town houses** (W 138th & 139th Sts, btwn Frederick Douglass & Adam Clayton Powell Jr Blvds; **S**B, C to 135th St), former home to some of Harlem's greatest luminaries, like blues veteran WC Handy and singer-dancer Bill 'Bojangles' Robinson.

❹ Shrine

This **mainstay** (www.shrinenyc.com; 2271 Adam Clayton Powell Jr Blvd, btwn 133rd & 134th Sts; ⏱4pm-4am; **S**2/3 to 135th St) on Harlem's nightlife circuit hosts an incredible nightly lineup of music, from calypso, Afropunk and French electro to Latin jazz and straight-up soul.

❺ Apollo Theater

One of the best places to catch a **concert** (📞tickets 800-745-3000, tours 212-531-5337; www.apollotheater. org; 253 W 125th St, btwn Frederick Douglass & Adam Clayton Powell Jr Blvds; tickets from $24; **S**A/B/C/D, 2/3 to 125th St) in Harlem. Ella Fitzgerald debuted here in 1934, at one of the theater's earliest Amateur Nights; they still take place every Wednesday (February to November), notorious crowds and all.

❻ Flamekeepers Hat Club

Harlem's Gilded Age lives on at this friendly corner **boutique** (📞212-531-3542; www.flamekeepers hatclub.com; 273 W 121st St, at St Nicholas Ave; ⏱noon-7pm Tue & Wed, to 8pm Thu-Sat, to 6pm Sun; **S**A/C, B/D to 125th St) lined with elegant hats and caps. Can't decide? Seek Marc Williamson's keen eye.

❼ Minton's

Bebop was incubated at this formal **jazz-and-dinner club** (📞212-243-2222; www.mintonsharlem.com; 206 W 118th St, btwn St Nicholas Ave & Adam Clayton Powell Jr Blvd; $20-25 or $30 food purchase minimum; ⏱6-11pm Wed-Sat, noon-3pm & 6-10pm Sun; **S**B/C, 2/3 to 116th St), where greats like Thelonious Monk, Dizzy Gillespie and Charlie Parker were all regulars. Dress to impress and savor sweet grooves over decadent Southern fare.

Explore
Upper West Side & Central Park

Walking past brownstones on quiet Upper West Side streets, you may feel like you've stepped out of a movie. This noted family neighborhood still harbors vestiges of old communities, now being given new verve by artisan coffee shops and designer emporiums. Verdant Central Park stretches to the east, while arts hub Lincoln Center and several museums serve as cultural anchors.

The Short List

○ **Central Park (p204)** *Escaping the city's frantic urban madness picnicking, row-boating and strolling.*

○ **Lincoln Center (p219)** *Plunging into the sheer depth of artistic choices at this first-class arts center.*

○ **American Museum of Natural History (p210)** *Walking among some of the world's largest dinosaurs.*

○ **Nicholas Roerich Museum (p210)** *Taking a pilgrimage to Tibet via a beautiful 19th-century town house.*

○ **Riverside Park (p211)** *Strolling along the Hudson waterfront as the sun goes down over the far shore.*

Getting There & Around

Ⓢ Use the 1, 2 and 3 lines for between Broadway and the river; the B and C are best for museums and Central Park.

🚌 The M104 runs up Broadway; the M10 up the park's western edge. Crosstown routes at 66th, 72nd, 79th, 86th and 96th Sts head to the Upper East Side.

Neighborhood Map on p208

Lincoln Center (p219) EILEEN_10/SHUTTERSTOCK ©

Top Experience 📷
Explore Central Park

With more than 800 acres of picturesque meadows, ponds and woods, Central Park might seem to be Manhattan in its raw state. But the park, designed by Frederick Law Olmsted and Calvert Vaux, is the result of serious engineering: thousands of workers shifted 10 million cartloads of soil to transform swamp and rocky outcroppings into the 'people's park' of today.

◎ MAP P208, E4

www.centralparknyc.org

59th to 110th Sts, btwn Central Park West & Fifth Ave

🕐 6am-1am

Ⓢ A/C, B/D to any stop btwn 59th St-Columbus Circle & Cathedral Pkwy (110th St)

Strawberry Fields

This tear-shaped **garden** (at W 72nd St; **S** C, B to 72nd St) serves as a memorial to former Beatle John Lennon, who lived directly across the street in the **Dakota Building** (1 W 72nd St, at Central Park West; **S** B, C to 72nd St) and was fatally shot there. The garden, which was partially funded by his widow Yoko Ono, is composed of a grove of stately elms and a tiled mosaic that reads, simply, 'Imagine.' Visitors can listen to an audioguide to Strawberry Fields, narrated by Yoko, at www.centralparknyc.org/imagine.

Bethesda Terrace & the Mall

The arched walkways of **Bethesda Terrace** (66th to 72nd St; **S** B, C to 72nd St), crowned by the magnificent **Bethesda Fountain** at 72nd St, has long been a gathering area for New Yorkers. To the south is **the Mall** (featured in countless movies), a promenade shrouded in mature North American elms. The southern stretch, known as **Literary Walk**, is flanked by statues of famous authors.

Great Lawn & the Ramble

The **Great Lawn** (btwn 79th & 85th Sts; ⊙ Apr–mid-Nov; **S** B, C to 86th St) is a massive emerald carpet at the center of the park, surrounded by ball fields and London plane trees. (It's where Simon & Garfunkel played their famous 1981 concert.) Immediately to the southeast is Delacorte Theater (p219), home to an annual Shakespeare in the Park festival, as well as **Belvedere Castle** (at W 79th St; ⊙ 9am-7pm mid-Jun–mid-Aug, 10am-5pm mid-Aug–mid-Jun; **S** 1/2/3, B, C to 72nd St), a bird-watching lookout. Further south is the leafy **Ramble** (btwn 73rd & 78th Sts; **S** B,C to 81st St-Museum of Natural History), a popular birding destination. On the southeastern end is the **Loeb Boathouse** (☎ 212-517-2233; btwn 74th & 75th Sts; boating per hour $15, each additional 15min $3; ⊙ 10am-7pm;

★ **Top Tips**

⊙ Hit up Central Park Bike Tours (p211), just one block south of the park, for bike rentals and guided tours.

⊙ Avoid the carriage rides. They're a rip-off and the horses lead miserable lives.

✗ **Take a Break**

⊙ Consider packing a picnic from the assortment of gourmet goodies at Zabar's (p214), a few blocks from the park.

⊙ Inside the park you can class things up a bit with a meal in the elegant Loeb Boathouse (p216).

[🚶]; [S] B, C to 72nd St, 6 to 77th St), home to a waterside restaurant that offers rowboat rentals and gondola rides.

Central Park Zoo

This small **zoo** ([☎] 212-439-6500; www.centralparkzoo.com; 64th St, at Fifth Ave; adult/child $20/15, without 4D Theater $14/9; [🕐] 10am-5pm Mon-Fri, to 5:30 Sat & Sun Apr-Oct, 10am-4:30pm Nov-Mar; [S] N/R to 5th Ave-59th St), which gained fame for its part in the DreamWorks animated movie *Madagascar,* is home to penguins, snow leopards and lemurs. Feeding times in the sea lion and penguin tanks make for a rowdy spectacle. The attached petting zoo, **Tisch Children's Zoo**, has alpacas and mini-Nubian goats and is perfect for small children.

Jacqueline Kennedy Onassis Reservoir

The reservoir (at 90th St) takes up almost the entire width of the park and serves as a gorgeous reflecting pool for the city skyline. It is surrounded by a 1.58-mile track that draws legions of joggers in the warmer months. Nearby, at Fifth Ave and 90th St, is a statue of New York City Marathon founder Fred Lebow, peering at his watch.

Conservatory Garden

If you want a little peace and quiet (as in, no runners, cyclists or buskers), the 6-acre **Conservatory Garden** (Fifth Ave at E 105th St; [🕐] 8am-5pm Nov-Feb, to 6pm Mar & Oct, to 7pm Apr & Sep, to 7:30pm late Aug, to 8pm May–mid-Aug; [S] 6 to 103rd St)

View of Manhattan buildings from Central Park

NIELSKLIM/SHUTTERSTOCK ©

ALISON RIDGWAY/LONELY PLANET ©

View from Belvedere Castle (p205)

serves as one of the park's official quiet zones. And it's beautiful, to boot: bursting with crabapple trees, meandering boxwood and, in the spring, lots of flowers. Otherwise, you can catch maximum calm (and max birdlife) in all areas of the park just after dawn.

Summer Happenings

During the warm months, Central Park is home to countless cultural events, many of which are free. The two most popular are Shakespeare in the Park (p219), which is managed by the Public Theater, and SummerStage (p26), a series of free concerts.

Central Park Then & Now

In the 1850s, this area of Manhattan was occupied by pig farms, a garbage dump, a bone-boiling operation and an African American village. It took 20,000 laborers two decades to transform this terrain into a park. Today, Central Park has more than 24,000 trees, 136 acres of woodland, 21 playgrounds and seven bodies of water – and more than 38 million visitors a year.

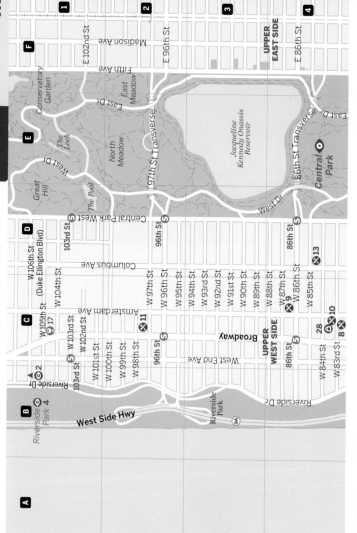

Hudson River

Metropolitan Museum of Art

E 79th St
E 72nd St
E 65th St
E 59th St

Madison Ave
Fifth Ave
5th Ave-59th St

Great Lawn
Turtle Pond

Conservatory Water

6 Central Park Conservancy
Conservatory Water

The Ramble
Bow Bridge

14

79th St Transverse
The Lake

Central Park West
72nd St

The Mall
Literary Walk

East Dr

7

The Pond
The Pond

Wollman Skating Rink

Museum of Natural History
81st St

American Museum of Natural History

New-York Historical Society

Columbus Ave

Central Park
72nd St

Sheep Meadow
Center Dr
65th St Transverse
West Dr

Center Dr
Central Park South

Central Park Bike Tours

24

1
3
30

W 82nd St
W 81st St
Zabar's
W 80th St
W 79th St
W 78th St
W 77th St
W 76th St
W 75th St
W 74th St
W 73rd St
W 72nd St
W 71st St
W 70th St
W 69th St
W 68th St
W 67th St
W 66th St
W 65th St
W 64th St
W 63rd St
W 62nd St
W 61st St
W 60th St
W 59th St

81st St
79th St
72nd St

20

18

19
15
29

26
27

5 American Folk Art Museum

16
12

21
25
22

66th St-Lincoln Center

Lincoln Center

59th St Columbus Circle

Columbus Circle

Broadway
Columbus Ave
Amsterdam Ave
West End Ave

Toga Bike Shop

Freedom Pl

West Side Hwy

500 m
0.25 miles

A B C D E F

5 6 7 8

For reviews see

◎ Top Experiences p204
◎ Sights p210
✕ Eating p213
◷ Drinking p216
◎ Entertainment p218
◎ Shopping p220

Sights

American Museum of Natural History
MUSEUM

1 ⊙ MAP P208, D5

Founded in 1869, this classic museum contains a veritable wonderland of more than 34 million artifacts – including lots of menacing dinosaur skeletons – as well as the **Rose Center for Earth & Space**, which has a cutting-edge planetarium. From October through May, the museum is home to the **Butterfly Conservatory**, a vivarium featuring 500-plus butterflies from all over the world that will flutter about and land on your outstretched arm. (📞212-769-5100; www.amnh.org; Central Park West, at W 79th St; suggested admission adult/child $23/13; ⏱10am-5:45pm; 🚼; 🅂C to 81st St-Museum of Natural History; 1 to 79th St)

Nicholas Roerich Museum
MUSEUM

2 ⊙ MAP P208, B1

This compelling little museum, housed in a three-story town house from 1898, is one of Manhattan's best-kept secrets. It displays 150 paintings by the prolific Nicholas Konstantinovich Roerich (1874–1947), a Russian-born poet, philosopher and painter. His most remarkable works are his stunning depictions of the Himalayas, where he and his family settled in 1928. Indeed, his mountainscapes are truly a wonder to behold: icy Tibetan peaks in shades of blue, white,

American Museum of Natural History

green and purple, channeling a Georgia O'Keeffe or Rockwell Kent vibe. (☎212-864-7752; www.roerich. org; 319 W 107th St, btwn Riverside Dr & Broadway; admission free; ⏰noon-5pm Tue-Fri, from 2pm Sat & Sun; Ⓢ1 to Cathedral Pkwy 110th St)

New-York Historical Society
MUSEUM

3 ◉ MAP P208, D5

As the antiquated hyphenated name implies, the Historical Society is the city's oldest museum, founded in 1804 to preserve historical and cultural artifacts. Its collection of more than 60,000 objects is quirky and fascinating and includes everything from George Washington's inauguration chair to a 19th-century Tiffany ice-cream dish (gilded, of course). However, it's far from stodgy, having moved into the 21st century with renewed vigor and purpose. (☎212-873-3400; www.nyhistory.org; 170 Central Park West, at W 77th St; adult/child $22/6, by donation 6-8pm Fri, library free; ⏰10am-6pm Tue-Thu & Sat, to 8pm Fri, 11am-5pm Sun; ♿; Ⓢ B, C to 81st St-Museum of Natural History)

Riverside Park
PARK

4 ◉ MAP P208, B1

A classic beauty designed by Central Park creators Frederick Law Olmsted and Calvert Vaux, this waterside spot, running north on the Upper West Side and banked by the Hudson River from W 59th

Cycling Central Park

The best way to cover all 840 acres of Central Park is to rent a bicycle. A full ride of the Central Park loop is 6.2 miles long, and takes in both hilly and flat terrain (the northern half is generally hillier than the south). You can see more information and a map of the park's paths at the Central Park Conservancy website (www.centralparknyc.org).

For rentals try **Central Park Bike Tours** (Map p208, E8; ☎212-541-8759; www.central parkbiketours.com; 203 W 58th St, btwn Broadway & 7th Ave; bike rentals per hour/day adult from $10.50/28, child $9/23; ⏰8am-8pm; ♿; Ⓢ1/2/3 to 59th St-Columbus Circle) and **Toga Bike Shop** (Map p208, C7; ☎212-799-9625; www.togabikes.com; 110 West End Ave, btwn W 64th & 65th Sts; rentals per 24hr hybrid/road bike $35/150; ⏰11am-7pm Mon-Wed & Fri, to 8pm Thu, 10am-6pm Sat, 11am-6pm Sun; Ⓢ1 to 66th St-Lincoln Center).

to 155th Sts, is lusciously leafy. Plenty of bike paths, playgrounds and dog runs make it a family favorite. Views from the park make the Jersey side of the Hudson look quite pretty. (www.riversideparknyc. org; Riverside Dr, btwn W 59th & 155th Sts; ⏰6am-1am; ♿; Ⓢ1/2/3 to any stop btwn 72nd & 125th Sts)

New York City on Page & Screen

New York has been the setting of countless works of literature, television and film. From critical commentaries on class and race to the lighter foibles of falling in love, these stories are not just entertainment but carefully placed tiles in NYC's diverse mosaic of tales.

Books

The Amazing Adventures of Kavalier & Clay (Michael Chabon; 2000) Touches upon Brooklyn, escapism and the nuclear family.

A Tree Grows in Brooklyn (Betty Smith; 1943) An Irish-American family living in the Williamsburg tenements in the 20th century.

Down These Mean Streets (Piri Thomas; 1967) Memoirs of tough times growing up in Spanish Harlem.

Invisible Man (Ralph Ellison; 1952) Poignant exploration of the situation of African Americans in the early 20th century.

Manhattan Beach (Jennifer Egan; 2017) Pulitzer Prize–winning author Egan's novel follows a young woman working in the Brooklyn Navy Yard during WWII.

Vanishing New York (Jeremiah Moss; 2017) Non-fiction work exploring gentrification and 21st-century NYC policy.

Films

Taxi Driver (1976) Martin Scorsese's story of a troubled Vietnam vet turned taxi driver.

Do the Right Thing (1989) Spike Lee's critically acclaimed comedy-drama probes the racial turmoil lurking just beneath the surface.

Requiem for a Dream (2000) Darren Aronofsky's unusual tale of a Brooklyn junkie and his doting Jewish mother.

Angels in America (2003) Mike Nichols' movie version of Tony Kushner's Broadway play recalls AIDS out of control in 1985 Manhattan.

Precious (Lee Daniels, 2009) Based on the novel *Push* by Sapphire; an unflinching tale of a Harlem teenager abused by her parents.

Margaret (2015) Kenneth Lonergan's second film explores the devastating effects of an accident on a Manhattan teen.

American Folk Art Museum
MUSEUM

5 ⦿ MAP P208, D7

This small institution offers rotating exhibitions in three small galleries. Past exhibits have included quilts made by 19th-century soldiers and sculptures by a celebrated Ghanaian coffin-maker of forts through which slaves were trafficked. The gift shop is a trove of unique, artsy items: books, jewelry, accessories, scarves, home decor etc. There's free music on Wednesdays (2pm) and Fridays (5:30pm). (☏212-595-9533; www.folkartmuseum.org; 2 Lincoln Sq, Columbus Ave, btwn W 65th & 66th Sts; admission free; ⊙11:30am-7pm Tue-Thu & Sat, noon-7:30pm Fri, noon-6pm Sun; ⑤1 to 66th St-Lincoln Center)

Central Park Conservancy
WALKING

6 ⦿ MAP P208, F8

The nonprofit organization that supports Central Park maintenance also offers a wide range of walking tours guided around the park. Some of the tours are free (such as the Heart of the Park tour, which takes in the park's highlights), while others cost $15 and require advance booking. The tours start from various points around the park; check the website for the schedule.

(☏212-310-6600; www.centralpark nyc.org/tours)

Wollman Skating Rink
SKATING

7 ⦿ MAP P208, E8

This rink is much larger than the Rockefeller Center skating rink, and not only does it allow all-day skating, its position at the southeastern edge of Central Park offers magical views. There's locker rental for $5 and a spectator fee of $5. Cash only. (☏212-439-6900; www. wollmanskatingrink.com; Central Park, btwn E 62nd & 63rd Sts; adult Mon-Thu $12, Fri-Sun $19, child $6, skate rentals $10; ⊙10am-2:30pm Mon & Tue, to 10pm Wed & Thu, to 11pm Fri & Sat, to 9pm Sun late Oct-early Apr; ⑤F to 57 St, N/R/W to 5th Ave-59th St)

Eating

Jin Ramen
JAPANESE $

8 ✕ MAP P208, C4

This buzzing little joint off Amsterdam Ave serves delectable bowls of piping hot ramen. *Tonkotsu* (pork broth) ramen is a favorite, though vegetarians also have tantalizing options. Don't neglect the appetizers: *shishito* peppers, pork buns and *hijiki* salad. The mix of rustic wood elements, exposed bulbs and red industrial fixtures gives the place a cozy vibe. (☏646-657-0755; www.jinramen.com; 462 Amsterdam Ave, btwn W 82nd & 83rd Sts; mains $13-19; ⊙lunch 11:30am-

Bagel with a Schmear, Please

A bastion of gourmet kosher foodie-ism, sprawling local market **Zabar's** (Map p208, C5; ☏212-787-2000; www.zabars.com; 2245 Broadway, at W 80th St; ⏰8am-7:30pm Mon-Fri, to 8pm Sat, 9am-6pm Sun; ⑤1 to 79th St) has been a neighborhood fixture since the 1930s. And what a fixture it is! It features a heavenly array of cheeses, meats, olives, caviar, smoked fish, pickles, dried fruits, nuts and baked goods, including pillowy, fresh-out-of-the-oven knishes (Eastern European–style potato dumplings wrapped in dough).

3:30pm, dinner 5-11pm Mon-Thu, to midnight Fri & Sat, to 10pm Sun; 🗸; ⑤1 to 79th St)

Barney Greengrass   DELI $$

9 🍴 MAP P208, C4

The self-proclaimed 'King of Sturgeon,' Barney Greengrass serves the same heaping dishes of eggs and salty lox, luxuriant caviar and melt-in-your-mouth chocolate babkas that first made it famous when it opened over a century ago. Fuel up in the morning at casual tables amid the crowded produce counters, or take lunch at the serviced cafe in an adjoining room. (☏212-724-4707; www.barneygreengrass.com; 541 Amster-

dam Ave, at W 86th St; mains $5.25-28, fish platters $37-67; ⏰deli 8am-6pm Tue-Sun, cafe 8:30am-4pm Tue-Fri, to 5pm Sat & Sun; ⑤1 to 86th St)

Cafe Lalo   DESSERTS $

10 🍴 MAP P208, C4

The vintage French posters and marble-topped tables make this longtime Upper West Side date spot feel like a Parisian cafe. But really, you're here for the mind-blowing array of desserts: choose (if you can) from over 30 different cakes, 23 flavors of cheesecake, 10 types of pie, a dozen kinds of fruit tart, cookies, pastries, zabaglione, chocolate mousse and more. (☏212-496-6031; www.cafelalo.com; 201 W 83rd St, btwn Amsterdam & Columbus Aves; desserts $5-10; ⏰8am-1am Mon-Thu, to 4am Fri, 9am-4am Sat, to 2am Sun; ⑤1 to 79th St, B, C to 81st St-Museum of Natural History)

Awadh   NORTH INDIAN $$

11 🍴 MAP P208, C2

This dark-toned, upscale North Indian gem harkens back to the culinary heritage of Lucknow and the cuisine of aristocratic Nawabs. Chef Gaurav Anand will transport you to the subcontinent with his transcendent *galouti* kebabs (melt-in-your-mouth minced lamb patties with spices, a Lucknow street-food legend) and anything cooked *dum phukt* style: meat and/or rice slow cooked inside a dough-sealed clay pot. (☏646-

861-3241; www.awadhnyc.com; 2588
Broadway, btwn W 97th & 98th Sts;
mains $13-26; ⏱5-11pm Mon-Fri,
noon-3pm & 5-11pm Sat & Sun;
⑤1/2/3 to 96th St)

Smith

AMERICAN $$$

12 MAP P208, D8

On a restaurant-lined strip across
from Lincoln Center, this always-
buzzing bistro serves high-end
comfort food with seasonal ac-
cents: grilled shrimp with quinoa
tabbouleh, burgers with raclette
and green peppercorn sauce, and
short rib ragù are a few recent
selections. There's also a raw
bar and myriad drink selections.
On warm days, there's open-air
seating in front. (☎212-496-5700;

https://thesmithrestaurant.com; 1900
Broadway, at W 63rd St; mains $18-47;
⏱7:30am-midnight Mon-Thu, to 1am
Fri, 9am-1am Sat, 9am-midnight Sun;
🛜; ⑤1 to 66th St-Lincoln Center, A/C,
B/D to 59th St-Columbus Circle)

Blossom on Columbus

VEGAN $$

13 MAP P208, D4

The elegantly modern surrounds
at this upscale vegan restaurant
elevate the plant-based menu to
a higher realm. Opt for something
veggie-forward like the roasted
red and yellow beet, chickpea and
cranberry kale salad, or else go
for something a bit, um, meatier
– pan-seared seitan cutlets with
white wine, lemon and capers.

Zabar's

(☎212-875-2600; www.blossomnyc.com; 507 Columbus Ave, btwn W 84th & 85th Sts; mains lunch $16-25, dinner $19-25; ⏱11:30am-3:30pm & 5-9:45pm Mon-Sat, from 10:30am Sun; 🖊; ⑤B, C, 1 to 86th St)

Lakeside Restaurant at Loeb Boathouse

AMERICAN $$$

14 ❌ MAP P208, E6

Perched on the northeastern tip of the Central Park Lake with views of the midtown skyline in the distance, the Loeb Boathouse provides one of New York's most idyllic spots for a meal. That said, you're paying for the setting. While the food is generally good (crab cakes are the standout; $21), the service can be indifferent. (☎212-517-2233; www.thecentralparkboathouse.com; Central Park Lake, Central Park, near E 74th St; mains lunch $26-38, dinner $30-46; ⏱restaurant noon-3:45pm Mon-Fri, from 9:30am Sat & Sun year-round, 5:30-9:30pm Mon-Fri, from 6pm Sat & Sun Apr-Nov; ⑤B, C to 72nd St, 6 to 77th St)

Gray's Papaya

HOT DOGS $

15 ❌ MAP P208, C6

It doesn't get more New York than bellying up to this classic stand-up joint – founded by a former partner of crosstown rival Papaya King (p192) – in the wake of a beer bender. The lights are bright, the color palette is 1970s and the hot dogs are unpretentiously good. (☎212-799-0243; www.grayspapaya

nyc.com; 2090 Broadway, at W 72nd St, entrance on Amsterdam Ave; hot dogs $2.95; ⏱24hr; ⑤1/2/3, B, C to 72nd St)

Drinking

Empire Rooftop

ROOFTOP BAR

16 🍺 MAP P208, D8

Sprawled across the top of the Empire Hotel, this stylish rooftop bar is one of New York's most expansive drinking spaces in the sky at 8000 sq ft. A bright, glass-roofed wing strewn with palms and sofas is perfect for winter and has a retractable roof for summer, and there's a handful of outdoor terraces. (www.empirehotelnyc.com; 44 W 63 St, at Broadway; ⏱3pm-1am Mon-Wed, to 2am Thu & Fri, 11am-2am Sat, to 1am Sun; 📶; ⑤1 to 66th St-Lincoln Center)

Plowshares Coffee

COFFEE

17 🍺 MAP P208, C1

Plowshares got in the specialty coffee game way back in 2008, when this small-but-exquisite espresso haven opened in the Bloomingdale district of the UWS. Your coffee is pulled from the Pagani of espresso machines: an $18,000 hand-built Slayer, of which just about as many exist as do the aforementioned made-to-order Italian car. A connoisseur's delight. (www.plowsharescoffee.com; 2730 Broadway, btwn W 104th & 105th

Gray's Papaya

Sts; ⏰7am-7pm Mon-Fri, from 8am Sat & Sun; Ⓢ1 to 103rd St)

Owl's Tail
COCKTAIL BAR

18 Ⓜ MAP P208, C6

A snazzy neighborhood cocktail bar that feels more downtown than UWS with its cozy banquet sofa seating, tiled flooring and industrially bent lighting. Owl art, from Northwest Coast style to wooden carvings to a stupendous mural, pepper the place. The highly social L-shaped bar is your perfect perch for popular beat-the-heat cocktails like Bicycle Thief (Campari, gin, grapefruit, lemon, simple syrup and seltzer). (www.owlstail.com; 215 W 75th St, btwn Broadway & Amsterdam Ave; ⏰4:30pm-1am Mon-Thu, 4pm-2am Fri, 11:30am-2am

Sat, 11:30am-1am Sun; 🛜; Ⓢ1/2/3 to 72nd St)

Gebhard's Beer Culture
CRAFT BEER

19 Ⓜ MAP P208, C6

One of two locations in the city (the other is Hell's Kitchen), cozy Gebhard's is one of the most serious hophead havens on the Upper West Side. You'll find 16 taps of New York–heavy craft, but brews can flow from anywhere from California to Canada. Wash it all down with burgers, tacos, hot dogs and other alcohol-absorbing pub grub. (www.beerculture.nyc/gebhards; 228 W 72nd St, btwn West End Ave & Broadway; ⏰4pm-2am Mon, from 11:30am Tue-Sun; Ⓢ1/2/3 to 72nd St)

Dead Poet

BAR

20 MAP P208, C5

This narrow, mahogany-paneled pub is a neighborhood favorite. It takes its Guinness pours seriously, and features cocktails tht are named after deceased masters of verse, including a Walt Whitman Long Island Iced Tea ($14) and a Pablo Neruda spiced-rum sangria ($13). Feeling adventurous? Order the signature cocktail ($15), a secret recipe of seven alcohols – you even get to keep the glass. (www.thedeadpoet. com; 450 Amsterdam Ave, btwn W 81st & 82nd Sts; ⊘noon-4am; 🛜; S 1 to 79th St)

Entertainment

Metropolitan Opera House

OPERA

21 ⭐ MAP P208, C8

New York's premier opera company is the place to see classics such as *La Boheme, Madame Butterfly* and *Macbeth*. It also hosts premieres and revivals of more contemporary works, such as John Adams' *The Death of Klinghoffer*. The season runs from September to May. Tickets start at $25 and can get close to $500. (🎫tickets 212-362-6000, tours 212-769-7028; www.metopera.org; Lincoln Center, Columbus Ave at W 64th St; tickets $25-480; ⊘box office 10am-10pm Mon-Sat, noon-6pm Sun; S 1 to 66th St-Lincoln Center)

David H Koch Theater, home to the New York City Ballet

BUMBLE DEE/SHUTTERSTOCK ©

New York City Ballet

DANCE

22 ⭐ MAP P208, C8

This prestigious company was first directed by the renowned Russian-born choreographer George Balanchine in the 1940s. Today, it's the largest ballet organization in the US, performing 23 weeks a year at Lincoln Center's David H Koch Theater. Rush tickets for those under age 30 are $30. During the holidays the troupe is best known for its annual production of *The Nutcracker* (tickets go on sale in September: book early). (📞212-496-0600; www.nycballet. com; Lincoln Center, Columbus Ave at W 63rd St; tickets $39 to $204; ⏱box office 10am-7:30pm Mon, to 8:30pm Tue-Sat, 4:30am-7:30pm Sun; 🚻; ⑤1 to 66th St-Lincoln Center)

New York Philharmonic

CLASSICAL MUSIC

23 ⭐ MAP P208, C7

The oldest professional orchestra in the US (dating to 1842) holds its season every year at David Geffen Hall; music director Jaap van Zweden took over from Alan Gilbert in 2017. The orchestra plays a mix of classics (Tchaikovsky, Mahler, Haydn) and contemporary works, as well as concerts geared toward children. (📞212-875-5656; www.nyphil.org; Lincoln Center, Columbus Ave at W 65th St; tickets $29-125; 🚻; ⑤1 to 66 St-Lincoln Center)

Lincoln Center

The stark arrangement of gleaming modernist temples that is **Lincoln Center** (📞212-875-5456, tours 212-875-5350; www.lincolncenter.org; Columbus Ave, btwn W 62nd & 66th Sts; tours adult/student $25/20; ⏱tours 11:30am & 1:30pm Mon-Sat, 3pm Sun; 🚻; ⑤1, 2, 3 to 66th St-Lincoln Center, A/C or B/D to 59th St-Columbus Circle) houses some of Manhattan's most important performance companies: the **New York Philharmonic**, the **New York City Ballet** and the **Metropolitan Opera**. The lobby of the iconic Opera House is dressed with brightly saturated murals by painter Marc Chagall. Various other venues are tucked in and around the 16-acre campus, including a theater, two film-screening centers and the renowned Juilliard School for performing arts.

Delacorte Theater

THEATER

24 ⭐ MAP P208, E5

Every summer the Public Theater (p79) heads here to present its fabulous free productions of **Shakespeare in the Park** (www. publictheater.org/free-shakespeare-in-the-park; Central Park; ⏱Jun-Aug; ⑤A/B/C to 81st St-Museum of Natural History), which founder Joseph Papp began back in 1954,

Metropolitan Opera House (p218)

(📅 box office 212-875-5232; adult/ student $15/12), a more intimate, experimental venue, or the **Walter Reade Theater**, with wonderfully wide, screening-room-style seats. (📞212-875-5610; www.filmlinc. com; W 65th St, Lincoln Center, btwn Broadway & Amsterdam Ave; 🚇1 to 66th St-Lincoln Center)

Shopping

Icon Style   VINTAGE

26 🔒 MAP P208, D7

This tiny gem of a vintage shop specializes in antique fine and costume jewelry dating from the 1700s to 1970s, but also stocks carefully curated dresses, gloves, bags and hats. Half of the shop is covered in strikingly restored apothecary units, with the goods displayed in open drawers. Stop by and indulge your inner Grace Kelly. (📞212-799-0029; www. iconstyle.net; 104 W 70th St, near Columbus Ave; 🕙11am-8pm Tue-Fri, to 7pm Sat, noon-6pm Sun; 🚇1/2/3 to 72nd St)

before the lovely, leafy, open-air theater was even built. Productions are usually superb and it's a magical experience: waiting in line for tickets is a rite of passage for newcomers to the city. (www. publictheater.org; Central Park, enter at W 81st St; 🚇B, C to 81st St-Museum of Natural History)

Film at Lincoln Center   CINEMA

25 ⭐ MAP P208, C8

Film at Lincoln Center is one of New York's cinematic gems, providing an invaluable platform for a wide gamut of documentary, feature, independent, foreign and avant-garde art pictures. Films screen in one of two facilities at Lincoln Center: the **Elinor Bunin Munroe Film Center**

T2   TEA

27 🔒 MAP P208, D7

Aficionados of the brewed leaf will find more than 150 varieties at this outpost of an Australian tea company: oolong, green, black, yellow, herbals, you name it. But you don't just have to go by smell – the staff will brew samples of anything you care to try on the spot. It also carries a selection of tea-related gifts. (📞646-998-5010;

www.t2tea.com; 188 Columbus Ave, btwn W 68th & 69th Sts; ⏱11am-7pm; Ⓢ1 to 66th St-Lincoln Center, B, C to 72nd St)

Magpie

ARTS & CRAFTS

28 🔒 MAP P208, C4

This charming little shop carries a wide range of ecofriendly objects: elegant stationery, beeswax candles, hand-painted mugs, organic-cotton scarves, recycled-resin necklaces, hand-dyed felt journals and wooden earth puzzles are a few things that may catch your eye. Most products are fair-trade, made of sustainable materials or locally designed and made. (www.magpienewyork.com; 488 Amsterdam Ave, btwn W 83rd & 84th Sts; ⏱11am-7pm Mon-Sat, to 6pm Sun; Ⓢ1 to 86th St)

Westsider Records

MUSIC

29 🔒 MAP P208, C6

Featuring more than 30,000 LPs, this shop has got you covered when it comes to everything from funk to jazz to classical, plus opera, musical theater, spoken word, film soundtracks and other curiosities. (Don't miss the $1 bins up front.) It's a good place to lose all track of time – as is its **bookstore** (📞212-362-0706; 2246 Broadway, btwn W 80th & 81st Sts; ⏱10am-9pm; Ⓢ1 to 79th St) further uptown. (📞212-874-1588; www.westsiderbooks.com; 233 W 72nd St, btwn Broadway & West End Ave; ⏱11am-7pm Mon-Thu, to 9pm Fri & Sat, noon-6pm Sun; Ⓢ1/2/3 to 72nd St)

Grand Bazaar NYC

MARKET

30 🔒 MAP P208, D5

One of the oldest open-air shopping spots in the city, browsing this friendly, well-stocked flea market is a perfect activity for a lazy Upper West Side Sunday morning. You'll find a little bit of everything here, including vintage and contemporary furnishings, antique maps, custom eyewear, hand-woven scarves, handmade jewelry and so much more. (📞212-239-3025; www.grandbazaarnyc.org; 100 W 77th St, near Columbus Ave; ⏱10am-5:30pm Sun; ⓈB, C to 81st St-Museum of Natural History, 1 to 79th St)

Explore

Brooklyn: Park Slope, Gowanus & Green-Wood Cemetery

Known for its graceful brownstone houses, Park Slope is Brooklyn's answer to Manhattan's Upper West Side, home to brunch places, boutiques and 585-acre Prospect Park, Brooklyn's most beautiful green space. To the west is quirky Gowanus, home to hip bars and music venues. South lie the rolling hills of historic, picturesque Green-Wood Cemetery.

The Short List

o **Prospect Park (p226)** *Wandering through acres of woodlands, meadows, lakes and more.*

o **Green-Wood Cemetery (p226)** *Marveling at a gorgeous sculpture park and notable necropolis.*

o **Celebrate Brooklyn! Festival (p232)** *Lounging on the grass with a picnic and listening to global sounds.*

o **Barbès (p231)** *Feeling the rhythm all night from North African grooves at this jazzy little club.*

o **Eclectic Shopping (p232)** *Snapping up quirky souvenirs at shops like Brooklyn Superhero Supply Co.*

Getting There & Around

Ⓢ The 2/3, R, F and G run along the edges of Park Slope and Gowanus. The 4/5, B/D and N/Q stop at transit hub Atlantic Ave-Barclays Center.

Neighborhood Map on p224

Brooklyn: Park Slope, Gowanus & Green-Wood Cemetery

Washington Ave

PROSPECT HEIGHTS

For reviews see	
Sights	p226
Eating	p227
Drinking	p230
Entertainment	p231
Shopping	p232

500 m
0.25 miles

N
0
0

Underhill Ave

St Johns Pl

Eastern Pkwy-
Brooklyn
Museum **S**

Eastern Pkwy S

Brooklyn
Botanic
Garden

Vanderbilt Ave

Sterling Pl

Park Pl

**Grand Army
3 Plaza**

Flatbush Ave

Flatbush Ave

**Grand Army
Plaza S**

Plaza St West

Plaza St

**1 Prospect
Park**

Long
Meadow

Prospect Park W

Dean St

Bergen St

Carlton Ave

Flatbush Ave S

Bergen St

S

7th Ave S

St Marks Pl

6th Ave

5th Ave

St Johns Pl

Lincoln Pl

Berkeley Pl

Union St

President St

Carroll St

Fiske Pl

8th Ave

7th Ave

X 8

Warren St

Baltic St

Butler St

Douglass St

Degraw St

Sackett St

Union St

4th Ave S

X 9

20

25

S Union St

13

22

12 X

Garfield Pl

1st St

2nd St

3rd St

4th St

5th St

6th St

7th St

8th St

6th Ave

5th Ave

21

14

**PARK
SLOPE**

9th St

18

23

**4th Ave-
9th St S**

Nevins St

X 7

Gowanus Canal

Carroll St

Denton
Pl

4th Ave

X 11

3rd Ave

GOWANUS

Degraw St

President St

Carroll St

1st St

2nd St

3rd St

Sackett St

Hoyt St

Bond St

16

Gowanus Canal

4th Ave

5th Ave

2nd Ave

6 X

19

4th St

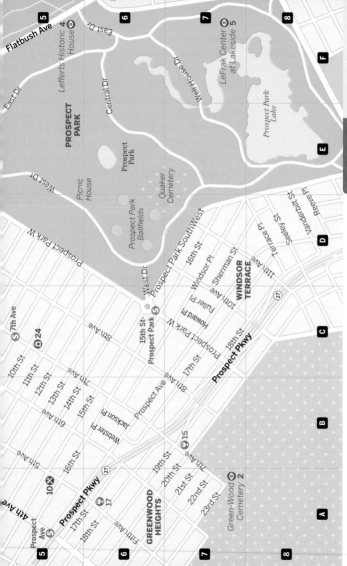

Flatbush Ave

Lefferts Historic House 4

East Dr

East Dr

WellHouse Dr

Central Dr

PROSPECT PARK

LeFrak Center at Lakeside 5

Prospect Park Lake

Prospect Park

Picnic House

West Dr

Prospect Park Ballfields

Quaker Cemetery

Reeve Pl

Vanderbilt St

Sherman St

Seeley St

Terrace Pl

11th Ave

Prospect Park SouthWest

16th St

Windsor Pl

Fuller Pl

Howard Pl

10th Ave

18th St

WINDSOR TERRACE

West Dr

Prospect Park W

Prospect Ave

17th St

Prospect Pkwy

7th Ave

24

8th Ave

15th St–Prospect Park

Prospect Park W

Prospect Ave

Jackson Pl

Webster Pl

8th Ave

7th Ave

10th St

11th St

12th St

13th St

14th St

15th St

6th Ave

16th St

5th Ave

19th St

20th St

21st St

22nd St

23rd St

15

7th Ave

Prospect Pkwy

10

27

Prospect Ave

17

17th St

18th St

Fifth Ave

4th Ave

GREENWOOD HEIGHTS

Green-Wood Cemetery 2

Sights

Prospect Park

PARK

1 ◉ MAP P224, E4

Brooklyn is blessed with a number of historic, view-laden and well used green spaces, but its emerald is Prospect Park. The designers of the 585-acre park – Frederick Law Olmsted and Calvert Vaux – considered it an improvement on their other New York project, Central Park, and between rambling its tree-fringed walkways and sighing at ornamental bridges, you might agree. (📞718-965-8951; www.prospectpark.org; Grand Army Plaza; ⏰5am-1am; 🚇2/3 to Grand Army Plaza, F, G to 15th St-Prospect Park, B, Q to Prospect Park, Q to Parkside Ave)

Green-Wood Cemetery

CEMETERY

2 ◉ MAP P224, A7

If you want to enjoy a slice of scenic Brooklyn in total peace and quiet, make for Green-Wood Cemetery. This historic burial ground set on the borough's highest point covers 478 hilly acres with more than 7000 trees (many of which are over 150 years old); its myriad tombs, mausoleums, lakes and patches of forest are connected by a looping network of roads and footpaths, making this a perfect spot for some aimless rambling. (📞718-768-7300; www.green-wood.com; 500 25th St, at Fifth Ave, Greenwood Heights; admission free; ⏰8am-5pm Oct-Mar, 7am-7pm Apr-Sep; 🅿; 🚇R to 25th St)

Grand Army Plaza

MONUMENT

3 ◉ MAP P224, E3

The grand entryway to Prospect Park, where Flatbush Ave meets the beginning of Eastern Pkwy, is a ceremonial arch created by visionary designer Calvert Vaux. Today part of a traffic circle, it's slightly removed from the park but the 1890s-built arch, formally known as the Soldiers' and Sailors' Monument, is a photogenic memorial to Union soldiers who fought in the Civil War. (Flatbush Ave & Eastern Pkwy, Prospect Park; ⏰6am-midnight; 🚇2/3 to Grand Army Plaza, B, Q to 7th Ave)

Lefferts Historic House

HISTORIC SITE

4 ◉ MAP P224, F5

Inside Prospect Park, this 18th-century Dutch farmhouse has period rooms festooned with farm implements, bouquets of herbs and antique ceramics, with a working garden outside. The former home of army lieutenant Pieter Lefferts, the house was moved here in the early 20th century from its original location on Flatbush Ave, in a neighborhood now called Prospect Lefferts Gardens. The house was closed for renovations from Spring 2020. (📞718-789-2822; www.prospectpark.org/lefferts; near Flatbush Ave & Empire Blvd, Prospect Park; adult/child $3/free; ⏰noon-5pm Thu-Sun Apr-Jun, Sep & Oct, to 6pm

The Gowanus Canal

Brooklyn's Gowanus Canal snakes east of the elevated Smith-9th Sts subway station, surrounded by former industrial blocks...but you may just smell it before you see it. Once a creek named after Gouwane, a chief of the indigenous Canarsee people, for many years the canal was used by merchant ships for unloading goods. Then local industry began dumping untreated waste into it, leading to a heavy sludge of congealed coal tar (called 'black mayonnaise') along the bottom. A purplish sheen on the surface – attractively iridescent, as long as you don't dwell on its origins – led to its nickname, 'the Lavender Lake.' The Environmental Protection Agency (EPA) declared the canal a Superfund site in 2009; a massive clean-up project is projected to finish in 2022.

As dredging continues, the canal's allure is increasing for local photographers (and the tangy odor is less pronounced than it once was). After rezoning efforts in the 2000s, the eponymous low-rent area that stretches north to Baltic St and east to Fourth Ave became home to artists' studios and music venues in large, postindustrial spaces. This led to more restaurants and bars – including one cheekily resurrecting the canal's former moniker (p231), and eventually to apartments and a huge branch of gourmet grocer Whole Foods – making Gowanus one of Brooklyn's most rapidly changing neighborhoods.

Jul & Aug, to 4pm Sat & Sun Nov & Dec; 🚻; S B, Q to Prospect Park)

LeFrak Center at Lakeside   BOATING

5 📍 MAP P224, F7

The most significant addition to Prospect Park since its creation, the LeFrak is a 26-acre ecofriendly playground. In winter there's ice skating, in summer there's roller skating and a sprinkler-filled water-play area for kids to splash about in. Pedal boats and kayaks are also available (usually late March to mid-October), and a va-

riety of bikes can be rented to tour the park. (📞 718-462-0010; www.lakesideprospectpark.com; 171 East Dr, near Ocean & Parkside Aves, Prospect Park; skating $7.25-10, skate rental $7, boat rental per hr $16-36, bike rental per hr $13-38; ⏱ hours vary; 🚻; S Q to Parkside Ave)

Eating

Four & Twenty Blackbirds   BAKERY $

6 ❌ MAP P224, A3

Inspired by their grandma, sisters Emily and Melissa Elsen use local

Smorgasburg Market

Every Sunday from April through October, Brooklyn's favorite open-air food hall **Smorgasburg** (www.smorgasburg.com; mains from $10; ◷Prospect Park 11am-6pm Sun) sets up shop in Prospect Park on Breeze Hill (south of the boathouse), with dozens of vendors selling an incredible array of goodness: Afghan comfort food, ramen burgers, Colombian arepas, Indian flatbread tacos, vegan Ethiopian dishes, sea-salt caramel ice cream, lavender lemonade, craft beer and much more.

fruit and organic ingredients to create NYC's best pies, hands down. Any time is just right to drop in for a slice – salted-caramel apple, lavender-honey custard or other seasonally changing flavors – and a cup of Stumptown coffee. (☏718-499-2917; www.birdsblack.com; 439 Third Ave, cnr 8th St, Gowanus; slices $6, whole pies $42; ◷8am-8pm Mon-Fri, from 9am Sat, 10am-7pm Sun; 🛜; 🅂R to 9th St)

Ample Hills Creamery
ICE CREAM $

 7 ⊗ MAP P224, B2

Though Ample Hills' Red Hook location now churns the ice cream, this scoop shop serves the small chain's magnificently creative flavors – honeycomb, butter cake, vegan-friendly mango and cherry-lime, plus 'It Came From Gowanus,' a chocolatey swirl of cookies and brownies, inspired by the dark depths of the Gowanus canal. Grab a cone and head up to the roof deck. (☏347-725-4061; www.amplehills.com; 305 Nevins St, at Union St, Gowanus; ice cream from $4.75; ◷noon-11pm Sun-Thu, to midnight Fri & Sat; 🛜🖍; 🅂R to Union St, F, G to Carroll St)

Skylce
THAI $$

8 ⊗ MAP P224, D1

Just when you thought the outstanding Thai food was reason enough to visit – sirloin yellow curry, scorching but refreshing papaya salad, mouthwatering *tom yum* soup – Skylce knocks it out of the park with a considerable dessert menu of parfaits, mango sticky rice and ice creams with flavors like lychee rose and durian. (☏718-230-0910; https://skyice.net; 63 Fifth Ave, at St Marks Pl, Park Slope; mains $11-18; ◷noon-10:30pm Sun, Mon, Wed & Thu, 4:30-10:30pm Tue, noon-11pm Fri & Sat; 🖍; 🅂2/3 to Bergen St, B, Q to 7th Ave)

Insa
KOREAN $$

9 ⊗ MAP P224, C1

Kimchi dumplings, spicy ribs and tofu *bibimbap* (stone bowl of veggies and rice) are highlights at tucked-away Insa, though it's most fun to barbecue squid, rib-eye or pork belly at your table. Amp it up by booking a small karaoke room ($30 to $60 per hour) or joining the free open-mic nights (from 10pm on the third Thursday of the month). (📞718-855-2620; www. insabrooklyn.com; 328 Douglass St, btwn Third & Fourth Aves, Gowanus; mains $16-29, barbecue for 2 $31-45; ⏱restaurant 5:30-10:30pm Mon-Thu, 5:30-11:30pm Fri, 3-11:30pm Sat, 3-10:30pm Sun, bar to 1am Mon-Thu, to 2am Fri & Sat, to midnight Sun; 🚇; S R to Union St)

Sidecar   AMERICAN $$

10 ✖ MAP P224, A5

Upscale American cuisine is beautifully conceived at Sidecar, an atmospheric spot with stamped-tin ceiling and leather boot seating. Classic dishes are given a modern touch, such as buttermilk fried chicken served with a savory root mash, and a club salad that mud-dles gruyère and tart apple into its medley of turkey and sun-dried tomato. (📞718-369-0077; www. sidecarbrooklyn.com; 560 Fifth Ave, btwn 15th & 16th Sts, Park Slope; mains $14-27; ⏱6pm-1am Mon, 11am-1am Tue-Thu & Sun, 11am-3am Fri & Sat; S R to Prospect Ave)

Baba's Pierogies   POLISH $

11 ✖ MAP P224, B2

Granny's recipes have been passed down to these Brooklyn purveyors of plump *pierogi* (Polish dumplings), whose soft dough is stuffed with cheese and potato, feta and spinach, or even mac 'n' cheese, before being boiled to perfection. There are vegan options, too, like dumplings crammed with sauerkraut or potato. (📞718-222-0777; www.babasbk.com; 295 Third

Smorgasburg

Ave, at Carroll St, Gowanus; 5/9 dumplings from $9/11; ⏱11:30am-10pm Tue-Sat, to 9pm Sun & Mon; 🔨; **S** R to Union St)

Luke's Lobster

SEAFOOD $

12 🦞 MAP P224, C2

Spreading across NYC (and far beyond) from the East Village, this chain of seafood 'shacks' works directly with fishers to ensure the provenance of its crustacea. Favorites include the lobster bisque, the clam and lobster chowders, and the staple lobster roll (a quarter crustacean on bread with mayonnaise and lemon butter). (☎347-457-6855; www.lukeslobster. com; 237 Fifth Ave, btwn Carroll & President Sts, Park Slope; lobster roll from $17, chowder $7-12; ⏱noon-10pm Mon-Thu, from 11am Fri-Sun; 🚼; **S** R to Union Ave)

Drinking

Union Hall

BAR

13 🚇 MAP P224, C2

Anyone seeking an authentically Brooklyn night out should look no further than Union Hall. This bar and event space is located in a converted warehouse and boasts a double-sided fireplace, towering bookshelves, leather couches and two full-size indoor bocce courts (a ball game similar to boules). Head to the basement for live music and comedy. (☎718-638-4400; www.unionhallny.com; 702 Union St, near Fifth Ave, Park Slope; ⏱4pm-4am

Mon-Fri, 1pm-4am Sat & Sun; **S** R to Union St)

The Gate

PUB

14 🚇 MAP P224, C3

The Gate is an amiable, locally loved pub that feels immediately comfortable. Facing the oasis of Washington Park, it offers two-dozen interesting craft beers, plus a social, central bar of scuffed wood, plenty of indoor niches, and outdoor seating for good weather. Good musical selections and genuine bar staff make this a dream local. (☎718-768-4329; www. thegatebrooklyn.com; 351 Fifth Ave, at 3rd St, Park Slope; ⏱3pm-4am Mon-Fri, from 1pm Sat & Sun; 📶; **S** F, G, R to 4th Ave-9th St)

Greenwood Park

BEER GARDEN

15 🚇 MAP P224, B7

Only in Brooklyn is a beer garden easily mistaken for an auto scrap yard...and all the better for it. Around the corner from Green-Wood Cemetery (p226), this 13,000-sq-ft indoor/outdoor beer hall in an open, industrial setting is a clever reconfiguration of a former gas station and mechanic's shop, with a rockin' soundtrack. Family-friendly by day, strictly 21-and-over after 7pm. Cash only. (☎718-499-7999; www.greenwood parkbk.com; 555 Seventh Ave, btwn 19th & 20th Sts, Greenwood Heights; ⏱noon-1am Sun-Thu, to 3am Fri & Sat, shorter hours in winter; 📶🚼; 🚌B67, B69 to 18th St, **S** F, G to 15th St-Prospect Park)

Lavender Lake

PUB

16 MAP P224, A2

Named after the colorfully polluted Gowanus Canal (p227), this popular local haunt is set in a former stable. Lavender Lake serves carefully selected craft beers and deceptively named cocktails with unorthodox ingredients like hibiscus mezcal and strawberry-infused tequila. The lumber-decked garden is a brilliant spot in summer. Weekday happy hour runs from 4pm to 7pm (and all day on Mondays). (347-799-2154; www.lavenderlake.com; 383 Carroll St, btwn Bond St & Gowanus Canal, Gowanus; 4pm-midnight Mon-Thu, 2pm-1am Fri, noon-2am Sat, noon-10pm Sun; F, G to Carroll St, R to Union St)

Freddy's

BAR

17 MAP P224, A6

This old-time bar with fascinating Prohibition-era history is located just past the southern fringe of Park Slope. Tip one back at the vintage mahogany bar while admiring the crazy art videos that are made by co-owner Donald O'Finn. There's also free live music (uke jams, honky-tonk), comedy nights and the odd film screening. A true New York classic. (718-768-0131; www.freddys bar.com; 627 Fifth Ave, btwn 17th & 18th Sts, Greenwood Heights; noon-4am; R to Prospect Ave)

Entertainment

Barbès

LIVE MUSIC

18 MAP P224, C4

This compact bar and performance space, named after a neighborhood in Paris with a strong North African flavor, is owned by French musicians (and longtime Brooklyn residents). There's live music all night, every night: an impressively eclectic lineup including Balkan brass, contemporary opera, Afro-Peruvian grooves, West African funk and other diverse sounds. (347-422-0248; www.barbesbrooklyn.com; 376 9th St, at Sixth Ave, Park Slope; requested donation for live music $10; 5pm-2am Mon-Thu, 2pm-4am Fri & Sat, 2pm-2am Sun; F, G to 7th Ave, R to 4th Ave-9th St)

Bell House

LIVE PERFORMANCE

19 MAP P224, A3

This 1920s warehouse in the light-industrial grid of Gowanus showcases high-profile live music and variety, spanning indie rockers, DJ nights, comedy shows, burlesque parties and more. The handsomely converted performance area holds up to 500 beneath its timber rafters, and the little Front Lounge has flickering candles, leather armchairs and plenty of beers behind the long oak bar. No under-21s. (718-643-6510; www.thebellhouse ny.com; 149 7th St, btwn Second & Third Aves, Gowanus; 5pm-late; F, G, R to 4th Ave-9th St)

Celebrate Brooklyn!

The multifaceted **Celebrate Brooklyn! Festival** (📞718-683-5600; www.bricartsmedia.org; Prospect Park Bandshell, near Prospect Park W & 11th St, Park Slope; ⏰ Jun–mid-Aug) has been going strong each summer for more than 40 years, with a stellar lineup of concerts, films, spoken-word shows and dance performances at the bandshell in the southwestern corner of Prospect Park (p226). Shows have a global feel, representing artists from Europe, the Middle East, the Caribbean and beyond, and many have free admission.

Littlefield   LIVE PERFORMANCE

20 ⭐ MAP P224, C2

This performance and art space occupying a 6200-sq-ft former textile warehouse showcases a wide range of live music and other shows, including comedy, storytelling, theater, dance, film screenings and trivia nights. Mondays bring a riotous comedy lineup; other regular events include the groan-inducing game show *Punderdome 3000,* oddball variety shows and trivia competition *Nerd Nite.* No under-21s. (www.littlefieldnyc.com; 635 Sackett St, btwn Third & Fourth Aves, Gowanus; tickets from $8; Ⓢ R to Union St)

Puppetworks   PUPPET THEATRE

21 ⭐ MAP P224, C4

In a tiny theater in Park Slope, this nonprofit outfit stages delightful marionette shows that earn rave reviews from pint-size critics. Catch puppet adaptations of classics like *Beauty and the Beast, The Frog Prince* and (of course) *Pinocchio.* Most shows happen on Saturday and Sunday at 12:30pm and 2:30pm. Check the website for schedules. Cash only. (📞718-965-3391; www.puppetworks.org; 338 Sixth Ave, at 4th St, Park Slope; adult/child $11/10; ⏰ office 10am-2:30pm; 🚼; Ⓢ F, G to 7th Ave)

Shopping

Diana Kane   FASHION & ACCESSORIES

22 🔒 MAP P224, C2

This beautifully curated boutique is brimming with locally made art, jewelry, women's clothing, candles and more. It's an inviting place to browse feminist greeting cards, paintings of iconic artists and one-of-a-kind gifts. (📞718-638-6520; www.dianakane.com; 229b Fifth Ave, btwn Carroll & President Sts, Park Slope; ⏰ noon-7pm Mon-Fri, 11am-8pm Sat, 11am-6pm Sun; Ⓢ R to Union Ave)

Brooklyn Superhero Supply Co   GIFTS & SOUVENIRS

23 🔒 MAP P224, B3

This curious shop sells capes, masks, utility belts, invisibility goggles, buckets of antimatter and other essentials for budding

Celebrate Brooklyn! Festival

superheroes...but the on-sale items are a mere distraction from the behind-the-scenes heroism. All sales provide support for 826NYC, a nonprofit that helps students improve their writing and literacy skills (the classroom area is concealed behind one of the shelves). (☏718-499-9884; www.superhero supplies.com; 372 Fifth Ave, btwn 5th & 6th Sts, Park Slope; ◷noon-6pm Tue-Sun; 🚼; Ⓢ F, G, R to 4th Ave-9th St)

Leroy's Place   ARTS & CRAFTS

24 🔒 MAP P224, C5

Is it a gallery, boutique or event space? No matter: inside whimsical Leroy's Place, you'll pose inside art installations, browse gifts from fine jewelry to zany T-shirts and keep the kids amused with over-sized monster puppets. (☏718-369-4200; www.leroysplace.com; 353 Seventh Ave, btwn 10th & 11th Sts, Park Slope; ◷noon-7pm Wed-Sun; 🚼; Ⓢ F, G to 7th Ave)

No Relation Vintage   VINTAGE

25 🔒 MAP P224, C2

Looking for a sports jersey? What about a piece of vintage designer clothing? There are many thrift stores in NYC, but few have quite this range. This gigantic vintage shop in the Gowanus area has a staggering inventory (you'll need to spend some time here), with great deals for bargain hunters. (☏718-858-4906; www.ltrainvintage nyc.com; 654 Sackett St, near Fourth Ave, Gowanus; ◷noon-7:45pm; Ⓢ R to Union St)

Walking Tour 🚶

Brooklyn: Williamsburg

The nightlife epicenter of Brooklyn, Williamsburg owes its growth to working-class communities of Latinx, Italian and Polish migrants, followed by starving artists – who then moved to Bushwick for cheaper rents, leaving gleaming condos and refurbished brownstones to professionals and hip young families. There's lots to explore, from vintage-cocktail dens to shops selling unique creations from local artisans.

Getting There

Williamsburg is in northern Brooklyn, just one stop from Manhattan and about 5 miles from Times Square.

S L to Bedford Ave.

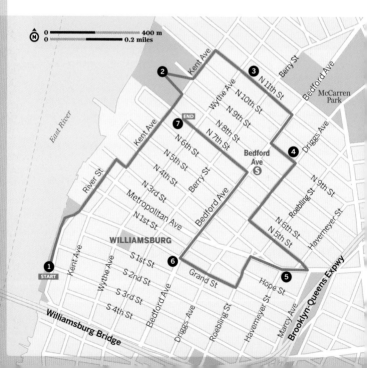

❶ Domino Park

This new, industrial-styled **park** (www.dominopark.com; River St, btwn Grand & S 5th Sts; 6am-1am; ; B32, Q59 to Kent Ave/S 1st St) has bocce, a kids' playground and an elevated walkway with marvelous Manhattan views.

❷ East River State Park

A 10-minute walk north is this open **green space** (718-782-2731; www.parks.ny.gov/parks/155; Kent Ave, btwn N 7th & N 9th Sts; 9am-9pm May-Sep, to 7pm Oct-Apr; B32 to Kent Ave/N 6th St) that offers picnicking and occasional concerts in the summer.

❸ Brooklyn Brewery

Continuing the long local beer-brewing tradition, this **brewery** (718-486-7422; www.brooklyn brewery.com; 79 N 11th St, btwn Berry St & Wythe Ave; tours Mon-Thu $18, Sat & Sun free; tasting room 5-11pm Mon-Thu, 5pm-midnight Fri, noon-midnight Sat, noon-8pm Sun, tours 1-6pm Sat & Sun, reserve ahead Mon-Fri) serves rich ales and hoppy IPAs and offers 45-minute tours.

❹ Buffalo Exchange

Create your own fashion mix of repurposed vintage and trendy recents at this beloved **resale shop** (718-384-6901; www.buffalo exchange.com; 504 Driggs Ave, at N 9th St; 11am-8pm Mon-Sat, noon-7pm Sun).

❺ City Reliquary

Browse curious objects from the past in this full-to-bursting **museum** (718-782-4842; www. cityreliquary.org; 370 Metropolitan Ave, near Havemeyer St; adult/child $7/free; noon-6pm Thu-Sun; G to Metropolitan Ave, L to Lorimer St) of NYC relics, from vintage postcards to exhibits on the 1939 World's Fair.

❻ Maison Premiere

Crank that time machine back one more notch at this **retro bar** (347-335-0446; www.maisonpremiere.com; 298 Bedford Ave, btwn S 1st & Grand Sts; 2pm-2am Sun-Wed, to 4am Thu-Sat) featuring bespoke cocktails, oysters and other treats with a smart Southern vibe.

❼ Artists & Fleas

On weekends, shop this **crafts warren** (917-488-4203; www. artistsandfleas.com; 70 N 7th St, btwn Wythe & Kent Aves; 10am-7pm Sat & Sun) of more than 75 booths featuring locally made jewelry, artworks, cosmetics, housewares and vintage records and clothes.

Survival Guide

Taxis outside Grand Central Terminal (p158) BLACKMAC/SHUTTERSTOCK ©

Before You Go

Book Your Stay

○ Expect high prices and small spaces.

○ Rates waver by availability, not by high-season or low-season rules. You'll pay dearly during holidays.

○ Accommodations fill quickly, especially in summer and December.

○ Brooklyn and Queens offer better value. A few hostels are scattered throughout NYC.

Useful Websites

NYC (www.nycgo.com/hotels) Listings from the NYC Official Guide.

Lonely Planet (lonelyplanet.com/usa/new-york-city/hotels) Hotel reviews and bookings.

Best Budget

Local (www.thelocalny.com) Affordable dorms and doubles with rooftop views and a great Long Island City location.

Harlem Flophouse (www.harlemflophouse.com) A charming

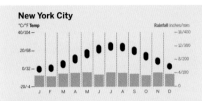

New York City

When to Go

Summer (June to August) Can be scorchingly hot, but brings a packed lineup of festivals and events.

Winter (December to February) Cold, sometimes with blizzards, but festive fun draws crowds.

Spring (Mar–May) Cafes drag their patio furniture out at the first hint of warm weather. One of the best times to explore the city.

Fall (Sep–Nov) Bursts of red and gold illuminate the city's parks, with still-warm days and cool nights.

townhouse in the heart of Harlem.

Carlton Arms (www.carltonarms.com) Divey, atmospheric, art-filled inn just a few blocks east of Madison Square Park.

NY Moore Hostel (www.nymoorehostel.com) Clean and friendly, on the doorstep of fab nightlife in Brooklyn's Williamsburg.

Best Midrange

Freehand New York (www.freehandhotels.com/new-york) Budget-conscious, design-forward rooms near the

Flatiron District.

Boro Hotel (www.borohotel.com) High design with panoramic views in Long Island City.

Arthouse Hotel NYC (www.arthousehotelnyc.com) Trendy lounge, light-filled rooms and sumptuous marble bathrooms close to the Lincoln Center.

Citizen M (www.citizenm.com) Contemporary, high-tech rooms near Times Square.

TWA Hotel (www.twahotel.com) Stay at JFK? Sure, if it means a neo-futurist hotel where you can spot planes from the pool.

At Home in Brooklyn (www.athomeinbrooklyn.com) A sumptuous breakfast to match the elegant styling of this parkside B&B.

Best Top End

Greenwich Hotel (www.thegreenwichhotel.com) Inner courtyards, individually designed rooms and a lantern-lit pool grace Robert De Niro's hotel.

Gramercy Park Hotel (www.gramercyparkhotel.com) Richly colored rooms sit above a sumptuous arty lobby with jazz-filled bars.

Knickerbocker (www.theknickerbocker.com) A luxurious Midtown option with a fabulous rooftop bar.

NoMad Hotel (www.thenomadhotel.com) Beaux-arts delight with apartment-style rooms, Parisian flair and a coveted restaurant and bar.

Bowery Hotel (www.theboweryhotel.com) Old-school elegance finds modern expression in the East Village.

Wythe Hotel (www.wythehotel.com) Upscale design and nostalgic touches in Williamsburg, Brooklyn's trendiest neighborhood.

Arriving in NYC

John F Kennedy International Airport (JFK)

○ The AirTrain ($5) links to the subway ($2.75) or the LIRR.

○ Express buses to Grand Central or Port Authority cost $19.

○ Taxis cost a flat $52, excluding tolls, tip and rush-hour surcharge.

Destination	Best Transport
Brooklyn	S LIRR to Atlantic Terminal
Lower East Side	S J/Z line
Lower Manhattan	S A line
Midtown	S LIRR to Penn Station
Greenwich Village	S A line
Upper West Side	S A line
Upper East Side	S E, then 4/5/6 lines
Harlem	S E, then B or C lines

LaGuardia Airport (LGA)

○ Bus ride ($2.75) includes one free transfer to the subway within two hours.

○ Express buses to Midtown cost $16.

○ Taxis range from $35 to $55, excluding tolls and tip.

Destination	Best Transport
Harlem	🚌 M60
Upper East Side	🚌 M60 & S 4/5/6 line
Midtown	🚌 Q70 & S F, 7 or E lines
Union Square	🚌 Q70 then S R line
Greenwich Village	🚌 Q70 then S F line
Brooklyn	Taxi

Newark Liberty International Airport (EWR)

○ About the same distance from Midtown as JFK (16 miles), Newark is a hub for United Airlines.

○ Take the AirTrain to Newark Airport train station, and board any train bound for Penn Station ($13).

○ Taxis range from $50 to $70 (plus $15 toll), excluding tip.

Getting Around

Subway

○ Inexpensive, efficient and operates around the clock, though navigating lines can be confusing.

○ A single ride is $2.75 with a MetroCard (or the expanding OMNY contactless system). Includes one free transfer to a bus within two hours.

Taxi & Rideshare

Yellow Taxis There are set fares for rides (which can be paid with credit or debit card). It's $2.50 for the initial charge (first one-fifth of a mile), 50¢ for each additional one-fifth mile as well as per 60 seconds in slow/non-moving traffic, $1 peak surcharge (weekdays 4pm to 8pm), and a 50¢ night surcharge (8pm to 6am), plus an MTA State surcharge of 50¢ per ride. Passengers must pay all bridge and tunnel toll charges. Tips are expected to be 10% to 15%, but give less if you feel in any way mis-

Subway Cheat Sheet

Numbers, letters, colors Color-coded subway lines are named by a letter or number, and carry a collection of two to four trains on their tracks.

Express & local lines A common mistake is accidentally boarding an 'express train' and passing by a local stop you want. Know that each color-coded line is shared by local trains and express trains; the latter make only select stops in Manhattan (indicated by a white circle on subway maps). For example, on the red line, the 2 and 3 are express, while the slower 1 makes local stops. If you're covering a greater distance – say from the Upper West Side to Wall St – you're better off transferring to the express train (usually just across the platform from the local) to save time.

Getting the right entrance Many stations in Manhattan have separate entrances for downtown or uptown lines (read the sign carefully). If you swipe in at the wrong one, re-enter the station (usually across the street) and plead ignorance to the station attendant; hopefully they'll buzz you through without having to swipe again, but if that doesn't work the alternative is to lose the $2.75 and just swipe in again. Also look for the green and red lamps above the stairs at each station entrance; green means that it's always open, while red means that particular entrance will be closed at certain hours, usually late at night.

Weekends All the rules switch on weekends, when some lines combine with others, some get suspended, some stations get passed, others get reached. Locals and tourists alike stand on platforms confused, sometimes irate. Check www.mta.info for weekend schedules, as sometimes posted signs aren't visible until after you reach the platform.

treated; be sure to ask for a receipt and use it to note the driver's license number.

Boro Taxis These apple-green taxis operate in the outer boroughs and Upper Manhattan. These allow folks to hail a taxi on the street in neighborhoods where yellow taxis rarely roam. They have the same fares and features as yellow cabs, and are a good way to get around the outer boroughs (from, say, Astoria to Williamsburg, or Park Slope to Red Hook). Drivers are reluctant (but legally obligated) to take passengers into Manhattan as they aren't legally allowed to take fares going out of Manhattan south of 96th St.

Passenger rights The TLC keeps a Passenger's Bill of Rights, which gives you the right to tell the driver which route you'd like to take, or ask your driver to turn off an annoying radio station. Also, the driver does not have the right to refuse you a ride based on where you are going. Tip: get in first, then say where you're going.

How to Take a Taxi

○ To hail a yellow cab, look for one with its roof light lit (if it's not lit, the cab is taken).

○ Stand in a prominent place on the side of the road and stick out your arm.

○ Once inside the cab, tell them your destination (it's illegal for drivers to refuse you a ride).

○ Pay your fare at the end, either with cash or credit card (via the touch screen in back). Don't forget to tip 10% to 15%.

○ If you download the smartphone app Curb, you can book a taxi to come pick you up, like any other ride-sharing service.

Private car These services are a common taxi alternative in the outer boroughs. Fares differ depending on the neighborhood and length of ride, and must be determined beforehand, as they have no meters. These 'black cars' are quite common in Brooklyn and Queens, but it's illegal if a driver simply stops to offer you a ride – no matter what borough you're in. A couple of car services in Brooklyn include **Northside** ([☎] 718-387-2222; www.northsidecarservice.com) in Williamsburg and **Arecibo** ([☎] 718-783-6465; www.arecibocc.com) in Park Slope.

Ride-sharing App-based car-hailing services have taken over the streets of the five boroughs. They're both convenient, indispensable for some, and of course adding to the already terrible traffic problem. Still, the city council has imposed limits on the number of ride-share vehicles cruising Manhattan, in an attempt to curb congestion, and the cap looks likely to endure. Tipping is encouraged.

Bus

○ A handy way to cross Manhattan east–west or to cover short distances when you don't want to bother going underground.

○ Rides cost the same as subway ($2.75 per ride), and you can use your Metrocard or pay in cash (exact change required).

○ If you pay with a Metrocard, you get one free transfer from bus to subway, bus to bus, or subway to bus. If you pay in cash, ask for a transfer (good only for a bus to bus transfer) from the driver when paying.

○ Look for the route on the small sign mounted on the pole of the bus stop.

Bicycle

○ NYC has hundreds of miles of designated bike lanes. The excellent bike-sharing network Citi Bike (www.citibike nyc.com) has kiosks all over Manhattan and parts of Brooklyn and Queens.

○ You can get a Citi Bike for a single ride ($3), or buy a pass (24-hour/three-day passes $12/24 including tax) at any kiosk station; during that pass period you can use the bikes for unlimited 30-minute periods.

○ Helmets aren't required by law for adults but are strongly recommended. You'll need to bring your own. They are required for children 13 and under.

○ Find bike lanes for every borough on NYC Bike Maps (www. nycbikemaps.com). Free bike maps are also available at most bike shops.

○ NYC auto traffic can be fierce. For your safety and that of others, obey traffic laws.

Boat

NYC Ferry (www. ferry.nyc; one-way $2.75) Operating in the East River, these boats link Manhattan, Brooklyn, Queens and the Bronx. Only $2.75 a ride ($1 more to bring a bicycle on board) and with charging stations and mini convenience stores on board.

NY Water Taxi (www. nywatertaxi.com) Zippy yellow boats that provide hop-on, hop-off services with four stops around Manhattan (Pier 83 at W 42nd St; Battery Park; Pier 16 near Wall St) and Brooklyn (Pier 1 in Dumbo). At

$37 for an all-day pass, though, it's priced more like a sightseeing cruise than practical transport.

Staten Island Ferry (Map p50; www.siferry. com; Whitehall Terminal, 4 Whitehall St, at South St, Lower Manhattan; ⏱ 24hr; Ⓢ 1 to South Ferry, R/W to Whitehall St, 4/5 to Bowling Green) Free, commuter-oriented ferry to Staten Island makes constant journeys across New York Harbor. Great for the views even if you just turn around and come right back.

Essential Information

Accessible Travel

○ Much of the city is accessible with curb cuts for wheelchair users.

○ All the major sites (like the Met museum, the Guggenheim, the National September 11 Memorial & Museum, and the Lincoln Center) are also accessible.

○ Some, but not all, Broadway venues have

provisions for theater-goers with disabilities.

○ Unfortunately, only about 100 of New York's 468 subway stations are fully wheelchair accessible. In general, the bigger stations have access, such as 14th St-Union Sq, 34th St-Penn Station, 42nd St-Port Authority Terminal, 59th St-Columbus Circle, and 66th St-Lincoln Center.

○ For a complete list of accessible subway stations, visit http://web.mta.info/accessibility/stations.htm. Also visit www.nycgo.com/accessibility.

○ All of NYC's MTA buses are wheelchair accessible, and are often a better option than negotiating cramped subway stations.

○ Order an accessible taxi through **Accessible Dispatch** (☏646-599-9999; http://accessible dispatch.org); there's also an app that allows you to request the nearest available service.

○ Download Lonely Planet's free Accessible Travel guides from https://shop.lonelyplanet.com/categories/accessible-travel.com.

Business Hours

Standard business hours are as follows:

Banks 9am–6pm Monday–Friday, some also 9am–noon Saturday

Bars 5pm–4am

Businesses 9am–5pm Monday–Friday

Clubs 10pm–4am

Restaurants Breakfast 6am–11am, lunch noon to 3pm, and dinner 5pm–11pm. Weekend brunch 10am–4pm.

Shops 10am to around 7pm weekdays, 11am to around 8pm Saturday; Sunday can be variable – some stores stay closed while others keep week-day hours. Stores stay open later in the neigh-borhoods downtown, such as SoHo.

Discount Cards

New York CityPASS (www.citypass.com) Buys you admission to six major attractions (including the Empire State Building) for $132 ($108 for kids), saving more than 40% than if purchased separately.

The New York Pass (www.newyorkpass.com) This pass gives you one-day access

to some 100 different sites, including the Empire State Building, for $134 (or $99 for children). Multiday passes also available (from two to 10 days).

Go City (www.gocity.com) A pass that lets you choose three to 10 attractions for discount-ed admission. You pick the sites from more than 90 options, including MoMA, the 9/11 Memo-rial and Museum, Top of the Rock and activities like Central Park bike rental and walking tours. Prices start at $94 for three sites, up to $270 for 10 sites.

Electricity

Type A
120V/60Hz

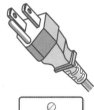

Type B
120V/60Hz

Emergency & Important Numbers

Local Directory ☏411

Municipal offices & NYC information ☏311

Fire, police & ambulance ☏911

Etiquette

Politeness It's common courtesy to greet nearby staff when entering or leaving a shop, cafe or restaurant.

Seating Systems When entering a restaurant, whether it's a diner or top-end table, hover until you are seated by waitstaff. The same applies in

some upscale bars, too. Coffee places and casual bars are self-service; cafes can be either.

Lively Debate Politics is loudly and enthusiastically discussed by New Yorkers, but like religion it's a topic that can quickly reveal allies...or enemies.

Transport Allow passengers to exit the subway car before entering; don't block the doors.

Gratuity Not optional in restaurants or bars; don't forget to tip.

Internet Access

○ Most public parks in the city now offer free wi-fi. Some prominent Manhattan spots include the High Line, Bryant Park, Battery Park, City Hall Park, Madison Square Park and Tompkins Square Park.

○ For other city hot spots, check www.nycgovparks.org/facilities/wifi.

○ Museums also often offer free wi-fi, as do all subway stations and public libraries.

○ Look for LinkNYC (www.link.nyc) around

town – these free, internet-connected kiosks also offer charging USB ports and wi-fi access.

○ Most cafes offer wi-fi for customers, as do the ubiquitous Starbucks around town.

Legal Matters

○ If you are arrested, you have the right to remain silent. There is no legal reason for you to speak to a police officer if you don't wish to – especially since anything you say 'can and will be used against you' – but never walk away from an officer until given permission (politely ask if you are free to leave).

○ All persons who are arrested have the legal right to make one telephone call. If you don't have a lawyer or family member to help you, call your consulate. The police will give you the phone number upon request.

Money

ATMs widely available; credit cards accepted at most hotels, stores and restaurants. Farmers markets and some food trucks, restaurants and bars are cash-only.

ATMs

o ATMs are on practically every corner. You can either use your card at banks – usually in a 24-hour-access lobby – or opt for the machines in delis, restaurants, bars and grocery stores, which charge service fees that average $4 but can go higher than $5.

o Most New York banks are linked by the New York Cash Exchange (NYCE) system, and you can use local bank cards interchangeably at ATMs – for an extra fee if you're banking outside your system.

Changing Money

Banks and money changers, found all over New York City (including all three major airports), will give you US currency based on the current exchange rate, often with a fee. Travelex has a branch in Times Square but considerable fees apply.

Credit Cards

o Major credit cards

Money-saving Tips

o MetroCards are valid on subways, buses, ferries and the aerial tram to Roosevelt Island. If you're staying more than a couple of days, buy a 7-Day Unlimited Pass ($33).

o Browse our list of free attractions (p27).

o Many museums offer free admission regularly. Check their websites for admission info.

o Save on theater tickets by buying them at the TKTS booth at Times Square or in Lower Manhattan (p61).

o Stock up on picnic goodies at the many outdoor farmers markets and gourmet grocers.

---

are accepted at most hotels, restaurants and shops throughout New York City. Certain transactions, such as purchasing tickets to performances and renting a car, can't be done without one.

o Visa, MasterCard and American Express are the cards of choice here. Places that accept Visa and MasterCard also accept debit cards. Be sure to check with your bank to confirm that your debit card will be accepted in other states or countries – debit cards from large commercial banks can often be used worldwide.

o If your cards are lost or stolen, contact your bank immediately.

Taxes & Refunds

o Restaurants and retailers never include the sales tax – 8.875% – in their prices, so don't order the $9.99 lunch special if you only have $10.

o Hotel rooms in New York City are subject to a 14.75% tax, plus a flat $3.50 occupancy tax per night.

o Several categories of so-called luxury services, including rental cars, carry an additional city surcharge (for rental cars it's 11%, so you wind up paying an extra 19.875% in total for this service).

o Clothing and footwear purchases under $110 are tax free; anything

Dos & Don'ts

∘ Hail a cab only if the roof light is on. If it's not lit, the cab is taken, so put your arm down already!

∘ New Yorkers don't always obey 'walk' signs, simply crossing when there isn't oncoming traffic. If you follow suit, look carefully!

∘ When negotiating pedestrian traffic on the sidewalk think of yourself as a vehicle – don't stop short, follow the speed of the crowd around you and pull off to the side if you need to take out your map or umbrella. Most New Yorkers are respectful of personal space, but they will bump into you – and not apologize – if you get in the way.

∘ Stand to the side of the doors to let disembarking passengers off first, then hop on (assertively, so the doors don't close in front of you).

∘ In New York you wait 'on line' instead of 'in line.' For telling time, you'll hear 'quarter of' rather than 'quarter to.'

∘ Oh, and Houston St is *How*-sten, not *Hugh*-sten, got it?

over that amount will incur the sales tax.

∘ Since the US has no nationwide value-added tax (VAT), foreign visitors cannot make 'tax-free' purchases.

Tipping

Tipping is *not* optional; only withhold tips in cases of outrageously bad service.

Restaurant servers 18–20%

Bartenders Minimum per drink $1, $2 for specialty cocktail or 15–20% overall

Taxi drivers 10–15%, rounded up to the next dollar

Airport & hotel porters $2 per bag, minimum per cart $5

Hotel cleaners $2–4 per night, envelope or card may be provided

Public Holidays

New Year's Day January 1

Martin Luther King Day Third Monday in January

Presidents' Day Third Monday in February

Memorial Day Late May

Independence Day July 4

Labor Day First Monday in September

Veterans Day November 11

Thanksgiving Fourth Thursday in November

Christmas Day December 25

Responsible Travel

Covid-19

∘ Covid-19 protocols are subject to change. Always check the latest requirements for travel to/within the USA at the CDC website (www.cdc. gov/coronavirus) and www.canitravel.net.

∘ NYC Covid protocols can be found at www.nyc. gov/coronavirus. Many indoor venues (theatres, bars, restaurants etc) may require proof of vaccination to enter.

Buy Local

○ Support New Yorkers by spending your money at locally owned shops, bars and restaurants instead of corporate chains. **Made In NYC** (www. madeinnyc.org) and **Black-Owned Brooklyn** (www.black ownedbrooklyn.com) offer curated listings.

Safe Travel

NYC is one of the USA's safest cities, but it's best to take a common-sense approach:

○ Don't walk alone at night in unfamiliar, sparsely populated areas.

○ Beware of pickpockets in the city, particularly in very busy areas like Times Square or Penn Station.

○ While it's generally safe to ride the subway after midnight, you may want to take a taxi, especially when alone (ride in the back).

○ Avoid pressure sales for show tickets and boat cruises; book your tickets online or at official vendors.

Smoking

○ Smoking is strictly forbidden in any location that's considered a public place, including subway stations, restaurants, bars, taxis and parks.

○ A few hotels have smoking rooms, but the majority are entirely smoke-free.

Toilets

○ Public restrooms can be found in transport hubs like Grand Central Terminal, Penn Station and Port Authority Bus Terminal, and in parks, including Madison Square Park, Bryant Park, Battery Park, Tompkins Square Park, Washington Square Park and Columbus Park in Chinatown, plus several places scattered around Central Park.

○ Your best bet is to pop into a Starbucks or a department store.

Tourist Information

NYC Information Center (Map p156, D5; www.nycgo.com; 151 W 34th St, at Broadway;

⊘10am-10pm Mon-Sat, to 9pm Sun; Ⓢ B/D/F/M, N/Q/R/W to 34th St-Herald Sq) Located at Macy's department store in Midtown.

Visas

○ The US Visa Waiver Program (VWP) allows nationals of 38 countries to enter the US without a visa, but you must fill out an ESTA (Electronic System for Travel Authorization; www.cbp.gov/travel/ international-visitors/ esta) application before departing.

○ There is a $14 fee for registration; when approved, it is valid for two years or until your passport expires, whichever comes first (unless your name, gender or citizenship changes).

○ If you hold a passport from a non-VWP country, are planning to stay longer than 90 days in the US or are planning to work or study here, you must obtain a visa from a US embassy or consulate in your home country.

Behind the Scenes

Send Us Your Feedback

We love to hear from travelers – your comments help make our books better. We read every word, and we guarantee that your feedback goes straight to the authors. Visit **lonelyplanet.com/contact** to submit your updates and suggestions.

Note: We may edit, reproduce and incorporate your comments in Lonely Planet products such as guidebooks, websites and digital products, so let us know if you don't want your comments reproduced or your name acknowledged. For a copy of our privacy policy visit lonelyplanet.com/privacy.

Acknowledgements

Cover photograph: Guggenheim Museum, Luigi Vaccarella/ 4 Corners Images ©

Back cover photograph: 42nd street, mbbirdy/Getty Images ©

Photographs pp34–5 (clockwise from top left): Songquan Deng; Marcio Jose Bastos Silva; Photo Spirit; Jeff Whyte; Michael Urmann/Shutterstock ©

Ali's Thanks

Thanks to Trisha Ping and Lauren Keith, to Dawn Hopper at Dutchess Tourism and Stacey-Ann Hosang at the Empire State Building, and to my co-authors, especially Anita Isalska and Ma-Sovaida Morgan. Thanks also to Mark Batt and to Michael and Ellen Korney for their love and support. My chapters are dedicated to the memories of my two favorite New Yorkers, Toni Halbreich and Albert Lemer.

This Book

This 8th edition of *Pocket New York City* was curated by Ali Lemer and researched and written by Ali Lemer, Anita Isalska, MaSovaida Morgan and Kevin Raub.

Destination Editors
Lauren Keith, Bailey Freeman

Senior Product Editors
Daniel Bolger, Martine Power

Product Editors
Grace Dobell, Alison Ridgway

Cartographers Alison Lyall, Julie Sheridan

Book Designers
Hannah Blackie, Fergal Condon

Assisting Editors
Hannah Cartmel, Kate Chapman, Kate Kiely, Jodie Martire, Kristin Odijk, Monique Perrin, Mani Ramaswamy

Cover Researcher
Meri Blazevski, Gwen Cotter

Thanks to William Allen, Imogen Bannister, Carolyn Boicos, Catherine Naghten, David Nelson, Kirsten Rawlings, Emily Ridgway, Jason Ridgway, Angela Tinson, Amanda Williamson

Index

See also separate subindexes for:

- 😵 **Eating p252**
- 🍷 **Drinking p253**
- ⭐ **Entertainment p254**
- 🛍 **Shopping p254**

Sights 000

Map Pages **000**

Our Writers

Ali Lemer

Ali has been a Lonely Planet writer and editor since 2007, and has authored guidebooks and articles on Russia, Germany, NYC, Chicago, Los Angeles, Melbourne, Bali, Hawaii, Japan and Scotland, among others. A native New Yorker, Ali has also lived in Melbourne, Chicago, Prague and the UK, and has traveled extensively around Europe, North America, Oceania and Asia.

Anita Isalska

Anita Isalska is a travel journalist, editor and copywriter. After several merry years as a staff writer and editor – a few of them in Lonely Planet's London office – Anita now works freelance between San Francisco, the UK and any Baltic bolthole with good wi-fi. Anita specialises in Eastern and Central Europe, Southeast Asia, France and off-beat travel.

MaSovaida Morgan

MaSovaida is a travel journalist whose wayfaring tendencies have taken her to more than 50 countries across all seven continents. As a Lonely Planet author, she contributes to guidebooks on destinations throughout Southeast Asia, the Middle East, Europe and the Americas. Prior to going freelance in 2018, MaSovaida spent four years at Lonely Planet's Nashville office as a Destination Editor, where she oversaw the company's content on South America and Antarctica.

Kevin Raub

An Atlanta native, Kevin started his career as a music journalist in New York, working for *Men's Journal* and *Rolling Stone* magazines. He ditched the rock 'n' roll lifestyle for travel writing and has written more than 95 Lonely Planet guides, focused mainly on Brazil, Chile, Colombia, USA, India, Italy and Portugal. Raub also contributes to a variety of travel magazines in both the USA and UK.

Published by Lonely Planet Global Limited
CRN 554153
8th edition – Feb 2022
ISBN 978 1 78701 746 7
© Lonely Planet 2022   Photographs © as indicated 2022
10 9 8 7 6 5 4 3 2 1
Printed in Singapore

Although the authors and Lonely Planet have taken all reasonable care in preparing this book, we make no warranty about the accuracy or completeness of its content and, to the maximum extent permitted, disclaim all liability arising from its use.